AMS SHORT COURSE LECTURE NOTES

Introductory Survey Lectures

published as a subseries of

Proceedings of Symposia in Applied Mathematics

Proceedings of Symposia in
APPLIED MATHEMATICS

Volume 62

Public-Key Cryptography

American Mathematical Society
Short Course
January 13–14, 2003
Baltimore, Maryland

Paul Garrett
Daniel Lieman
Editors

American Mathematical Society
Providence, Rhode Island

LECTURE NOTES PREPARED FOR THE
AMERICAN MATHEMATICAL SOCIETY SHORT COURSE
PUBLIC-KEY CRYPTOGRAPHY
HELD IN BALTIMORE, MARYLAND
JANUARY 13–14, 2003

The AMS Short Course Series is sponsored by the Society's Program Committee for National Meetings. The series is under the direction of the Short Course Subcommittee of the Program Committee for National Meetings.

2000 *Mathematics Subject Classification.* Primary 54C40, 14E20, 14G50, 11G20, 11T71, 11Yxx, 94Axx, 46E25, 20C20.

Library of Congress Cataloging-in-Publication Data

Public-key cryptography / Paul Garrett, Daniel Lieman, editors.
p. cm. — (Proceedings of symposia in applied mathematics ; v. 62)
Papers from a conference held at the 2003 Baltimore meeting of the American Mathematical Society.
Includes bibliographical references and index.
ISBN 0-8218-3365-0 (alk. paper)
1. Computers—Access control—Congresses. 2. Public key cryptography—Congresses. I. Garrett, Paul, 1952– II. Lieman, Daniel, 1965– III. American Mathematical Society. IV. Series.

QA76.9.A25P82 2005
005.8′2—dc22 2005048178

∞ The paper used in this book is acid-free and falls within the guidelines
established to ensure permanence and durability.
Visit the AMS home page at `http://www.ams.org/`

10 9 8 7 6 5 4 3 2 1 10 09 08 07 06 05

Contents

Preface

For the Baltimore 2003 meeting of the A.M.S. Daniel Lieman organized an expository and tutorial conference on public-key cryptography for mathematicians. This volume is the collection of papers that grew out of that conference.

By contrast to a number of lower-level introductory texts aimed at undergraduates, and which therefore necessarily dilute discussion of specific cryptographic issues with discussion of elementary mathematics, the aim here was to provide a survey and introduction to public-key cryptography assuming considerable mathematical maturity and considerable general mathematical knowledge. Thus, we hoped to make clearer the cryptographic issues that fall outside the scope of standard or typical mathematics.

The papers are mostly expository, with the mathematical level of the exposition meant to be palatable to experienced mathematicians not already too much acquainted with this subject.

An important part of the context is the extra-mathematical aspect. That is, many motivations and crucial issues for genuine cryptography are difficult or impossible to understood purely in terms of formal algorithmic or other mathematical notions. (And the very validity of that last assertion is a subject of debate.) It is necessary to have some idea of the complications entailed by real-life implementations of cryptographic systems. In particular, and in considerable contrast to formal mathematics, we cannot assume that everyone plays by the rules. Further, indeed, by contrast to most mathematical and scientific research contexts wherein there is no antagonist other than a merely disinterested Nature, the presence of an *active antagonist* is a singular aspect of the practice of cryptography.

Some of the authors of the papers are academic mathematicians, some are professional cryptographers outside academe, and some have been in both situations. All the papers were reviewed for literal correctness and for aptness for our espoused purposes.

Paul Garrett

Proceedings of Symposia in Applied Mathematics
Volume **62**, 2005

Cryptographic Primitives

Paul Garrett

Abstract. An overview of cryptographic primitives, emphasizing public-key (asymmetric) ciphers and fundamental algorithms from computational number theory. Examples of protocol sketches.

A **symmetric** or **private-key** cipher is one in which knowledge of the *encryption* key is explicitly or implicitly equivalent to knowing the *decryption* key. An **asymmetric** or **public-key** cipher is one in which the *encryption* key is effectively public knowledge, without giving any useful information about the *decryption* key. Until 30 years ago all ciphers were private-key. The very possibility of public-key crypto did not exist until the secret work Ellis-Cocks-Williamson at the UK's CESG-at-GCHQ in the 1960's, and public-domain work of Merkle, Diffie-Hellman, and Rivest-Shamir-Adleman in the 1970's. Even more significant than the *secrecy* achievable by public-key ciphers is the variety of effects achievable that were (and continue to be) simply impossible with even the best symmetric-key ciphers. *Key exchange* and *signatures* (authentication) are the most notable among well-established uses. Further examples are given in section 6.

Other articles in this volume address specific aspects of public-key cryptography at greater length. D. Lieman's article [Lie] concerns refinements of protocols appropriate to genuine practical implementations. N. Howgrave-Graham [HG] treats proofs of security. J. Silverman's [Sil3] discusses elliptic curves. W. Whyte's [Wh] and W.D. Banks' [Ba] articles consider the problem of designing faster cryptosystems of various sorts. And I. Shparlinski [Shp2] discusses design and attacks upon systems based upon various hidden-number problems. Given these, we will emphasize algorithms related mostly to RSA, primality testing, and factoring attacks, as opposed to discrete logs and/or elliptic curves, and give only simple naive forms of protocol-ideas rather than refined forms.

By now there are many introductory texts on cryptography. Many of them are reviewed in [L3].

1991 *Mathematics Subject Classification.* Primary 54C40, 14E20; Secondary 46E25, 20C20.

Key words and phrases. Cryptography, public key ciphers, RSA, trapdoor, Diffie-Hellman, key exchange, signatures, zero-knowledge proofs, primes, factorization, primality testing, pseudoprimes, probable primes, computational number theory, complexity, probabilistic algorithms, Monte Carlo methods, protocols, DES, AES, Rijndael.

1 Prototypes

Several points which occur either literally or figuratively throughout discussions of public-key ciphers are already nicely illustrated in the case of the Rivest-Shamir-Adleman cipher, RSA, from [RSA], together with the Diffie-Hellman key exchange [DH]. Subordinate algorithmic issues will be made more precise in the sequel. A relevant notion is that of **trapdoor**: a computation which runs much more easily in one direction than back. A prototypical example is that *multiplication* of large integers is easy, while *factoring* of large integers is difficult (to the best of our knowledge). And then there is the question of how to make such an irreversible process into a useful one. Another apparently comparably difficult task, relevant to both RSA and Diffie-Hellman, is computation of discrete logarithms modulo primes, while exponentiation (by the square-and-multiply algorithm (4.3)) is easy.

A key point is that while *factoring* large numbers into primes appears to be difficult, merely *testing* large numbers for primality is definitely easy (e.g., by Miller-Rabin (4.13)).

A critical but often tacit issue is the generation of sufficiently many high-quality random bits incidental to generation of random primes.

And here might be the time to introduce a common computer-language notation

$$x \,\%\, n = x \textbf{ reduced} \text{ modulo } n$$

This notation allows us to easily make a distinction between reduction and equivalence classes or equalities modulo n.

1.1 RSA cipher.

For Alice to set things up so that Bob (or other people without prior contact with her) can send her messages that cannot be decrypted by an eavesdropper Eve, Alice proceeds as follows. *(But it must be disclaimed at once that this is a naive and very incomplete implementation of RSA!)*

First, there are one-time set-up computations. Alice generates two large random primes p and q (at least $> 2^{512}$, and probably $> 2^{1024}$), and computes her **RSA modulus** $n = pq$. Alice will keep the primes p and q secret, while she will make n public. Alice chooses an **encryption exponent** $e > 2$. Often the Fermat prime $e = 2^{16} + 1 = 65537$ is used, for reasons that will become clearer subsequently. The encryption exponent e is made public. Alice computes the **decryption exponent** d with the property that

$$ed = 1 \bmod (p-1)(q-1)$$

Alice keeps the decryption exponent d secret. This ends Alice's set-up. The encryption key e is the **public key** and the decryption key d is the **private key**. Integers n of the form $n = pq$ with p and q distinct primes are called **RSA moduli**, or sometimes **Blum integers** if both primes are 3 modulo 4.

For Bob to send a message to Alice that only Alice can read, he proceeds as follows. Note that Bob's procedure requires no prior contact or arrangment with Alice, in particular, no pre-existing secret shared by the two of them. For simplicity, we assume that the plaintext x is an integer in the range $1 < x < n$. The **encoding** step $x \to E_{n,e}(x)$ is

$$E_{n,e}(x) = x^e \,\%\, n$$

This produces a **ciphertext** $y = x^e \,\%\, n$ in the range $0 < y < n$. Bob sends this over a (probably insecure) channel to Alice.

Alice decrypts Bob's message as follows. The **decryption** step $y \to D_{n,d}(y)$ is

$$D_{n,d}(y) = y^d \,\%\, n$$

This blunt description shows the simplicity of set-up and operation, but several things need clarification:

Why is it feasible for Alice to find two large random primes?
Why is it feasible for Bob to compute x^e reduced mod n?
Why is it feasible for Alice to compute $d = e^{-1} \bmod (p-1)(q-1)$?
Why is it feasible for Alice to compute y^d reduced mod n?
Why does the decryption step decrypt, that is, why is $y^d \bmod n = x$?
Why is it *not* feasible for Eve (the eavesdropper) to compute d from n and e?
Why is it *not* feasible for Eve to compute x from $x^e \bmod n$?
How do we get a good supply of *random numbers*?

The decryption step decrypts: At first glance, possibly the least obvious fact is that the decryption step really does recover the plaintext. For the decryption step to genuinely decrypt, recovering the plaintext, the two keys e, d must have the property that

$$(x^e)^d = x \bmod n$$

for integers x. **Euler's theorem** (4.5) asserts in general that if $\gcd(x, n) = 1$, then

$$x^{\varphi(n)} = 1 \bmod n$$

where φ is the Euler totient function

$$\varphi(n) = \text{number of integers } 1 \le \ell \le n \text{ with } \gcd(\ell, n) = 1$$

Thus, e and d should be mutual **multiplicative inverses modulo** $\varphi(n)$

$$d \cdot e = 1 \bmod \varphi(n)$$

For integers n of the form $n = p \cdot q$ with distinct primes p, q it is easy to see that

$$\varphi(p \cdot q) = (p-1)(q-1)$$

Then one can easily verify that the encryption and decryption really work for $\gcd(x, n) = 1$: let $ed = 1 + \ell(p-1)(q-1)$. Then

$$D_{n,d}(E_{n,e}(x)) = (x^e)^d = x^{ed} \bmod n$$

$$= x^{1+\ell\cdot(p-1)(q-1)} = x \cdot (x^{\varphi(n)})^\ell = x \bmod n$$

by invoking Euler's theorem.

Euler's theorem requires that x be prime to n. The probability that a random x in the range $1 < x < n$ would be divisible by p or q is

$$\frac{1}{p} + \frac{1}{q} - \frac{1}{pq}$$

which is sufficiently tiny that we ignore it. In any case, testing for this is easy, via the Euclidean algorithm. And we note that a systematic ability to choose such messages would be (therefore) tantamount to being able to systematically factor large integers. And the encryption exponent e must be prime to $\varphi(n) = (p-1)(q-1)$ so that it will have a multiplicative inverse modulo $\varphi(n)$. Failure in this regard would be detected in set-up.

The security of RSA depends upon the difficulty of *factoring* integers into primes, or at least factoring integers $n = pq$ which are the product of two primes: if Eve can factor n into p and q she knows as much as Alice about the set-up. Eve can compute $\varphi(n) = (p-1)(q-1)$ and compute the decryption exponent d just as Alice (probably by the extended Euclidean algorithm (4.2)). Factoring is not *provably* difficult, though no polynomial-time public-domain algorithm exists.

Given $n = pq$ the product of two big primes p, q (with the primes secret), it seems hard to compute $\varphi(n)$ when only n is given. Once the factorization $n = p \cdot q$ is known, it is easy to compute $\varphi(n)$ as

$$\varphi(n) = \varphi(pq) = (p-1)(q-1)$$

In fact, for numbers $n = pq$ of this special form, knowing both n and $\varphi(n)$ *gives* the factorization $n = p \cdot q$ with little computation. Indeed, p, q are the roots of the equation

$$x^2 - (p+q)x + pq = 0$$

Already $pq = n$, so if $p + q$ is expressed in terms of n and $\varphi(n)$, we have the coefficients of this equation expressed in terms of n and $\varphi(n)$, giving an easy route to p and q separately. Since

$$\varphi(n) = (p-1)(q-1) = pq - (p+q) + 1 = n - (p+q) + 1$$

rearrange to get

$$p + q = n - \varphi(n) + 1$$

Therefore, p and q are the roots of the equation

$$x^2 - (n - \varphi(n) + 1)x + n = 0$$

Computing roots: Also, even more obviously, the security of RSA also depends upon the difficulty of computing e^{th} *roots* modulo n: if Eve can compute e^{th} roots modulo n, then she can compute the plaintext as the eth root of the ciphertext $y = x^e \,\%\, n$. While computing roots modulo *primes* is easy (4.17), computing roots modulo composite numbers appears to be hard (without factoring).

Common modulus: The *users* of a system with modulus n (the product of two secret primes p, q), public key e, and private key d *do not need to know the primes* p, q. Therefore, one might envisage the scenario in which a **central agency** uses the same modulus $n = pq$ for several different users, only with different encryption/decryption exponents e_i, d_i. However, compromise of one key pair e_1, d_1 compromises the others to a degree, since

$$\varphi(n) \mid (e_1 d_1 - 1)$$

and $\varphi(n) < n$, greatly reducing the search space for $\varphi(n)$. But, in fact, the situation is far worse: the user with keypair e_1, d_1 need not determine $(p-1)(q-1)$ exactly, since an inverse $D = e_2^{-1} \bmod N$ for N any multiple of $(p-1)(q-1)$ also works as a decryption exponent for encryption exponent e_2. That is, a multiplicative inverse modulo a multiple of $(p-1)(q-1)$ is a multiplicative inverse modulo $(p-1)(q-1)$, even if it is needlessly larger. And, of course, two collaborating users with encryption/decryption pairs e_1, d_1 and e_2, d_2 can compute, together,

$$\gcd(e_1 d_1 - 1, e_2 d_2 - 1)$$

of which $\varphi(n)$ is a divisor, even more sharply reducing the search space for $\varphi(n)$.

Fast exponentiation: Naively, raising large numbers to large powers is slow, so from a naive viewpoint it may be unclear why the algorithms in authorized execution of RSA are any faster than a hostile attack. In fact, the required exponentiation can be arranged to be much faster than prime factorizations for numbers in the relevant range. That is, to compute x^e we do *not* compute all of $x^1, x^2, x^3, \ldots, x^{e-1}, x^e$. The *square-and-multiply* exponentiation algorithm (4.3) is a simple example of a fast exponentiation algorithm, consisting of a systematization of the idea of using a binary expansion of the exponent to reduce the total number of operations. For example,

$$x^{17} = x^1 \cdot ((((x^2)^2)^2)^2)$$

Key generation: To set up $n = pq$ from secret primes p, q, and to determine a key pair e, d with $ed = 1 \bmod \varphi(n)$, requires two large primes p, q. Since the security of RSA is based upon the intractability of factoring, it is fortunate that primality testing is much easier than factorization. That is, we *are* able to obtain many 'large' primes $p, q >> 2^{512}$ *cheaply*, despite the fact that we cannot generally factor 'large' numbers $n = pq >> 2^{1024}$ into primes. The Fermat pseudoprime test (4.13) combined with the Miller-Rabin strong pseudoprime test (4.13) provide one efficient test for primality.

Relative difficulty of factoring: The various modern factorization tests, such as Pollard's rho (8.2), or even the better subexponential sieve methods (8.4), while vastly better than antique trial division (4.7), are still too slow to compete, for sufficiently large modulus n. Again, there is no proof that factoring is more difficult than primality testing.

Padding: From a mathematical viewpoint, it is obvious that if an attacker knows the encryptions y_1, y_2 of two different plaintexts x_1, x_2 (with the same public key), then the attacker knows the encryption of $y_1 y_2 \% n$, where n is the RSA modulus. This sort of **leakage** of information may seem obscure, but can be systematically exploited. Thus, in reality, with most public-key ciphers, plaintexts must be *padded* with various amounts of random material.

It seems that attacks on RSA will succeed only when RSA is **improperly implemented**, for example, with too-small modulus. The key size (the size of the RSA modulus $N = pq$) must not be too small, or a brute-force attempt to factor n may succeed in a time smaller than one would want. E.g., in 1999 Adi Shamir designed a specialized computer 'Twinkle' which speeded up execution of certain factorization attacks by a factor of 100 or 1000. To break the RSA *function* means to invert the function

$$x \to x^e \% N$$

without being given the decryption exponent d in advance. To break the RSA *cipher* means something with more possibilities than breaking the RSA function: it means to recover all or part of a plaintext without being given the decryption exponent. Unbreakability of the cipher, rather than of the function, is **semantic security**.

Both $p-1$ and $q-1$ should have at least one very large prime factor, since there are factorization attacks against $n = pq$ that are possible if $p-1$ or $q-1$ have only smallish prime factors (Pollard's $p-1$ attack (8.3)). The primes p and q should not be 'close' to each other, since there are factorization attacks on n that succeed in this case (Fermat, etc.). The ratio p/q should not be 'close' to a rational number with smallish numerator and denominator, or else D. H. Lehmer's Continued Fraction factorization attack on $n = pq$ will succeed. If quantum computers ever become a reality, 1993 work of Peter Shor [Sho1], [Sho2] shows that there is a fast *quantum* algorithm to factor large numbers.

Forward search attack. If the collection of all possible messages is known, and is relatively small, then the attacker need only encrypt all the messages until a match is found. For example, if the message is known to be either 'yes' or 'no', then only one encryption need be computed to know which is the plaintext. To defend against this, messages should be *padded* by adding random bits at front and/or back.

Small decryption exponent attack: To save some computation time, one might try to arrange so that the decryption exponent is small. But if $d < \frac{1}{3}N^{1/4}$, then there is an efficient algorithm to recover this decryption exponent! See [Wie]. In [Bo] it is speculated that using a decryption modulus less than $\sqrt{N}$ may be vulnerable to such attacks.

Small public exponent attacks: A traditional choice of encryption exponent $e = 3$ is insecure. Suppose that Alice wishes to send the same secret message to several different people. If she does the obvious thing, encrypting the message using each of their public keys and sending, then eavesdropper Eve collects all the encrypted messages. *If the number of messages is greater than or equal the encryption exponent e, then Eve can recover the message.* For example, if $e = 3$ then just 3 different encryptions are sufficient to recover the message. More sophisticated attacks of this sort are **Hastad's broadcast attack** and **Coppersmith's short pad attack** [Co2]. If the larger $e = 2^{16} + 1 = 65537$ is used, these vulnerabilities seem to be eliminated.

Partial disclosure: When the (public) encryption exponent is small, **partial disclosure** of the decryption key breaks RSA: [Bo]. From [BDF], the $n/4$ least significant bits of the (private) decryption key d, the entire decryption key can be recovered in time linear in $e \log_2 e$. This is related to a factorization result: given either the $n/4$ highest or $n/4$ lowest bits of p, one can efficiently factor $n = pq$ [Co2].

Timing, power attacks. Especially in situations such as smart cards where an adversary may have virtually unlimited opportunities to do known-plaintext attacks and measurements, naive forms of RSA are vulnerable to **timing attacks**, where the adversary *times* the computation, thereby finding the number of exponentiations occuring in a decryption, thereby getting information on the decryption exponent [Ko]. Similarly, power attacks measure power consumption to acquire information about sizes of keys.

1.2 Diffie-Hellman key exchange.

The discovery [DH] of the possibility of a **key exchange** procedure was a great surprise, even more so than the notion of public-key *cipher*. The goal is that Alice and Bob, who have not met previously, establish a *shared secret* using only an insecure channel to communicate. The eavesdropper Eve has greater computing power than Alice and Bob, and hears everything that passes between them. We do suppose that Eve cannot actively disrupt the communications, but, rather, is a passive eavesdropper.

Typically the shared secret would be used to create a *session key*, that is, a key for a faster symmetric cipher, to be used just during the current communication session.

Again, a crucial mathematical point is that computing *discrete logarithms* modulo primes is relatively difficult, while exponentiating integers modulo large primes is relatively easy. And, again, it is relatively easy to find large primes in the first place. And there is the often-tacit assumption that we can generate sufficiently many high-quality random numbers.

Alice and Bob agree on a large random prime p (at the very least $\sim 2^{1024}$) and a random *base* g in the range $1 < g < p$. These are public knowledge. Alice secretly chooses a random a in the range $1 < a < p$ and computes $A = g^a \,\%\, p$. Similarly, Bob secretly chooses a random b in the range $1 < b < p$ and computes $B = g^b \,\%\, p$. Alice sends A over the channel, and Bob sends B over the channel. So Alice knows p, g, a, A, B, Bob knows p, g, A, b, B, and Eve knows p, g, A, B.

Alice computes $K_A = B^a \,\%\, p$

Bob computes $K_B = A^b \,\%\, p$

They have computed the same thing, since

$$K_A = (B^a) = (g^b)^a = (g^a)^b = A^b = K_B \bmod p$$

Alice and Bob have a shared secret which it is apparently *infeasible* for Eve to obtain.

The feasibility for Alice and Bob follows from the feasibility of exponentiating via the square-and-multiply algorithm, and the feasibility of probabilistic methods (e.g., testing for primality via Miller-Rabin (4.13)) for finding large primes. The infeasibility for the eavesdropper Eve depends (at least) upon the (apparent) infeasibility of computing discrete logarithms.

2 Complexity

It is apparently unreasonable to demand *absolute* unbreakability of ciphers. It is far more reasonable, and sufficient for real use, to require that it be *infeasible* for an attacker to break a system. As one would anticipate, this is a context-dependent qualification.

2.1 Polynomial-time algorithms.

A common description of the **complexity** of a computation is as *runtime complexity*, the number of **bit operations** it takes. A **bit** is a 0 or a 1. A bit operation is the application of either one of the $2^2 = 4$ functions that takes two bits as input and produces a single bit as output, or one of the 2 functions that takes a single bit as input and produces a single bit output. The abstract model of a bit operation ignores the cost and/or difficulty of reading and writing, and of moving bits among registers.

An algorithm is **polynomial-time** if the run-time is at most polynomial in the number of bits in the input (with a polynomial independent of the input). This means that *even in the worst-case scenario* (for possibly tricky or nasty inputs) the estimate must hold. It is entirely possible that most often even less time is used, but the worst-case scenario is accounted for in this traditional terminology. Questions with polynomial-time algorithms to answer them make up class **P**.

If the *correctness of a guess* at an answer to a question can be proven or disproven in polynomial time, then the question is in class **NP**. This class of questions certainly contains the class **P**. It is widely believed that the class **P** is strictly smaller than the class **NP**, but this is the main open question in complexity theory. Problems in **P** are considered **easy**, and those in **NP** but not in **P** are considered **hard**. Ironically, since we don't have a proof that **P** is strictly smaller than **NP**, for now we have no proof that there are *any* hard problems in this sense.

A question A is *reducible* to another question B (in polynomial time) if there is a polynomial-time algorithm to answer question A (for a given input) from an answer to question B (with related input). In this context, a possibly unknown and unspecified process to answer B is an **oracle** for B. Surprisingly, it has been shown that there are problems C in **NP** so that *any* problem in **NP** can be reduced to to C in polynomial time. Such problems are **NP-hard** or **NP-complete**. (Finer distinctions can be made which make these two phrases mean different things.)

In effect, Turing, Church, Post, Kleene, and others verified that *computability* is machine-independent (given a sufficiently complicated computing machine). Similar considerations indicate that the notion of polynomial time is machine-independent. Nevertheless, for practical purposes, the degree of the polynomial and the constants appearing can have a great practical impact.

To avoid misunderstanding, it might be mentioned that discussion of manipulation of integers typically tacitly assumes that they are re-written in binary. This re-writing, and conversion back to decimal, are both polynomial-time, so this conversion does not affect qualitative conclusions about run-time.

It is easy to verify that the usual arithmetic algorithms involving Hindu-Arabic numerals are polynomial-time. Especially for large-ish integers, there are several algorithms for multiplication which are faster than the method taught in grade school. See [Kn]. However, the speed-ups don't occur until the integers are considerably larger than those used by schoolchildren. Indeed, direct experimentation seems to indicate that the overhead for clever algorithms makes these inferior to optimized machine-code implementations of classical algorithms, until the integers become larger than current cryptographic uses demand.

It is more common to worry about *time* (i.e., runtime) rather than *space* (i.e., memory used), but this concern may be simply an artifact of the apparent fact that in practice most bottlenecks are run-time rather than memory.

If an algorithm does not (in its worst case) run in polynomial time, then (by default) we say it runs in **exponential time**. Note that this is measured in terms of input size.

Thus, for example, recall that the naive trial-division test for primality of a number N uses roughly $\sqrt{N}$ steps to prove that N is prime (if it is). The *size* n of N as input is $n = \log_2 N$, and

$$\sqrt{N} = 2^{\log_2 N/2} = 2^{n/2}$$

This grows faster than any polynomial in n. That is, trial division is an exponential algorithm.

2.2 Probabilistic algorithms.

The notion that an algorithm could have random elements is surprising. Even more surprising is that for some important problems there are *much* faster probabilistic algorithms than deterministic ones. There is some charming and colorful terminology for probabilistic algorithms. A **Monte Carlo** algorithm *always* yields an answer (in polynomial time), but this answer has only a *probability* of being correct. It is **yes-biased** if a 'yes' answer is true with some probability, but a 'no' answer is always correct. (Similarly for **no-biased** Monte Carlo algorithms.) A Monte Carlo algorithm is either yes-biased or no-biased, so 'half' its answers are *certain*.

The pseudo-primality tests mentioned in 4.13 are yes-biased Monte Carlo algorithms, since a 'yes' answer (asserting primality) may be wrong, but a 'no' answer (asserting compositeness) is always correct. This holds for the simplest test, the Fermat test, and also for the Miller-Rabin test for strong pseudoprimality.

A **Las Vegas** algorithm has *expected* run time which is polynomial, so may occasionally fail to give an answer (in polynomial time). But if it *does* give an answer for a particular input (after whatever time) then the answer is *correct*.

A less standard usage is that an **Atlantic City** algorithm gives a correct answer at least $3/4$ of the time, and runs in polynomial time. (The number $3/4$ can be replaced with any probability above $1/2$.) Atlantic City algorithms are *two-sided* versions of Monte Carlo algorithms.

There is notation for these classes of algorithms. The class **ZPP** consists of questions answerable by a (polynomial-time) Las Vegas algorithm. The class **RP** consists of those questions answerable in polynomial time by a Monte Carlo method. Questions answerable by polynomial-time Atlantic City algorithms are in **BPP**.

2.3 Subexponential algorithms.

At this time, the best known algorithms for factoring integers into primes, for computing discrete logarithms, and for other important computations, are *not* polynomial-time, but are nevertheless significantly faster than literal exponential-time. We can quantify this distinction. The class of $L(a, b)$ of algorithms consists of those whose runtime for input of size n is

$$O(\, e^{(b+o(1))\,\cdot\, n^a\ (\ln n)^{1-a}})$$

with $b \geq 0$, $0 \leq a \leq 1$. The union

$$\bigcup_{0<a<1,\ 0<b} L(a, b)$$

for all $0 < a < 1$, $0 < b$ is the collection of **subexponential algorithms**.

E.g., for $b \geq 0$ $L(0, b)$ is the collection of polynomial-time algorithms with runtimes $O(n^b)$. On the other hand, $L(1, b)$ is genuinely exponential-time algorithms with runtimes $O(e^{bn})$.

Currently, the best algorithms currently known for *factoring* and the best algorithms for computing *discrete logarithms* in $\mathbb{Z}/p^e$ (p prime) are (conjecturally) in a class

$$L(\frac{1}{3},\, 1.923)$$

See [Co1] for factoring and [A] for discrete logs in $\mathbb{Z}/p^e$. These run-time estimates are *conjectural* since they rely upon plausible but unproven hypotheses on the distributions of various special sorts of integers. It is a striking coincidence that the two conjectural runtimes are the same. For less elementary abstract discrete logarithm problems, such as on *elliptic curves*, no runtime this low is known. This gives a technical advantage to elliptic curve ciphers, and this margin is important in practice.

2.4 Kolmogoroff complexity.

Solomonoff, Chaitin, and Kolmogorov independently developed a version of complexity, **program (-length) complexity**, which emphasizes *program length* rather than *runtime*. This notion of complexity affords a useful perspective on *(pseudo) random numbers*.

The idea is that a rather special string of characters such as

$$110110110110110110110110110110110110110110110110110$$

can be described much more briefly than by listing the characters, as '17 copies of 110'. By contrast, the string

$$111011110111010111111111110001000110000010011000110$$

admits no obvious simpler description than to just list all the characters directly.

From a probabilistic viewpoint, one might pretend that every string of (for example) 51 0's and 1's is equally likely to be chosen 'at random'. However, this is naive. For example, of the two strings above, the second is plausibly 'random', but the first is not. That is, we would not be suspicious if we were told that the second one was chosen 'at random' (whatever this means). However, the first is 'too structured' and we would doubt that it was 'chosen at random'.

We can modify our notion of 'random string of characters of length n' to incorporate the idea that a *truly random object* should not have a description any simpler than the thing itself. This makes more legitimate our objection to the 17 copies of the string 110, while still admitting the other string as random, since no simpler description string is obvious.

An informal definition of the **Kolmogorov complexity** of an object is the *length of the shortest description of the object.* Here the object itself *is* a description of itself. The issue is whether there is a *shorter* description of it than just it itself, where 'description' certainly may include a program (in *some* language, running on *some* machine) which generates the thing.

Of course this pseudo-definition makes sense only in relation to a given descriptive apparatus. Otherwise we are vulnerable to the usual paradoxes concerning such things as 'the putative first integer not describable in fewer than twelve words'.

It can be proven, not surprisingly, after making things more precise, that 'most' strings of characters of a given length n have no description significantly shorter than n, so that the shortest description of a typical one is achieved just by writing it out. A counting argument essentially suffices.

A necessary preliminary to a serious treatment of this subject is proof that program/description length only depends in a rather shallow manner upon the machine or descriptive apparatus. [LV] gives a thorough introduction to many facets of this subject, with historical and conceptual background.

2.5 Linear complexity, LFSRs, LCGs.

The family of LFSRs (linear feedback shift registers) and LCGs (linear congruential generators) generate potentially infinite streams

$$b_0, b_1, b_2, \ldots$$

of values b_i from a fixed finite alphabet, specified by very simple rules and short lists of parameters. This sharply circumscribed model of generation of an output stream can be viewed as a much simpler restricted cousin of Kolmogoroff (program) complexity. These LFSRs and LCGs incidentally give examples of pRNGs (pseudo-random number generators) unsuitable for cryptographic uses, though useful in other situations if used carefully.

For example, a **linear feedback shift register** (LFSR) most often uses alphabet $\mathbb{Z}/2$, is specified completely by a **length** n and coefficients $c_1, c_1, \ldots, c_n \in \mathbb{Z}/2$, and the values b_i with $i \geq n$ are produced by a recursion

$$b_i = c_1 b_{i-1} + c_2 b_{i-2} + \ldots c_n b_{i-n}$$

Thus, the *seed* consisting of the first n values

$$\text{seed} = (b_0, b_1, \ldots, b_{n-1})$$

together with the n coefficients c_i completely determine the output stream. In this simple case of alphabet $\mathbb{Z}/2$, the non-zero coefficients are necessarily 1, so it suffices to tell merely the indices i such that $c_i \neq 0$. Engineering terminology of circuit diagrams often refers to indices with non-zero coefficients as *taps*.

The elementary features of LFSRs are easily analyzed by linear algebra: the matrix giving the linear recurrence relation

$$\begin{pmatrix} c_1 & c_2 & c_3 & \ldots & c_{n-1} & c_n \\ 1 & 0 & 0 & \ldots & 0 & 0 \\ 0 & 1 & 0 & \ldots & 0 & 0 \\ 0 & 0 & 1 & \ldots & 0 & 0 \\ \vdots & \vdots & \vdots & & \vdots & \vdots \\ 0 & 0 & & & 0 & 0 \\ 0 & 0 & & \ldots & 1 & 0 \end{pmatrix} \begin{pmatrix} b_i \\ b_{i-1} \\ \\ \\ \vdots \\ b_{i-n+2} \\ b_{i-n+1} \end{pmatrix} = \begin{pmatrix} b_{i+1} \\ b_i \\ \\ \\ \vdots \\ b_{i-n+3} \\ b_{i-n+2} \end{pmatrix}$$

has (as usual) characteristic polynomial

$$P(x) = x^n + c_1 x^{n-1} + c_2 x^{n-2} + \ldots + c_{n-1} x + c_n$$

where we take advantage of the fact that the characteristic is 2 to ignore signs.

Since the internal state

$$(b_{i-n+1}, b_{i-n+2}, \ldots, b_{i-1}, b_i)$$

has $2^n - 1$ possible non-zero values when all b_j are in $\mathbb{F}_2$, this internal state will return to its initial state in at most $2^n - 1$ steps. This maximum is achieved when the degree-n characteristic polynomial $P(x)$ is *primitive*, meaning that

$$x^{2^n - 1} = 1 \bmod P(x)$$

but

$$x^\ell \neq 1 \bmod P(x)$$

for $1 \leq \ell < 2^n - 1$. Since the multiplicative group $\mathbb{F}_q^\times$ of a finite field $\mathbb{F}_q$ is cyclic, the primitive polynomials $P(x)$ in $\mathbb{F}_2[x]$ are exactly the irreducibles (over $\mathbb{F}_2$) of generators for $\mathbb{F}_{2^n}^\times$. There are $\varphi(2^n - 1)$ such generators (with Euler's totient function φ (4.5)), and thus there are $\varphi(2^n - 1)/n$ such primitive polynomials of degree n. Similar counting arguments apply generally.

The further issue of finding *sparse* primitive polynomials (i.e., with very few non-zero coefficients) is of obvious interest for speed-up of computation. The extreme case of trinomials is already non-trivial. See [Go].

The **linear complexity** of a stream of outputs in $\{0, 1\}$ is the smallest value of n such that the outputs can be produced by a length n LFSR.

Unlike other notions of complexity which are not effectively computable, the linear complexity of a stream of bits is computable in polynomial time (for given length of bit stream). This is the *Massey-Berlekamp* algorithm [Ma], which computes the constants for a LFSR of length n given just $2n$ initial bits. Since presumably any LFSR used in practice would be essentially primitive, the output bitstream would give $2^n - 1$ bits before repeating. Thus, the number (i.e., $2n$) of (initial) bits needed to determine the constants is polynomial in the logarithm of the size of the output (i.e., $2^n - 1$). The procedure of finding a LFSR to generate a given bit stream is also called *shift register synthesis*.

Linear congruential generators (LCGs) generate streams of values

$$b_0, b_1, \ldots$$

in a finite field $\mathbb{F}_q$ given the initial state b_0 and given structure constants A, B in $\mathbb{F}_q$, by

$$b_i = Ab_{i-1} + B$$

Since

$$\begin{pmatrix} A & B \\ 0 & 1 \end{pmatrix} \begin{pmatrix} b_i \\ 1 \end{pmatrix} = \begin{pmatrix} b_{i+1} \\ 1 \end{pmatrix}$$

these also admit an elementary analysis by linear algebra, and, therefore, are inappropriate for cryptographic use.

2.6 Quantum algorithms.

One should be aware that *quantum cryptography* and *quantum computing* are very different things. Quantum crypto is already feasible, if not widely used. Quantum computing is not yet publicly known to be feasible. The practical impact of the feasibility of quantum cryptography is modest, given its complication and given the efficacy of other more familiar cryptographic schemes.

That is, it *does* appear that practical **quantum channels** can be and are being used to communicate with absolute security, in a certain qualified sense. In very rough terms, these are channels designed to be very sensitive to quantum effects, such as changes in state due to observation. The idea is that if anyone eavesdrops on (observes) the channel, this will alter the message for reasons of basic quantum mechanics. Thus, detection of eavesdropping is certain.

A less practical but more dramatic sort of quantum cryptography is **quantum teleportation**, i.e., using the Einstein-Podolsky-Rosen effect [EPR], related to Bell's theorem [Be]. The idea is that if two particles have quantum states which are 'entangled', and then they are separated widely in space, a change of state in one (perhaps caused by an observation being made) *instantly* causes a corresponding change of state in the other. Information has traveled faster than light, and without interaction with any intervening medium. If we could really do this reliably, quantum teleportation would provide absolutely secure communication of a novel type.

There is only very primitive progress (in the public domain, at least) toward building a *quantum computer.* While transistors make use of quantum effects, designers intend for these circuits to behave compatibly with macroscopic objects, *avoiding* the peculiarities of quantum behavior. But by the 1980s *exploitation* rather than *avoidance* of quantum effects had been explicitly considered. For example, R. Feynman noted the infeasibility of using classical computers to efficiently simulate quantum events.

The possible impact of hypothetical quantum computers was unclear until about 1993, at which time Peter Shor's algorithm for factoring large numbers quickly on a quantum computer [Sho1], [Sho2] decisively illustrated the cataclysmic changes that could occur in computation. For example, RSA would be irretrievably broken. Similarly, the discrete log problem in $(\mathbb{Z}/p)^\times$ (p prime) has a polynomial-time quantum algorithm.

Another example of a quantum algorithm which transcends human intuition based on macroscopic processes is Grover's algorithm, which allows a search of an unstructured collection of n things in $\sqrt{n}$ time. Even for ciphers not dependent upon number theoretic issues with polynomial-time quantum algorithms, widespread availability of Grover's algorithm would speed up brute-force attacks, necessitating substantial increases in key lengths in all ciphers.

In the early 1990s enthusiasts were optimistic, but (public-domain) progress toward building a sufficiently large quantum computer has been much slower than hoped. For example, in 2000 [KLMT] reported successful manipulation of 3 qubits, then 5 qubits, and now 7 qubits. In all cases they used nuclear magnetic resonance (NMR).

Even if we imagine that quantum computers will be constructed some time soon, low-level traditional computational techniques must be rebuilt. For example, from [PB], it is impossible to delete a copy of an arbitrary quantum state perfectly. While a classical computer can delete information, and can undo the deletion using a copy, a quantum computer cannot delete quantum information.

A technical issue which has effectively disappeared for classical computers is (internal) *error correction*, and *fault-tolerant* computing. Nowadays classical computers are sufficiently reliable (in hardware) that little internal redundancy is built in. By contrast, the very nature of quantum effects exploited by (hypothetical) quantum computers will require development of quantum error-correction techniques. As a sample, see [CS].

It is unclear whether there will ever be quantum computers accessible to ordinary people. Indeed, one might speculate upon whether ordinary people would be *allowed* to own them.

3 Background on Symmetric Ciphers

Until the 1960's, the only ciphers were **symmetric ciphers**, meaning that knowledge of the encryption key is equivalent to knowledge of the decryption key (modulo feasible computations). It is worthwhile to see why certain old symmetric ciphers fail, as these failures illustrate possible difficulties for the asymmetric (public-key) cipher situation as well. Further, Many contemporary applications of public-key ciphers also make substantial use of (modern) symmetric ciphers, so it would be naive to discuss public-key ciphers without some acknowledgment of symmetric ciphers.

3.1 Bad Old Symmetric Ciphers.

Cryptograms (substitution ciphers), are broken by analysis of letter frequences and small words in English (or other alphabet-based natural languages). The fact that these occur in many newspapers as puzzles should already suggest that they are completely insecure. Shift ciphers and affine ciphers are special cases of cryptograms. Cryptograms give an immediate example of a cipher in which the key space (i.e., set of all possible keys) is fairly large ($26! \sim 4 \cdot 10^{26}$) but the cipher is nevertheless insecure.

Anagrams (permutation ciphers) can be broken by *multiple anagramming.* This means to consider two (or more) ciphertexts encrypted with the same key, to attempt *simultaneous* decryption, rejecting rearrangements if prohibited pairs or triples of letters occur in *either* putative decryption. In a language such as English where many letter combinations are rare or effectively prohibited, this procedure is surprisingly effective. Again, anagrams are ciphers with unlimited key space but nevertheless insecure.

It is worth noting that a fatal systemic weakness in many classical ciphers is that they admit *incremental* or *gradual* decryption, wherein information about the key or plaintext is found a little bit at a time. A good cipher does not allow this, as it is a fatal weakness. And note that various forms of information leakage in naive implementations of modern ciphers give an opening to incremental decryption. From the viewpoint of computational feasibility, a cipher which permits incremental decryption in effect allows an attacker to replace a search through an unstructured set of (for example) 2^n possible decryptions with a search through a binary tree with 2^n leaves, eliminating *branches* of the tree at each step, rather than single leaves. Thus, rather than the 2^n steps for the unstructured case, an attacker may face only n steps to break the cipher.

Vigenère ciphers are interesting **polyalphabetic** ciphers, meaning that they may encrypt the same plaintext character differently depending upon its position. They do not change the position of characters in the plaintext. A Vigenère cipher encrypts a stream

$$x_0 \, x_1 \, x_2 \, \ldots$$

from an alphabet $\mathbb{Z}/N$ using a key $k_0, \ldots, k_{n-1}$ of length n (from $\mathbb{Z}/N$) to the ciphertext

$$\ldots, \; y_i = (x_i + k_{i \,\%\, n}), \; \ldots$$

That is, a potentially infinite sequence is made from the key material by forcing it to repeat, and then the plaintext sequence and periodic key sequence are added termwise. These ciphers do not admit quite so obvious an attack as cryptograms and anagrams, but, nevertheless, are completely broken. An attack using trigrams due to Kasiski as early as 1880 breaks the cipher, as does the even-stronger Friedman attack from the early 20th century (see [G] or [St], for example), unless the key is random and nearly as long as the plaintext itself. Again, Vigenère ciphers have an indefinitely large key space, but this fails to assure security.

Enigma and **Purple** ciphers were WWII ciphers which were broken due to a combination of key distribution flaws, human error, and modest keyspace size. It is worth noting that the break would have been impossible without Alan Turing's innovations in automated computing. One broader lesson from those episodes is that, even though a hardware or software improvement may not convert an exponential-time computation to a polynomial-time computation, reduction by a large constant factor may be decisive in practical terms.

3.2 One-time pads and their failure modes.

The OTP (One-Time Pad) seems to be the only cipher provably secure in absolute terms, i.e., not relative to any unproven assumptions about feasibility of computation. An OTP for a message of length $\leq n$ in alphabet $\mathbb{Z}/2$ uses a *random* key

$$k_0, k_1, \ldots, k_{n-1}$$

of length n, and encrypts a binary plaintext

$$x_0, x_1, \ldots, x_{n-1}$$

to ciphertext

$$\ldots, y_i = x_i + k_i, \ldots \qquad \text{(all in } \mathbb{Z}/2)$$

Each key can be used *only once*. This set-up obviously admits variation. The binary case is sometimes called a **Vernam cipher**.

The proof of security is simply that the *conditional* probability that the plaintext is a particular message *given* the ciphertext is the same as the unconditional probability of the message (i.e., without knowing the ciphertext). In effect, this is the definition of the *randomness* of the key. Intuitively, an attacker learns nothing about the plaintext from seeing the ciphertext.

The operational difficulty is the non-reusability of the key(s), and the requirement that the key(s) be random. Indeed, the **failure modes** of the OTP are catastrophic. For example, if a *periodic* key is used then the OTP becomes a Vigenère cipher, and is broken. If a key is reused, the two messages together effectively create a Vigenère cipher, again creating a break. For that matter, creating securely-random keys is a non-trivial task (9.6).

Thus, **key distribution** and **key generation** are critical bottlenecks for use of OTPs. Nevertheless, because of the security when used properly, OTPs *are* used in critical applications such as nuclear launch security, and highest-level diplomatic communications. The infrastructure costs are too high for more mundane uses.

3.3 DES and AES.

The DES (Digital Encryption Standard) from 1976 was a stop-gap measure which accidentally became a *de facto* standard for 30 years, at least in the United States. It is a symmetric cipher whose antecedent *Lucifer* was designed at IBM, and subsequently tweaked at NSA for reasons which were not explained at the time, and perhaps never quite explained fully. The role of the NSA (perhaps unduly) compromised the world's opinion of this modern cipher. It was never publicly broken structurally, but its too-small keyspace made it obsolete by rendering it vulnerable to brute-force attacks [EFF]. [L1] is a more substantial review of the story of DES.

The new standard, the AES (Advanced Encryption Standard), Rijndael, was chosen in late 2000 as a replacement, from among finalists *MARS* from IBM, *RC6* from RSA Laboratories, *Rijndael* from Joan Daemen and Vincent Rijmen [DR], *Serpent* from Ross Anderson, Eli Biham, and Lars Knudsen, *Twofish* from Bruce

Schneier, John Kelsey, Doug Whiting, David Wagner, Chris Hall, and Niels Ferguson [ST]. The NIST (National Institute of Standards) had stipulated that any patent rights to a candidate cipher would have to be relinquished if the cipher were chosen as the new standard. [L2] discusses AES in a fashion parallel to the discussion of DES in [L1].

DES uses a 64-bit key, of which 8 bits are error-check bits, so it actually has a 56-bit key. The new standard, AES, was mandated by NIST to have 128-bit, 192-bit, and 256-bit keys, and available block sizes of 128, 192, and 256 bits. DES encrypts blocks of 64 bits of plaintext at a time. The AES encrypts blocks of 128, 196, or 256 bits, as mandated.

It is not unreasonable to suppose that the NSA was ahead of public cryptanalytic technique, and in particular was aware of two 'modern' cryptanalytic attacks: **differential cryptanalysis** and **linear cryptanalysis**, beyond brute-force attacks. Very roughly, differential cryptanalysis makes a systematic study of how small changes in plaintext affect the ciphertext. Linear cryptanalysis tries to approximate the effect of encryption by *linear* functions. These and other attacks can be viewed as aiming to effectively demonstrate that the complexity of a cipher is significantly lower than intended. In either case, any detectable pattern allows an attacker increased efficiency. See [St] for a readable account of both these techniques. Differential cryptanalysis was developed by Biham and Shamir [BS1], [BS2], [BS3]. Linear cryptanalysis by Matsui [Mat1], [Mat2]. The analysis of Twofish in [ST] also gives clear examples of these attacks.

We give a rough description of DES for contrast both to AES and to public-key ciphers. A DES encryption consists of 16 **rounds**, meaning repetitions of a simpler process. Each round is **Feistel network**, described just below. Many modern symmetric ciphers are composed of *rounds* each of which is a Feistel network. Rijndael is unusual in that its rounds are *not* Feistel networks.

A **Feistel network** is simple and gives a function *guaranteed to be invertible* and *to be its own inverse.* Fix a positive integer n, which would be 32 in the case of DES. Given a string of $2n$ bits, break them into two parts, the *left* and *right* halves, L and R. View L and R as **vectors** of length n with entries in $\mathbb{F}_2 = \mathbb{Z}/2$. For *any* function f that accepts as inputs n bits and produces an output of n bits, the corresponding Feistel network F_f takes two n-bit pieces L and R as inputs, and produces $2n$ bits of output by

$$F_f(L, R) = (L + f(R), R)$$

where $+$ is vector addition in $\mathbb{F}_2^n$. The key property of a Feistel network is the obvious feature that F_f is invertible and is its own inverse. Each **round** of DES is an enhanced version of the Feistel network we just described, with a specific choice of the function f, depending on the key.

In DES, at the very outset, the 64-bit key has every eighth bit removed, leaving just 56 bits of key material. An important feature of DES (as with most symmetric ciphers) is that each round uses a different 48-bit **subkey** of the 56-bit key. The description of the round subkeys is **key scheduling**, and is a critical feature of any cipher. For each round of DES, the key is broken into two 28-bit halves, each of which is shifted left (with wrap-around) by either 1 or 2 bits, depending upon which round we're in, by an irregular pattern which we'll suppress. Then the *shifted* batch of 56 bits is mapped to 48 bits by a **'compression permutation'** (it's not invertible). The compression permutation is the same for each round, though we won't give it here. So the result of the initial key permutation, with the round-dependent shifts by 1 or 2 bits, followed by the compression permutation, produces a 48-bit **subkey** for each of the 16 rounds.

As indicated above, each round of DES manipulates halves of the text, in a manner that depends on the round subkey. Let L_i be the left half in the ith round, and let R_i be the right half in the ith round. The formula to get from one round to the next is of the form

$$(L_i, R_i) = (R_{i-1}, L_{i-1} + f(R_{i-1}))$$

where f depends on the ith subkey. That is, in addition to the Feistel trick we *interchange* halves of the text, so that both halves will get obscured in the course of several rounds. We must describe the function f and how it depends on the round subkey.

For each round, the right half R_{i-1} has applied to it a fixed (rather simple) **'expansion permutation'** or **E-box**, which accepts 32-bit inputs and creates 48-bit outputs, given by a random-looking formula we'll suppress. The pattern is *not* very complicated, but does have the critical effect of allowing one bit of the text to affect more than one bit of the expanded version. This is an **avalanche effect**. At each round, the 48-bit output from the E-box is added to the 48-bit subkey for that round, both treated as vectors in $\mathbb{F}_2^{48}$.

The most serious and mysterious part of DES, critical to security, is the application of the **substitution boxes**, or **S-boxes** to the 48 bits coming from adding the subkey to the output from the E-box. There are 8 S-boxes, each of which takes a 6-bit input and produces a 4-bit output. The 48 bits are broken into 8 pieces of 6 bits each and fed to the S-boxes. The outputs are concatenated to give a 32-bit output. Each of the S-boxes is given by an input-output table. (The explicit listing of these would be unenlightening, and we resist the temptation to prove the point.)

After all 16 rounds, *not* exchanging left and right halves after the last (16th) round, a *final permutation* is applied to the text. The output is the completed ciphertext. Happily, because of the Feistel network property, and by the relatively simple choice of the initial and final permutation, exactly the same process (with the same key) **decrypts**.

The details we've suppressed seem to admit no simple description, which is to say that there appears to be no clarifying underlying pattern offering an explanation. While possibly frustrating from a certain viewpoint which effectively believes in unlimited compressibility of description, from a Kolmogoroff (program) complexity viewpoint the situation is reasonable, or even desirable in terms of resistance to cryptanalytic attacks. That is, it might be argued that the ineffability of the *details* of DES (as opposed to its broad description as 16 rounds of a Feistel network) is essential to its security.

Once more, it appears that DES eventually failed only because its keyspace was too small, *not* because of any (public-knowledge) structural weakness. It is also true that its block size was small enough so that, with vastly increased machine capabilities, one could contemplate dictionary attacks if DES were operated in the most naive mode (which no cipher should be).

AES, Rijndael: Of all the AES candidates, Rijndael is/was the most mathematically structured. Rijndael can accommodate key sizes of 128, 192, or 256 bits (versus 56 for DES). It acts on plaintexts of block sizes 128, 192, or 256 bits. Rijndael is composed of *rounds*, with 10, 12, or 16 rounds depending on the key size. Each round, rather than being a Feistel network, has four parts:

$$\text{State} \longrightarrow \text{ByteSub(State)} = \text{Affine(Inverse(State))}$$

$$\text{State} \longrightarrow \text{ShiftRow(State)}$$

$$\text{State} \longrightarrow \text{MixColumn(State) (except in the final round)}$$

$$\text{State} \longrightarrow \text{AddRoundKey(State)}$$

described in more detail below. (These names are used in the semi-official Java description/implementation of Rijndael.)

First, whatever the block size, the 128, 196, or 256 bits are grouped into bunches of 8 bits as *bytes*, and then read into a 4-by-n matrix, where n is 4, 6, or 8, respectively.

The *ByteSub* operation acts on each byte of the text, and is the analogue of the *S-boxes* in DES and many other ciphers. The *Inverse* operation is inversion in the finite field $\mathbb{F}_{2^8}$ with 2^8 elements, modeled as $\mathbb{F}_2[x]$ modulo the irreducible ('Rijndael') octic

$$x^8 + x^4 + x^3 + x + 1$$

and taking representatives which are polynomials of degree less than 8. The 8 bits are taken as the coefficients in $\mathbb{F}_2$ of such a representative polynomial. The *Affine* map is the second half of Rijndael's *S-box*, consisting of the $\mathbb{F}_2$-affine map

$$x \longrightarrow Ax + b$$

on $\mathbb{F}_2^8$ where

$$A = \begin{pmatrix} 1 & 0 & 0 & 0 & 1 & 1 & 1 & 1 \\ 1 & 1 & 0 & 0 & 0 & 1 & 1 & 1 \\ 1 & 1 & 1 & 0 & 0 & 0 & 1 & 1 \\ 1 & 1 & 1 & 1 & 0 & 0 & 0 & 1 \\ 1 & 1 & 1 & 1 & 1 & 0 & 0 & 0 \\ 0 & 1 & 1 & 1 & 1 & 1 & 0 & 0 \\ 0 & 0 & 1 & 1 & 1 & 1 & 1 & 0 \\ 0 & 0 & 0 & 1 & 1 & 1 & 1 & 1 \end{pmatrix} \qquad b = \begin{pmatrix} 1 \\ 1 \\ 0 \\ 0 \\ 0 \\ 1 \\ 1 \\ 0 \end{pmatrix}$$

and now a byte is viewed as an element of $\mathbb{F}_2^8$. Note that A is a circulant matrix.

The *ShiftRow* and *MixColumn* operations are more elementary *diffusion* operations. *ShiftRow* acts on the 4-by-n matrix of bytes by leaving the top row alone, shifting the second row to the right by 1 (with wrap-around), shifting the third row to the right by 2 (with wrap-around), and the bottom row by 3 (with wrap-around). The *MixColumn* operation acts on each column of the 4-by-n matrix of bytes, by left multiplication by the (circulant) matrix

$$\begin{pmatrix} 02 & 03 & 01 & 01 \\ 01 & 02 & 03 & 01 \\ 01 & 01 & 02 & 03 \\ 03 & 01 & 01 & 02 \end{pmatrix}$$

where the entries are in hexadecimal (i.e., base 16).

The *AddKey* operation is, as usual, simply an addition of the text with the round subkey (as vectors over $\mathbb{F}_2$). The non-trivial part of the keyed part of each round is *key scheduling*. In the case of Rijndael, key scheduling is the least comprehensible and least obviously structured of the whole, using an irregular recursion which invokes hard-coded constants. See the AES homepage [AES] for these details.

4 Review of Number Theory

The algorithms here are well-known and are discussed in many sources. We emphasize that the fundamental arithmetic operations, namely addition, subtraction, multiplication, and division-with-remainder, all require a number of single-digit operations (or, essentially equivalently, *bit-operations*) at most polynomial in the number of digits of the integers. Optimization of these operations is not our immediate concern, but can have a practical impact (see [Ber], [Kn]).

4.1 Euclidean algorithm. To compute *gcd*'s, and to compute $e^{-1} \bmod m$, use the familiar Euclidean algorithm. To compute $\gcd(x, y)$:

Initialize $X = x$, $Y = y$, $R = X \bmod Y$
while $R > 0$
    replace X by Y
    replace Y by R
    replace R by $X \bmod Y$
When $R = 0$, $Y = \gcd(x, y)$

To compute $\gcd(x, y)$ takes at most $2\log_2 y$ steps, if $x \geq y$, since one can readily show that in any *two* steps the sizes of the variables X, Y decrease by at least a factor of 2.

4.2 Extended Euclidean algorithm. To compute multiplicative inverses $e^{-1} \bmod x$ with $\gcd(e, x) = 1$, minimizing memory use, rewrite each of the steps in the previous as

$$\begin{pmatrix} 0 & 1 \\ 1 & 0 \end{pmatrix} \begin{pmatrix} 1 & -q \\ 0 & 1 \end{pmatrix} \begin{pmatrix} X \\ Y \end{pmatrix} = \begin{pmatrix} \text{new } X \\ \text{new } Y \end{pmatrix}$$

where $R = X - qY$ with $|R| < Y$. Thus, we obtain an integral matrix $\begin{pmatrix} a & b \\ c & d \end{pmatrix}$ with determinant ± 1 such that

$$\begin{pmatrix} a & b \\ c & d \end{pmatrix} \begin{pmatrix} x \\ e \end{pmatrix} = \begin{pmatrix} \gcd(x, e) \\ 0 \end{pmatrix}$$

When $\gcd(x, e) = 1$, we have

$$ax + be = 1$$

and thus

$$b = e^{-1} \bmod x$$

The two integers a, b with that property $ax + be = 1$ are useful in a computational form of **Sun-Ze**'s theorem (the so-called *Chinese Remainder Theorem*): given x and e relatively prime, and arbitrary s, t, the simultaneous system of congruences

$$\begin{cases} y &= s \bmod x \\ y &= t \bmod e \end{cases}$$

has a unique solution y modulo $x \cdot e$, given by

$$y = ax \cdot t + be \cdot s \bmod xe$$

4.3 Square-and-multiply fast exponentiation. To compute $x^e \,\%\, m$, keep track of a triple (X, E, Y) initialized to be $(X, E, Y) = (x, e, 1)$. At each step of the algorithm:

For E odd replace Y by by $(X \times Y) \,\%\, m$ and replace E by $E - 1$
For E even replace X by $(X \times X) \,\%\, m$ and replace E by $E/2$
When $E = 0$ the value of Y is $x^e \,\%\, m$

This algorithm takes at most $2 \log_2 E$ steps.

4.4 Fermat's Little Theorem. This asserts that for p prime, for an arbitrary integer b

$$b^p = b \bmod p$$

This has an elementary proof by induction on b, using properties of binomial coefficients, but also is a special case of Euler's theorem (4.5).

The converse of Fermat's theorem is false, but not *very* false. The only *non-prime* $n < 5000$ with $2^n = 2 \bmod n$ are

341, 561, 645, 1105, 1387, 1729, 1905, 2047

2465, 2701, 2821, 3277, 4033, 4369 4371, 4681

Requiring also $3^n = 3 \bmod n$ leaves

561, 1105, 1729, 2465, 2701, 2821

Requiring also $5^n = 5 \bmod n$ leaves

561, 1105, 1729, 2465, 2821

Compared with 669 primes under 5000, this is a *false positive* failure rate of less than 1%. We say that n is a **Fermat pseudoprime base** b if $b^n = b \bmod n$. There are only 172 non-prime Fermat pseudoprimes base 2 under 500,000 versus 41,538 primes, a false positive rate of less than 0.41% There are only 49 non-prime Fermat pseudoprimes base 2 and 3 under 500,000, a false positive rate of less than 0.118% There are only 32 non-prime Fermat pseudoprimes base 2, 3, 5 under 500,000:

561	1105	1729	2465	2821	6601	8911	10585
15841	29341	41041	46657	52633	62745	63973	75361
101101	115921	126217	162401	172081	188461	252601	278545
294409	314821	334153	340561	399001	410041	449065	488881

Sadly, adding more such requirements does not shrink these lists further. n is a **Carmichael number** if it is a *non-prime* Fermat pseudoprime to *every* base b. In 1994 Alford, Granville, and Pomerance [AGP] showed that there are infinitely-many Carmichael numbers. And it appears that among *large* numbers Carmichael numbers become more common. It is relatively elementary to prove that a Carmichael number must be odd, square-free, and divisible by at least three primes.

4.5 Euler's Theorem. This is a generalization of Fermat's Little Theorem to composite moduli. Let $\varphi(n)$ be Euler's *totient function*, which counts the integers ℓ in the range $1 \le \ell \le n$ which are relatively prime to n. For $\gcd(x, m) = 1$

$$x^{\varphi(n)} = 1 \bmod n$$

This is an immediate corollary of Lagrange's theorem, applied to the multplicative group $\mathbb{Z}/n^\times$ of $\mathbb{Z}/n$.

Euler's theorem proves that **RSA decryption works**, using $\varphi(pq) = (p-1)(q-1)$: with $y = x^e \bmod n$, letting $ed = 1 + M \cdot \varphi(n)$, all equalities modulo n,

$$y^d = (x^e)^d = x^{1+M\cdot\varphi(n)} = x \cdot (x^{\varphi(n)})^M = x \cdot 1^M = x \bmod n$$

4.6 Primitive roots, discrete logarithms. A primitive root b modulo m is a generator for the group $(\mathbb{Z}/m)^\times$. Existence of a primitive root modulo m is equivalent to the cyclic-ness of the multiplicative group $(\mathbb{Z}/m)^\times$. For p prime, $(\mathbb{Z}/p)^\times$ is cyclic, because $\mathbb{Z}/p$ is a field. Relatively elementary arguments then show that there are primitive roots modulo p^ℓ and $2p^\ell$ for $p > 2$ prime, and modulo 4. Non-existence of primitive roots for all other moduli is easier. This was understood by Fermat and Euler.

Because of the cyclic-ness of $(\mathbb{Z}/p)^\times$ for $p > 2$ prime, we have **Euler's criterion**: $b \in (\mathbb{Z}/p)^\times$ is a square modulo p if and only if

$$b^{(p-1)/2} = 1 \bmod p$$

An analogous result holds for q^{th} powers when p is a prime with $p = 1 \bmod q$.

Modulo a prime p, for a fixed primitive root b, for $x \in (\mathbb{Z}/p)^\times$ the **discrete logarithm** or **index** of x modulo p base g is the integer ℓ (uniquely determined modulo $p-1$) such that

$$x = b^\ell \bmod p$$

4.7 Futility of trial division. Trial division attempts to divide a given number N by integers from 2 up through $\sqrt{N}$. Either we find a proper factor of N, or N is prime. (If N has a proper factor ℓ larger than $\sqrt{N}$, then $N/\ell \le \sqrt{N}$.) The extreme case takes roughly $\sqrt{N}$ steps. A crude estimate shows the hopelessness of factoring integers by trial division in the range relevant to public-key cryptography. If $N \sim 10^{200}$ is prime, or if it is the product of two primes each $\sim 10^{100}$, then it will take about 10^{100} trial divisions to discover this. (Minor clevernesses do not seriously reduce this number.) If we could do 10^{12} trials per second, and if there were a 10^{12} hosts on the internet, with $< 10^8$ seconds per year, a massively parallel trial division would take 10^{68} years. Even if CPU speeds were to increase by a factor of 10^{10}, this would still leave 10^{58} years.

Concrete examples of trial division runtimes. Someone who had not been paying attention might still think that trial division does succeed. Some very specific examples, done on a 2.44 Gigahertz machine, coded in C++ using GMP:

1002904102901	has factor	1001401	('instantaneous')
100001220001957	has factor	10000019	(3 seconds)
10000013000000861	has factor	100000007	(27 seconds)
1000000110000000721	has factor	1000000007	(4 minutes)

Nowhere near 10^{200}, and the runtimes are ballooning already.

4.8 Quadratic reciprocity. For an odd prime p, the **quadratic symbol** or **Legendre symbol** $(b/p)_2$ is

$$\left(\frac{b}{p}\right)_2 = \begin{cases} 0 & \text{if } \gcd(b,p) > 1 \\ 1 & \text{if } x^2 = b \bmod p \text{ has a solution } x \text{ and } \gcd(b,p) = 1 \\ -1 & \text{if } x^2 = b \bmod p \text{ has no solution } x \text{ and } \gcd(b,p) = 1 \end{cases}$$

For arbitrary integers n factored as

$$n = 2^{e_0} p_1^{e_1} \dots p_k^{e_k}$$

with odd primes p_i, the **extended quadratic symbol** or **Jacobi symbol** is

$$\left(\frac{b}{n}\right)_2 = \left(\frac{b}{p_1}\right)_2^{e_1} \cdots \left(\frac{b}{p_k}\right)_2^{e_k}$$

While for p prime the quadratic (Legendre) symbol $(b/p)_2$ tells whether or not b is a square modulo p, this is *not* the case for non-prime n. Thus, the Jacobi symbol is of interest mostly as an auxiliary gadget useful in computation of Legendre symbols. Its utility in this auxiliary role is due to the fact that Jacobi symbols *can be computed quickly* using quadratic reciprocity (4.8).

With this notation, Euler's criterion for b to be a square modulo prime p is

$$\left(\frac{b}{p}\right)_2 = b^{(p-1)/2} \bmod p$$

From this follows the basic multiplicative property of quadratic symbols (for prime p)

$$\left(\frac{ab}{p}\right)_2 = \left(\frac{a}{p}\right)_2 \cdot \left(\frac{b}{p}\right)_2$$

The multiplicative property for the Jacobi symbols is analogous: For arbitrary odd integer n, and for a and b relatively prime to n,

$$\left(\frac{ab}{n}\right)_2 = \left(\frac{a}{n}\right)_2 \cdot \left(\frac{b}{n}\right)_2$$

This follows directly from considering a prime factorization of n and invoking the multiplicativity of the Legendre symbol.

The **Law of Quadratic Reciprocity** is the first result of *modern* number theory. Lagrange had conjectured it in the late 18th century, but it was not proven until 1796, by Gauss. From a naive viewpoint, there is no reason why any such thing should be true. But, by now, 200 years later, this result has been well assimilated and is understood as the simplest representative of a whole family of *reciprocity laws*, themselves part of *classfield theory*, itself has been assimilated into the Langlands program. Quadratic reciprocity asserts that, for distinct odd primes p and q,

$$\left(\frac{p}{q}\right)_2 = (-1)^{(p-1)\cdot(q-1)/4} \left(\frac{q}{p}\right)_2$$

Also there are the *supplementary laws*

$$\left(\frac{-1}{p}\right)_2 = (-1)^{(p-1)/2}$$

$$\left(\frac{2}{p}\right)_2 = (-1)^{(p^2-1)/8}$$

Granting this, we have an algorithm for telling whether $x^2 = c \bmod p$ is solvable or not, although this does not *find* the square root if it exists. The difference between *proving existence* of the square root and the harder task of *finding it* is parallel to the difference between proving that a number *fails to be prime* and actually *finding a proper factor*. Indeed, apart from taking out powers of 2, there is no reason to factor into primes the inputs to these quadratic symbols! This is especially relevant for large integers.

As a corollary, we have *(Quadratic Reciprocity for Jacobi symbols)*: For m, n odd positive integers

$$\left(\frac{m}{n}\right)_2 = (-1)^{(m-1)(n-1)/4} \left(\frac{n}{m}\right)_2$$

4.9 The Prime Number Theorem. This theorem asserts that the number $\pi(x)$ of primes below x has the asymptotic property

$$\pi(x) \sim \frac{x}{\ln x}$$

meaning that

$$\lim_{x \to \infty} \frac{\pi(x)}{x/\ln x} = 1$$

This was proven independently in 1896 by Hadamard and de la Vallèe Poussin. The argument has been greatly simplified since then, but still makes essential use of the fact that the (analytically continued) Riemann-Euler zeta function

$$\zeta(s) = \sum_{n=1}^{\infty} \frac{1}{n^s}$$

is non-zero on the line $\mathrm{Re}(s) = 1$, at the edge of the region of convergence in the complex plane.

As a raw heuristic, from the Prime Number Theorem we imagine that roughly $1/\ln n$ of integers near n are prime. Equivalently, we expect to test about $\frac{1}{2}\ln n$ randomly chosen integers near n before finding a prime. Note that this is laughably unsupported without knowing an error term in the assertion of asymptotics of the prime-counting function $\pi(x)$. Nevertheless, it is useful to think of the primes as having *density* $1/\ln n$ near n.

4.10 The Riemann Hypothesis (RH). From 1858 or so, this is the conjecture that all the zeros of (the analytically continued) $\zeta(s)$ in the strip $0 < \mathrm{Re}(s) < 1$ actually lie on the middle *critical* line $\mathrm{Re}(s) = 1/2$. If this were true, then we would have a much better error term in the prime number theorem than any presently known, namely

$$\pi(x) = \mathrm{li}(x) + O(\sqrt{x}\ln x)$$

where

$$\mathrm{li}(x) = \int_2^x \frac{dt}{\ln t} \sim \frac{x}{\ln x}$$

differs slightly from $x/\ln x$, though is roughly asymptotic to it. (The proof that RH implies this error term took several decades of development in complex analysis.) If this were so, then there would be rigorous justification for the heuristic that primes have density $1/\ln n$ near n.

4.11 Dirichlet's Theorem. This theorem on primes in arithmetic progressions is that for $\gcd(a, N) = 1$ there are infinitely many primes in the arithmetic progression

$$\{a + N\ell : \ell = 1, 2, 3, \ldots\}$$

This can be proven simply for some special values of a, such as $a = 1$, but is best proven using the behavior of *Dirichlet L-functions*

$$L(s, \chi) = \sum_{n \geq 1} \frac{\chi(n)}{n^s}$$

where χ is a *Dirichlet character* modulo some N, meaning that $\chi(n)$ depends only upon n mod N, and that χ has the multiplicative property $\chi(mn) = \chi(m)\chi(n)$. A little more specifically, as Euler proved the infinitude of primes from the blowing-up of $\zeta(s)$ as $s \to 1^+$, Dirichlet proved this theorem from the fact that for χ taking values other than 1 the L-function $L(s, \chi)$ has a non-zero *finite* limit as $s \to 1^+$.

4.12 The Extended Riemann Hypothesis (ERH). This is a similar conjecture about the zeros of the (analytically continued) Dirichlet L-functions, that the only zeros of these L-functions in the strip $0 < \mathrm{Re}(s) < 1$ actually lie on the middle *critical* line $\mathrm{Re}(s) = 1/2$. This conjecture would imply a sharp error term for the asymptotics of primes in arithmetic sequences. Also, the ERH arises in many questions other basic questions, such as estimates relevant to a deterministic form of the Miller-Rabin pseudoprimality test (4.13).

4.13 Pseudoprimes, probable primes. We should substantiate the assertion that testing large integers for primality is feasible. First, any practical procedure to hunt for large primes typically uses Fermat's pseudo-primality testing base 2 as a first filter, given the simplicity of this test (and the square-and-multiply algorithm). Recently it has been shown [AKS], [Bor], [Ber] that there is a deterministic polynomial-time algorithm to test primality. However, it seems that the algorithm is slower than the best probabilistic algorithms, so will not replace them in the short run. About **terminology**: we will call an integer that has passed some primality test a *pseudoprime*. This usage is not universal. Sometimes the term *pseudoprime* is meant to refer only to a *non-prime* integer that has, nevertheless, passed a primality test, reserving the term *probable prime* for integers that have passed a test but whose actual primality is unknown.

The first probabilistic (pseudo-) primality test which admitted a useful analysis was that of Solovay and Strassen [So] from 1977. The provable result is that, if n were composite, then at least half the integers b in the range $1 < b < n$ would detect this via the Solovay-Strassen test. Specifically, an integer n passes the **Euler pseudoprime** (Solovay-Strassen) test base b if

$$b^{(n-1)/2} = \left(\frac{b}{n}\right)_2 \mod n$$

where the right-hand side is an extended (Jacobi) quadratic symbol.

A better test with provable behavior is the **Miller-Rabin** test [Ra], [M] for 'strong' pseudoprimes, from 1978–80. To explain why this test might work, first note that for $n = r \cdot s$ composite (with $\gcd(r, s) = 1$), by Sun-Ze's theorem there are at least 4 solutions to

$$x^2 = 1 \mod n$$

Namely, there are 4 choices of sign in

$$x = \pm 1 \mod r \quad x = \pm 1 \mod s$$

Thus, if we find $b \neq \pm 1 \bmod n$ such that $b^2 = 1 \bmod n$, n is definitely *not* composite. Roughly, the **Miller-Rabin test** (details shortly) looks for such extra square roots of 1 modulo n.

Theorem: (Miller-Rabin) For composite n, at least 3/4 of b in the range $1 < b < n$ will detect the compositeness (via the Miller-Rabin test).

Pseudo-corollary: If n passes the Miller-Rabin test with k random bases b, then

$$\text{'probability } n \text{ is prime'} \geq 1 - \left(\frac{1}{4}\right)^k$$

The **Miller-Rabin test base** b is

```
factor n − 1 = 2^s · m with m odd
replace b by b^m mod n
    if b = ±1 mod n stop: n is 3/4 prime
    else continue
set r = 0
while r < s
    replace b by b^2 mod n
    if b = −1 mod n stop: n is 3/4 prime
    elsif b = +1 mod n stop: n is composite
    else continue
    replace r by r + 1
if we fall out of the loop, n is composite.
```

If n passes this test it is a **strong pseudoprime base** b. The proof is not terribly difficulty, but is not short, and requires attention to detail. See [BS], [Ko1], [G]. In the course of the proof one also verifies that strong pseudoprimes base b are a subset of Euler pseudoprimes base b, which are themselves a subset of the Fermat pseudoprimes base b.

If the *Generalized Riemann Hypothesis* were true, then for composite n there would be $1 < b < 2\log^2 n$ such that n fails the test base b (see [M]). But even if we knew the truth of the Generalized Riemann Hypothesis, we would not use $2\log^2 n$ bases b in the Miller-Rabin test, since a mere 20 (or 50, or 100 would provide sufficient surety, and would take much less time.

Failure rate of Miller-Rabin? The fraction of b's which detect compositeness is apparently much greater than 3/4. For $n = 21311$ the detection rate is 0.9976. For 64777 the detection rate is 0.99972. For 1112927 the detection rate is 0.9999973. Under 50,000 there are only 9 non-prime strong pseudoprimes base 2, namely 2047, 3277, 4033, 4681, 8321, 15841, 29341, 42799, 49141. Under 500,000 there are only 33 non-prime strong pseudoprimes base 2. Under 500,000 there are *no* non-prime strong pseudoprimes base 2 and 3. In the range $100,000,000 < n < 101,000,000$ there are 3 strong pseudoprimes base 2 whose compositeness is detected base 3, namely 100463443, 100618933, 100943201.

4.14 Hunting for big primes. A naive but reasonable approach to find a (probable) prime above a lower bound $2n$, assuming no randomness properties are needed, is as follows. The test to which we will subject each candidate N is:

```
Trial division by a few small primes:
    if N passes, continue, else reject N at this point
Fermat pseudoprime test base 2
```

if N passes, continue, else reject N at this point
Miller-Rabin pseudoprime test base with bases
the first 20 primes

Then test $N = 2n + 1$. If it passes, we're done. If not, replace N by $N + 2$ and continue. Our heuristic from the Prime Number Theorem is that we expect to test roughly $\frac{1}{2} \cdot \frac{\ln n}{n}$ candidates near n before finding a prime.

As examples, we hunt using Fermat base 2, and then Miller-Rabin base 2, 3, 5, to find the next prime after some representative starting points. Even the 1000-digit computation took only 90 seconds.

First 'prime' after	10^{21}	is	$10^{21} + 117$
First 'prime' after	10^{50}	is	$10^{50} + 151$
First 'prime' after	10^{100}	is	$10^{100} + 267$
First 'prime' after	10^{200}	is	$10^{200} + 357$
First 'prime' after	10^{300}	is	$10^{300} + 331$
First 'prime' after	10^{1000}	is	$10^{1000} + 453$

4.15 Generating big random primes. When a cipher or protocol calls for a *random* prime above 2^{1024}, one should not pick the first (probable) prime above 2^{1024} each time, to say the least. Rather, for example, one could reasonably use 1024 random bits $b_0, b_1, \ldots, b_{1023}$ and start testing at

$$N = 2^{1024} + \sum_{i=0}^{1023} b_i \cdot 2^i$$

This leaves open the question of generating high-enough quality random bits for this purpose.

4.16 Continued fractions. For real x the recursion

$$\begin{array}{lllr} a_0 & = & \text{floor}(x) & x_1 = 1/(x - a_0) \\ a_1 & = & \text{floor}(x_1) & x_2 = 1/(x - a_1) \\ a_2 & = & \text{floor}(x_2) & x_3 = 1/(x - a_2) \\ & \ldots & & \end{array}$$

gives

$$x = a_0 + \cfrac{1}{a_0 + \cfrac{1}{a_1 + \cfrac{1}{a_2 + \ddots + \cfrac{1}{a_n + x_n}}}}$$

The usual notational relief is to write this as

$$x = a_0 + \frac{1}{a_1 +} \frac{1}{a_2 +} \cdots \frac{1}{a_n + x_n}$$

The **nth convergent** p_n/q_n is obtained by truncating

$$\frac{p_n}{q_n} = a_0 + \frac{1}{a_1 +} \frac{1}{a_2 +} \cdots \frac{1}{a_n}$$

where the numerator p_n and denominator q_n are relatively prime integers. For example, because

$$x = 1 + \frac{1}{1 + x}$$

has positive root $\sqrt{2}$

$$\sqrt{2} = 1 + \frac{1}{2+}\frac{1}{2+}\cdots$$

Similarly,

$$\frac{1+\sqrt{5}}{2} = 1 + \frac{1}{1+}\frac{1}{1+}\cdots$$

The recursion for the convergents in terms of the integers a_i appearing in the expansion is

$$p_i = a_i p_{i-1} + p_{i-2}$$

$$q_i = a_i q_{i-1} + q_{i-2}$$

In a similar vein, one can easily verify that

$$p_{n+1}/q_{n+1} - p_n/q_n = \frac{(-1)^n}{q_n\, q_{n+1}}$$

and x is always between successive convergents

$$p_{2n}/q_{2n} \le x \le p_{2n+1}/q_{2n+1}$$

These convergents are the best rational approximations to x for given size of denominator.

4.17 Square roots modulo primes. These can be computed quickly by a probabilistic algorithm. This is a necessary ingredient in the *quadratic sieve* (8.4). As a preamble, recall from above that for a prime p equal to 3 modulo 4, and for a square b mod p we have

$$\text{square root of } b \bmod p = b^{(p+3)/4} \bmod p$$

This (deterministic) formula is a special case of the following (probabilistic) algorithm.

Suppose that b is a square modulo p. This can be tested efficiently by Euler's criterion, or by quadratic symbol computations. Remove all the factors of 2 from $p-1$, giving

$$p - 1 = 2^s \cdot (\text{odd})m$$

Our first approximation at a square root of b mod p is

$$c = b^{(m+1)/2} \bmod p$$

Specifically, we claim that

$$c^2/b = 2^{s-1}\text{th root of unity mod } p$$

Indeed, modulo p,

$$(c^2/b)^{2^{s-1}} = ((b^{(m+1)/2})^2 \cdot b^{-1})^{2^{s-1}} = b^{(m+1)\cdot 2^{s-1}} \cdot b^{-2^{s-1}} = b^{(p-1)/2} = \left(\frac{b}{p}\right)_2$$

by Euler. So it remains to modify c by a 2^sth root of unity mod p to get the actual square root of b.

Let g be a *non-square* modulo p. Again, testing whether a randomly chosen g is a square or not is easy, and if one chooses unluckily one simply tries again, knowing that half the integers mod p are non-squares. Claim that $h = g^m \,\%\, p$ is a *primitive* 2^sth root of 1 modulo p. Indeed, by Fermat's Little Theorem it is *a* 2^sth root of unity. If h were a 2^{s-1}th root of unity, then (since primitive roots exist modulo p) h would be a square, which it is not.

Thus, we wish to determine an integer $0 \le j < 2^{s-1}$ such that

$$h^j \cdot c = \text{ square root of } b \bmod p$$

Write j in binary

$$j = j_0 + j_1 \cdot 2^1 + j_2 \cdot 2^2 + \ldots + j_{s-2} \cdot 2^{s-2}$$

with $j_i \in \{0, 1\}$. We recursively determine the coefficients j_i as follows. First, compute

$$(c^2/b)^{2^{s-2}} \% p$$

Above, we saw that the square of this is 1 mod p so it is ± 1. If it is $+1$, take $j_0 = 0$, and if it is -1, take $j_0 = 1$. Thus

$$(h^{j_0} c)^2/a \text{ is a } 2^{s-2}\text{th root of 1 mod } p$$

Inductively, suppose $j_0, \ldots, j_k$ have been chosen, such that

$$(h^{j_0 + \ldots + j_k 2^k} \cdot c)^2/b$$

is a 2^{s-k-2}th root of 1 mod p. Compute

$$\left((h^{j_0 + \ldots + j_k 2^k} \cdot c)^2/b\right)^{2^{s-k-3}} = \pm 1$$

If the value is $+1$, take $j_{k+1} = 0$, and take $j_{k+1} = 0$ if the value is -1. Thus, finally,

$$(h^{j_0 + \ldots + j_{s-2} 2^{s-2}} \cdot c)^2/b = 1$$

which is to say that

$$h^{j_0 + \ldots + j_{s-2} 2^{s-2}} \cdot c = \text{ square root of } b \bmod p$$

Example: To find a square root of $b = 2$ modulo $p = 401$, first take out the powers of 2 from $p - 1$

$$p - 1 = 401 - 1 = 2^4 \cdot 25$$

Thus, in the notation above, $m = 25$, and $s = 4$. Let

$$c = b^{(m+1)/2} = 2^{(25+1)/2} = 2^{13} = 172 \bmod 401$$

From above,

$$c^2/b = 172^2/2 = 172^2 \cdot 201 = 356 \bmod 101$$

is not 1, so $c = 172$ is not a square root of 2 mod 401. Test $g = 3$ to see whether or not it is a square mod 401: via the square and multiply algorithm gives

$$3^{(401-1)/2} = -1 \bmod 401$$

so $g = 3$ is a non-square. Thus, a primitive $2^s = 2^4$ root of unity mod p is

$$h = g^m = 3^{25} = 268 \bmod 401$$

Compute

$$(c^2/b)^{2^{s-2}} = (172^2/2)^4 = -1 \bmod 401$$

so take $j_0 = 1$. Next, compute

$$((h^{j_0} \cdot c)^2/b)^{2^{s-3}} = ((268 \cdot 172)^2/2)^2 = -1 \bmod 401$$

so $j_1 = 1$. According to the discussion, it should be that

$$h^{j_0+j_1 2} \cdot c = 268^{1+2} \cdot 172 = 348 \bmod 401$$

is a square root of 2 modulo 401, as indeed can be checked.

4.18 Hensel's lemma. This is an efficient device to find solutions of polynomial equations modulo p^{e+1} from solutions modulo p^e. It is an ingredient in the quadratic sieve, among many other things. It is an analogue of the Newton-Raphson method of approximating *real* roots of polynomials over $\mathbb{R}$, but works better.

Let $f(x)$ be a polynomial with integer coefficients, let p be a prime, and suppose that we have an integer x_0 such that for an integer exponent $e > 0$

$$f(x_0) = 0 \bmod p^e$$

while

$$f'(x_0) \neq 0 \bmod p$$

where f' is the usual derivative of f. Let $f'(x_0)^{-1}$ be an integer which is a multiplicative inverse to $f'(x_0)$ mod p. Then the simplest form of Hensel's lemma asserts that

$$x_1 = x_0 - f(x_0) \cdot f'(x_0)^{-1}$$

satisfies

$$f(x_1) = 0 \bmod p^{e+1}$$

For example to find a square root of 2 modulo 17^3, take $f(x) = x^2 - 2$, and begin with $x_0 = 6$, since $f(6) = 0 \bmod 17$. Here

$$f'(6) = 2 \cdot 6 = 12$$

for which an inverse modulo 17 is 10 (e.g., by extended Euclid). Thus,

$$x_1 = x_0 - f(x_0) \cdot f'(x_0)^{-1} = 6 - 34 \cdot 10 = 244 \bmod 17^2$$

For a square root x_2 modulo 17^3, we can re-use $f'(x_0)$, and continue to obtain

$$x_2 = x_1 - f(x_1) \cdot 10 = 244 - (244 \cdot 244 - 2) \cdot 10 = 4290 \bmod 17^3$$

which (as can be readily verified) is a square root of 2 modulo 17^3.

Solving equations $x^2 = n \bmod 2^e$ is slightly more complicated, and, at some point one certainly will view Hensel's lemma as a p-adic algorithm in order to fit the whole thing into a more stable world-view. But for our immediate purposes (e.g., the quadratic sieve (8.4)), observe that the only odd square modulo 4 is 1, and the only odd square modulo 8 is still 1. But for $n = 1 \bmod 8$, and with $x^2 = n \bmod 2^e$ with $e \geq 3$, the step becomes

$$\text{replace } x \text{ by } x - \frac{(x^2 - n)/2}{x} \bmod 2^{e+1}$$

Then $x^2 = n \bmod 2^{e+1}$.

5 More public-key ciphers

We briefly describe some other public-key ciphers, to illustrate the variety of trapdoors which have been exploited.

5.1 El Gamal Ciphers.

This idea appeared in [ElGamal 1985]. It is slightly more complicated than RSA, but still essentially elementary, and admits abstraction to arbitrary groups in place of $\mathbb{Z}/p^\times$. For example, the elliptic-curve cryptosystems are of this nature. See [Sil3], [Wh] in this volume, and many other sources concerning elliptic curves in cryptography, such as [Ko3], [KMV], [BSS]. **The hard task** here is **computation of discrete logs**, for example in the group $\mathbb{Z}/p^\times$ with p prime. The *easy* task is exponentiation (e.g., by square-and-multiply).

Note that computation of discrete logs is *not* necessarily difficult in every group: in the *additive* group $\mathbb{Z}/n$ computation of the discrete log of m for a base b amounts to solving for x in

$$x \cdot b = m \bmod n$$

That is, the problem becomes that of finding a multiplicative inverse, easily accomplished via the extended Euclidean algorithm.

Description of encryption and decryption. Alice chooses a large random prime $p > 10^{150}$, a primitive root b modulo p, and a random key k, and integer in the range $1 < k < p$. Alice computes $c = b^k \,\%\, p$ and publishes p, b, and c.

Bob, who has no prior contact with Alice, can send a message that only Alice can decrypt is as follows. We can assume that Bob's plaintext x is an integer in the range $0 < x < p$. Bob chooses an auxiliary random integer r, *a temporary secret known only to Bob*, and encrypts the plaintext x as

$$y = E_{b,c,p,r}(x) = (x \times c^r) \,\%\, p$$

Along with this encrypted message is sent the *header* $b^r \,\%\, p$.

Alice's decryption step requires knowledge of the discrete logarithm ℓ, but *not* the random integer r. First, from the header b^r the Alice computes

$$(b^r)^\ell = b^{r \cdot \ell} = (b^\ell)^r = c^r \bmod p$$

Then the plaintext is recovered by multiplying by the multiplicative inverse $(c^r)^{-1}$ of c^r modulo p:

$$D_{b,c,p,r,\ell}(y) = ((c^r)^{-1} \cdot y) \,\%\, p = (c^r)^{-1} \cdot c^r \cdot x \bmod p = x \bmod p$$

5.2 Knapsack ciphers.

There is no single knapsack cipher, but rather a family of ciphers using the same underlying mathematical problem, the *knapsack* or *subset sum problem.* Merkle and Hellman [MH] first made a cipher of this type. Adi Shamir [Sh] found a decisive attack. In fact, the progression of attacks and attempts to defeat them is representative of the iterative processes by which real ciphers come into existence. We describe the basic version here and briefly indicate the nature of Shamir's attack.

The **knapsack problem** is: given a list of positive integers $a_1, \cdots, a_n$, and given another integer b, find a subset $a_{i_1}, \cdots, a_{i_k}$ so that

$$a_{i_1} + \cdots + a_{i_k} = b$$

if this is possible. Each element a_i can be used at most once, although some of the values a_i may be the same. There are variants: one is to tell, for given a_i's and b, whether or not a solution *exists*. Or, granting that a solution exists, *find it.* All of these are provably NP-complete. Visibly, a brute-force search adding up all possible 2^n subsets of the a_i's rapidly becomes infeasible.

Call $a = (a_1, \ldots, a_n)$ the **knapsack vector**, and b the **size** of the knapsack. The a_i's which occur in a solution

$$b = a_{i_1} + \cdots + a_{i_k}$$

are **in the knapsack** of size b. A knapsack vector $a = (a_1, \ldots, a_n)$ of length n can be used to *encrypt* a vector $x = (x_1, \ldots, x_n)$ of bits (0's and 1's) by computing a function

$$b = f_a(x) = x_1\, a_1 + \cdots + x_n\, a_n$$

The knapsack vector a and the size b are transmitted. *Decryption* consists of finding a subset of the knapsack vector entries which add up to the size. Thus, the decryption step solves a knapsack problem. As it stands, authorized decryption would be no easier than unauthorized decryption.

There might be more than one possible decryption, which would be bad, so a knapsack vector with the property that for a given size there is *at most one* solution to the knapsack problem is called **injective**. The function

$$f_a(x) = x_1\, a_1 + \cdots + x_n\, a_n$$

above is injective if and only if the knapsack vector $a = (a_1, \ldots, a_n)$ is injective.

By the NP-completeness of the general knapsack problem, we might be confident of the difficulty of unauthorized decryption. But for the authorized decryptor to decrypt, we must arrange things so that the *authorized* decryption amounts to solving a much easier *subproblem.*

A knapsack vector $a = (a_1, \ldots, a_n)$ is **superincreasing** if each a_i is strictly greater than the sum of the preceding elements in the vector, that is, for every index i

$$a_1 + \cdots + a_{i-1} < a_i$$

If the knapsack vector $a = (a_1, \ldots, a_n)$ is superincreasing, then there is a much easier method for solving the knapsack problem with size b:

If $b < a_n$, then a_n *cannot* be in the knapsack of size b (it just won't fit)
If $b \geq a_n$, then a_n *must* be in the knapsack of size b

(since by the superincreasing property the other a_i's add up to less than a_n, so cannot add up to b.) In the first case, keep the same knapsack size b. In the second case, replace b by $b - a_n$. In either case, replace the knapsack vector by $(a_1, \ldots, a_{n-1})$. This converts the problem into a new knapsack problem with a shorter knapsack vector. The process terminates when we reach a_1. The problem will be solved in the affirmative if $a_1 = b$ (with the value of b at that time), and in the negative if $a_1 \neq b$. If the authorized decryptor can decrypt by solving a superincreasing knapsack problem, the decryption is acceptably easy.

On the other hand, if the knapsack were *visibly* superincreasing, then an unauthorized decryptor could do the same. So try to *disguise* the superincreasing property in a manner known to the authorized decryptor, but unknown to adversaries. Even if the list of knapsack items were wildly rearranged, sorting n things takes only $O(n \log n)$ steps if done slightly cleverly.

The first idea of hiding is by a secret multiplication and reduction modulo some modulus. Alice chooses a superincreasing knapsack vector $(a_1, \ldots, a_n)$, and chooses an integer (the **modulus**)

$$m > a_1 + \cdots + a_n$$

Choosing m to be larger than the sum of the a_i's is what causes this procedure sometimes to be called **strong modular multiplication**. Alice chooses another number (the **multiplier**) t relatively prime to m. Then Alice computes

$$c_i = (ta_i) \% m$$

This gives a new knapsack vector $c = (c_1, \ldots, c_n)$, which Alice publishes as her *public key*. Alice keeps t and m (and the inverse of t modulo m) secret. For Bob to encrypt an n-bit message x so that (supposedly) only Alice can read it, the encryption step is similar to what was done before, encrypting $x = (x_1, \ldots, x_n)$ as

$$b = f_c(x) = c_1x_1 + \cdots + c_nx_n$$

with altered knapsack vector c. Bob transmits ciphertext b to Alice. Alice's decryption procedure is to compute

$$t^{-1} \cdot b \% m = t^{-1}(c_1x_1 + \cdots + c_nx_n)$$

$$= (t^{-1}c_1)x_1 + \cdots + (t^{-1}c_n)x_n = a_1x_1 + \cdots + a_nx_n \bmod m$$

Since m is larger than the sum of all the a_i's, the equality modulo m is actually an equality of integers,

$$(t^{-1}b) \% m = a_1x_1 + \cdots + a_nx_n$$

Since Alice knows the superincreasing knapsack vector of a_i's, or can compute them from the c_i's by

$$a_i = (t^{-1} \cdot b_i) \% m$$

she can solve the knapsack problem and decrypt.

Big Problem: Although implicitly we might have thought that an adversary must find *the* secret t and m in order to convert the problem into a superincreasing knapsack problem, this turned out not to be so. Certainly if an adversary is lucky enough to find *any* t' and m' so that

$$a' = (t'^{-1}c_1 \% m', \ldots, t'^{-1}c_n \% m')$$

is superincreasing, this converts the problem to an easy one. Adi Shamir [Sh] found a way to find (t', m') in polynomial time to convert the published vector to a superincreasing one. This breaks this simplest knapsack cipher.

(Note, too, that as it stood this cipher was completely vulnerable to chosen-plaintext attacks.)

5.3 NTRU.

The NTRU cipher, invented in 1995 by J. Hoffstein, J. Pipher, and J. Silverman, [HPS], is mathematically more complicated than RSA or ElGamal, although it still uses only basic abstract algebra and number theory. W. Banks' article [Ba] in this volume discusses this cipher in more detail. The NTRU cipher is patented.

The hard task. The computational task which is presumed to be difficult, thereby presumed to assure the security of the NTRU cipher, is not as readily described as prime factorization or discrete logarithms: it must be hard to *find the smallest vector in a lattice* $\mathbb{Z}^n \approx \Lambda \subset \mathbb{R}^n$. There is a relatively good algorithm, the LLL (Lenstra-Lenstra-Lovasz) algorithm [LLL], improved in [SE], which *quickly* finds a short vector in a *typical* lattice. But when the smallest vector is near to or longer than the 'expected value' of sizes of shortest vectors, the LLL algorithm does not perform well. Parameter choices for NTRU must be made to play upon this effect.

Description of encryption and decryption. Fix positive integer parameters N, p, q, where p, q need not be prime but must be *relatively* prime, and probably $\gcd(N, pq) = 1$. Let R be the set of polynomials in x with integer coefficients and with degree strictly less than N, with the multiplication $\star$ that is polynomial multiplication followed by reduction modulo $x^N - 1$

$$x^i \star x^j = x^{i+j \,\%\, N}$$

That is,

$$\left(\sum_{0 \le i < N} a_i x^i\right) \star \left(\sum_{0 \le j < N} b_i x^i\right) = \sum_{i,j} a_i b_j \; x^{i+j \,\%\, N} = \sum_{0 \le k < N} \left(\sum_{i+j=k \,\%\, N} a_\ell b_k\right) x^k$$

The addition in R is addition of polynomials.

On R we also have reduction mod p and reduction mod q of the coefficients of polynomials. Write

$$f \,\%\, p = \text{polynomial } f \text{ with coefficients reduced mod } p$$

$$f \,\%\, q = \text{polynomial } f \text{ with coefficients reduced mod } q$$

Say that a polynomial f has an **inverse** F **mod** p if the polynomial F satisfies

$$(f \star F) \,\%\, p = 1$$

To create an NTRU key, Alice chooses two polynomials f and g of degrees $N - 1$, making sure that f has an inverse F_p mod p and an inverse F_q mod q. Alice's public key is

$$h = (F_q \star g) \,\%\, q$$

Alice's private key is f.

A *message* is a polynomial of degree $N - 1$ with coefficients reduced mod p (in the sense that they lie in the range $(-p/2, p/2]$). For Bob to encrypt a message x for Alice, he randomly chooses a polynomial φ of degree $N - 1$ and computes

$$y = (p\varphi \star h + x) \,\%\, q$$

and transmits this to Alice.

To decrypt, Alice computes

$$a = (f \star y) \,\%\, q$$

and then

$$x = (F_p \star a) \,\%\, p$$

It is not clear that the alleged decryption decrypts. Indeed, the parameters must be chosen properly in order to arrange that correct decryption occurs with high probability.

Why does decryption (mostly) work? The polynomial that Alice computes in the decryption step is

$$\begin{aligned} a &= f \star y \\ &= f \star (p\phi \star h + m) \,\%\, q && \text{(by definition of encryption)} \\ &= f \star (p\phi \star F_q \star g + m) \,\%\, q && \text{(by construction of } h\text{)} \\ &= (f \star p\phi \star F_q \star g + f \star m) \,\%\, q && \text{(by distributivity)} \\ &= (f \star F_q \star p\phi \star g + f \star m) \,\%\, q && \text{(by commutativity)} \\ &= (1 \star p\phi \star g + f \star m) \,\%\, q && \text{(by inverse property of } F_q \text{ mod } q\text{)} \\ &= (p\phi \star g + f \star m) \,\%\, q \end{aligned}$$

Alice shifts the coefficients by subtracting q if necessary to put them into the interval $(-q/2, q/2]$. By careful choices of parameters, it can be arranged that all the coefficients lie in the range $(-q/2, q/2]$ even before reduction modulo q, so that reduction mod q does nothing. So Alice is really computing

$$\begin{aligned} (a \,\%\, p) &= (p\phi \star g + f \star m) \,\%\, q \,\%\, p \\ &= (p\phi \star g + f \star m) \,\%\, p \\ &= 0 \star g + f \star h \,\%\, p && \text{(since } p\phi \,\%\, p = 0\text{)} \\ &= f \star m \,\%\, p \end{aligned}$$

Then the star-multiplication by F_p recovers the plaintext:

$$\begin{aligned} (f \star m) \star F_p \,\%\, p &= (f \star F_p) \star m \,\%\, p \\ &= 1 \star m \\ &= m \end{aligned}$$

The most serious type of attack on the NTRU cipher seems to be what are called *lattice attacks*, which view the key f as more or less the shortest vector in a special collection ('lattice') of vectors. The LLL algorithm will quickly find a short vector, unless it is frustrated by having the length of the shortest vector be close to or even larger than the expected value of such length (for suitably 'random' lattice). In order to break NTRU, however, the LLL algorithm would have to find one of the shortest vectors in a lattice where all the 'short' vectors have *moderate* length. Suitable parameter settings in NTRU seem to achieve the effect of frustrating LLL.

NTRU sends roughly $\frac{\ln q}{\ln p} > 1$ bits of ciphertext for each bit of plaintext, unlike many older ciphers, which send one bit of ciphertext for each bit of plaintext. For discussion of relative speeds of encryption/decryption, parameter setting, apparent security, and more details, see NTRU's home page at

http://www.ntru.com/

5.4 Arithmetica Key Exchange.

The Arithmetica key exchange of Anshel, Anshel, and Goldfeld, [AAG], is a new *key exchange mechanism* (and cipher). By extreme constrast with Diffie–Hellman, it plays upon sophisticated mathematics to make a plausible claim of security. Some general ideas about using word problems in groups to make ciphers appeared earlier in [WM]. A significant new idea in [AAG] is use of the *braid group*, or more generally Artin groups, making use of a new algorithm discovered in [BKL]. The Arithmetica key exchange is patented.

Let G be a group. For a fixed set of elements $S = \{s_1, \ldots, s_n\}$ in G, a **word** in S is any expression

$$s_{i_1}^{k_1} s_{i_2}^{k_2} \ldots s_{i_N}^{k_N}$$

where the exponents k_j are positive or negative integers. The set S *generates* G if every element of G is expressible as a word in the elements of S and their inverses.

The **word problem** in a group G with respect to a subset $S = \{s_1, \ldots, s_n\}$ is the question of determining whether or not two *words* in S are equal, as elements of G. The **conjugacy problem** in a group G with respect to S is the question of determining whether or not two words x, y in S are *conjugate* (meaning, as usual that there is $g \in G$ so that $gxg^{-1} = y$). It is known that in general the word problem is *undecidable*, and the conjugacy problem has a similar status. But note that, even for specific groups where there *is* an algorithm, the algorithm may be 'bad' in that it runs in exponential time in the length of the inputs.

So in general the word problem and conjugacy problem are hard. But in [BKL] a class of groups, the *braid groups* (see below), was distinguished in which the word problem has a polynomial-time solution, and seemingly the conjugacy problem does not. This suggests making a cipher in which authorized decryption requires solving such a word problem, and unauthorized decryption requires solving the conjugacy problem.

A **braid group** with n generators is a group G generated by a set $S = \{s_1, \ldots, s_n\}$ with relations

$$s_i s_{i+1} s_i = s_{i+1} s_i s_{i+1}$$

and

$$s_i s_j = s_j s_i \quad \text{for } |i - j| > 1$$

The definition of **Artin group** includes braid groups as a special case where all parameters m_i are 3 (see just below). An Artin group is a group G generated by a set $S = \{s_1, \ldots, s_n\}$ with relations

$$\underbrace{s_i s_{i+1} s_i \ldots s_i s_{i+1} s_i}_{m_i \text{ factors}} = \underbrace{s_{i+1} s_i s_{i+1} \ldots s_{i+1} s_i s_{i+1}}_{m_i \text{ factors}}$$

and

$$s_i s_j = s_j s_i \quad \text{for } |i - j| > 1$$

Coxeter groups are quotients of Artin groups, by additional relations

$$s_i^2 = e \quad \text{for all indices } i$$

The key exchange. Here Alice and Bob proceed as follows. The public information is a group G and two lists $S_A = \{a_1, \ldots, a_m\}$, $S_B = \{b_1, \ldots, b_n\}$ of elements of G. Alice chooses a secret word a in S_A, and Bob chooses a secret word b in S_B. Alice transmits to Bob the list

$$ab_1a^{-1}, \; a_2^b a^{-1}, \; \ldots, \; ab_n a^{-1}$$

and Bob transmits to Alice the list

$$ba_1b^{-1}, \; ba_2b^{-1}, \; \ldots, \; ba_m b^{-1}$$

(These must be disguised, *rewritten*, to make this secure.) Then the common key for Alice and Bob will be the expression (the *commutator* of a and b)

$$\text{common key } = aba^{-1}b^{-1}$$

which they can both compute, as follows.

Let

$$a^{-1} = a_{i_1}^{e_{i_1}} \ldots a_{i_N}^{k_{i_N}}$$

be an expression of the inverse a^{-1} of Alice's secret a in terms of Alice's a_i's. Then

$$\begin{aligned} ba^{-1}b^{-1} &= b(a_{i_N}^{e_{i_1}} \ldots a_{i_N}^{k_{i_N}})b^{-1} \\ &= (ba_{i_1}b^{-1})^{e_{i_1}} \ldots (ba_{i_N}b^{-1})^{k_{i_N}} \end{aligned}$$

These ba_jb^{-1} are exactly what Bob had sent to Alice, so she knows what they are. That is, Alice can compute $ba^{-1}b^{-1}$. And then, since she knows her own secret a, she can compute

$$a \cdot (ba^{-1}b^{-1}) = aba^{-1}b^{-1}$$

Symmetrically, Bob can compute aba^{-1}, and since he knows his own secret b (and its inverse b^{-1}), he can compute

$$(aba^{-1}) \cdot b^{-1} = aba^{-1}b^{-1}$$

Thus, Alice and Bob have a shared secret.

The above description did not depend upon specifics concerning the group G. But for the shared secret $aba^{-1}b^{-1}$ to be unambiguous, it must be convertible to some 'canonical' form. For braid groups this is in effect accomplished in [BKL].

Certainly the most obvious attack on such a cipher would solve the conjugacy problem. At this time the conjugacy problem is not known to have a fast algorithm for braid groups, for example.

6 Protocol Sketches

Beyond key exchanges, trapdoor mechanisms allow other important effects to be achieved. We give simple illustrations below, with the warning that these are (mostly) very naive versions and require considerable further refinement to achieve their stated goals. Typical weaknesses involve set-up, cheating, and issues about whether cheating can be *prevented*, or merely *detected*.

6.1 Signatures.

Signatures are as important an application as secrecy. For example, the RSA mechanism can be re-used, effectively run backward, to allow Bob to convince Alice that the message he sent her really came from him, as follows. We assume that Bob has published an RSA modulus n and encryption exponent e, with secret decryption exponent d. To convince Alice that the message x purporting to be from Bob really is from him, Bob computes

$$y = x^d \,\%\, n \text{ (yes, using the } \textit{decryption} \text{ exponent)}$$

and sends *this* to Alice, together with a little header in plain text explaining to Alice where she can look up Bob's public key e (and modulus n) to use to compute

$$x = y^e \,\%\, n$$

If this computation yields non-gibberish, since d is secret, Alice will believe that Bob sent the message (assuming, as usual, the difficulty of factoring, etc.). This does require that the collection of possible messages x be sufficiently structured, e.g., be in a natural language such as English. However, any eavesdropper can also decrypt. Thus, while this procedure makes a good attempt at **authentication**, it does not in itself provide *secrecy*.

There is also the **ElGamal signature** scheme [E], which has been adopted as the **Digital Signature Standard** (DSA) by the National Institute of Standards and Technology in 1994. To set this up, Bob chooses a large prime p and primitive root g mod p. Bob chooses a secret random private key k, and computes $h = g^k \% p$. The data p, g, h are the public key.

Given a message x which he wants to sign, Bob chooses an auxiliary random $n \in \mathbb{Z}/(p-1)^\times$, and computes

$$a = g^n \% p$$

$$b = (x - ka) \cdot n^{-1} \% p - 1$$

Bob sends x, a, and b to Alice (in addition to the public p, g, h). Alice computes

$$h^a \cdot a^b \% p$$

and

$$g^x \% p$$

If these are the same, Alice believes that Bob sent the message x. We can see directly that if a, b are computed propertly then these values will be the same. Indeed, in that case

$$h^a \cdot a^b = g^{ak} g^{nb} = g^{ak+nb} = g^{ak+n(x-ka)n^{-1}} = g^x \bmod p$$

Why can Eve not forge a signature in the El Gamal scheme? Clearly several approaches that Eve might take to compute a, b without knowing the key k involve computing a discrete log. There are, however, further possible attacks, such as the *existential* attack discussed in Stinson [St] chapter 7, wherein Eve manages to sign a random message.

And, as one might anticipate, the *nonce* n should not be used to sign two different messages, or Eve can do a feasible computation to break the scheme.

It must be emphasized that for real use, such as in long-lasting documents, considerable refinement of these basic ideas is necessary. Again, see Stinson's [St] chapter 7 for further discussion of signatures.

6.2 Thresh-hold schemes.

Also called **secret-sharing schemes**, these are arrangements by which a group of entities restrict access to a secret, so that the secret is inaccessible unless a sufficient number (but not necessarily all) of the entities cooperate.

Say that a secret is k-**shared** among t people if any k or more of them can learn the secret, but a group of fewer than k cannot learn the secret. The problem is: given a **secret** x to be k-**shared** among t people $A_1, A_2, \ldots, A_t$, give A_i a piece of information a_i so that A_i knows a_i (but not a_j for $j \neq i$), *no part* of the secret x can be recovered from any $k-1$ of the a_i, and the secret x can be computed (feasibly) from any k of the a_i's. For given t and x, a list of $a_1, \ldots, a_n$ accomplishing this is a (k,t)-**thresh-hold scheme**. A simple example uses Sun-Ze's theorem, as follows.

Let $m_1, \ldots, m_t$ be mutually relatively prime integers greater than 1. Let $a_1, \ldots, a_t$ be integers. Let $M = m_1 \ldots m_t$, $M_i = M/m_i$, and let $n_i = M_i^{-1} \bmod m_i$. Since m_i is relatively prime to m_j for $j \neq i$, m_i is also relatively prime to M_i, by unique factorization. Thus, the multiplicative inverse N_i exists and is computable, via Euclid. The family

$$x = a_i \bmod m_i \quad \text{for all } i$$

is equivalent to the single congruence

$$x = \sum_{i=1}^{t} a_i\, M_i\, n_i \mod M$$

Fix k with $1 < k \leq t$. Let H_k be the *smallest* product of k different m_i's, and let h_{k-1} be the *largest* product of $k-1$ different m_i's. We must assume that

$$H_k \geq (N+1) \cdot h_{k-1}$$

for some large positive integer N. For any **secret** number x in the range

$$h_{k-1} < x < H_k$$

let $a_i = x \,\%\, m_i$. Then the set $\{a_1, \ldots, a_t\}$ is a (k,t) thresh-hold scheme for x.

This is not hard to see. Suppose that $a_1, \ldots, a_k$ are known. Let $M' = a_1 \ldots a_k$, and $M'_i = M'/m_i$ for $1 \leq i \leq k$. Let $n'_i = M_i'^{-1} \mod m_i$ for $1 \leq i \leq k$. Let

$$x' = \sum_{i=1}^{k} a_i\, M'_i\, n_i \mod M'$$

Then

$$x' = x \mod M'$$

Since $M' \geq H_k > x$, the secret x is already reduced modulo M', so can be computed by

$$x = x' \,\%\, M'$$

On the other hand, suppose only $a_1, \ldots, a_{k-1}$ are known. Let $M' = a_1 \ldots a_{k-1}$, and $M'_i = M'/m_i$ for $1 \leq i \leq k-1$. Let $n'_i = M_i'^{-1} \mod m_i$ for $1 \leq i \leq k-1$. Let

$$x' = \sum_{i=1}^{k-1} a_i\, M'_i\, n_i \mod M'$$

Since $M' = m_1 \ldots m_{k-1}$,

$$x' = x \mod m_1 m_2 \ldots m_{k-1}$$

Also $m_1 m_2 \ldots m_{k-1} \leq h_{k-1}$. Since $h_{k-1} < x < H_k$ and

$$(H_k - h_{k-1})/h_{k-1} > N$$

there are at least N possibilities for $y \mod M$, so

$$x' = y \mod M'$$

Thus, knowledge of only $k-1$ of the a_i's is insufficient to discover the secret x.

6.3 Zero-knowledge proofs.

As a simple case, we look at a protocol for Peter (the prover) to prove to Vera (the verifier) that he knows the factorization of a large integer n which is the product of two large primes p, q (both equal to 3 modulo 4), without imparting to Vera the factorization itself. Our first attempt will fail, since it will allow Vera to cheat. However, this too-naive attempt is enlightening.

First, for prime $p = 3 \bmod 4$, and for $x \neq 0 \bmod p$, if x is a square modulo p then there is a distinguished square root b of x, the so-called **principal square root** of x, given by the formula

$$b = x^{(p+1)/4} \bmod p$$

This principal square root b is also characterized as the square root of x which is itself a square. And, indeed, *if* $x = a^2 \bmod p$, then a direct computation (using Fermat's little theorem) verifies that the formula works, and yields a value which is itself a square.

The (faulty) protocol is as follows. Vera chooses random integer x and sends $x^4 \% n$ to Peter. Peter computes the principal square root $y_1 = (x^4)^{(p+1)/2}$ of x^4 mod p and principal square root $y_2 = (x^4)^{(q+1)/2}$ of x^4 mod q, and uses Sun-Ze's theorem (via the Euclidean algorithm) to compute y so that $y = y_1 \bmod p$ and $y = y_2 \bmod q$. Peter sends this value back to Vera.

Since the principal square root of $x^4 \bmod p$ is certainly x^2 (modulo p), and similarly modulo q, Peter must have computed

$$y = x^2 \bmod pq$$

Since Vera already can compute x^2, Peter has imparted no new information to Vera. (But Vera can cheat! See below.)

Why should Vera be convinced that Peter can factor n into p and q? Because, in any case, being able to take square roots modulo n (a product of two secret primes p and q) by whatever means gives a probabilistic algorithm for factoring n, as follows. Given an **oracle** (an otherwise unexplained mechanism) which computes square roots mod n, repeatedly do the following: choose random x, compute $x^2 \% n$, and give the result to the oracle, which returns a square root y of x^2 modulo n. Since there are exactly two square roots of any nonzero square modulo a prime, by Sun-Ze there are exactly 4 square roots of any square modulo $n = pq$, and $\pm x$ are just 2 of them. Let the other two be $\pm x'$. Assuming that the original x really was 'random', the probability is 1/2 that the oracle will return $\pm x'$ as y. If so, then n does not divide either of $x \pm y$ (since $y \neq \pm x \bmod n$), but nevertheless n divides $x^2 - y^2$ (since $x^2 = y^2 \bmod n$). So p divides one of $x \pm y$ and q divides the other of the two. Therefore, $\gcd(x - y, n)$ (computed via Euclid) is either p or q. The oracle can be called repeatedly, with probability 1/2 that a factorization will be obtained at each step. So the probability that we fail to obtain a factorization after ℓ invocations of the oracle is $(1/2)^\ell$, which goes to 0 quickly. Thus, even if Peter did not know the factorization initially, his ability to take square roots modulo n would allow him to factor n.

But the fact that a square root oracle for n can be used to factor n also allows Vera to cheat, as follows. Instead of giving Peter fourth powers $x^4 \bmod n$ she chooses random x and gives Peter just the square $x^2 \bmod p$. If she can do this repeatedly then she is using Peter as a square-root oracle for n, and thus Vera can factor n, defeating the purpose of the protocol.

The following much-enhanced version of the above idea is the **Fiege-Fiat-Shamir** scheme. Again, Peter knows the factorization $n = p \cdot q$ with secret distinct primes p, q. He wishes to prove to Vera that he knows p and q, without divulging p and q. (Thus, by the way, such a proof would be *reproducible.*)

Peter chooses random (secret) v, and computes and publishes $s = v^2 \% n$. We already know that if one can compute square roots modulo n then one can (probabilistically) factor n. Thus, whoever can prove that they know v may reasonably claim that they are Peter.

To prove to Vera that he's Peter, Peter chooses $r_1, \ldots, r_k$ random, and sends to Vera the set of squares $s_1 = r_1^2 \% n, \ldots, s_k = r_k^2 \% n$. (Again, if anyone can find all the square roots mod n, then they can probably factor n.)

Vera chooses a partition of the set of indices $1, 2, \ldots, k$ into two sets S_1 and S_2, and sends these sets of indices back to Peter. For $i \in S_1$, Peters further sends $t_i = v \cdot r_i$ to Vera, and for $i \in S_2$ Peter sends r_i to Vera. Vera checks whether or not $t_i^2 = v \cdot s_i \bmod n$ and whether $r_i^2 = s_i \bmod n$. If so, she believes that Peter is himself, that is, that he knows the factorization.

6.4 Electronic money.

A drawback to conventional credit cards, as opposed to paper money, is that the credit card's value exists only insofar as it is connected to the identity of the cardholder. And, then, the cardholder's transactions are traceable. By contrast, traditional paper money has value *in itself*, and in particular has no connection to one's identity, so does not yield information about other transactions. Current electronic banking and commercial transactions have the same problem as credit cards, in that *someone* knows quite a lot about your on-line financial transactions, where you are when they are made, and your general spending patterns.

Ideally, *e-money* would have a value independent of the possessor's identity, would be *divisible*, would be *transferable*, would *not* be *reusable* (meaning that you could not spend the same dollar twice), would *not* depend upon a *central authority*, and transactions could take place *offline*. These requirements were laid out and met in [OO]. Systems meeting varying subsets of these desiderata appear in [Ch] and [CFN]. See also [Br], which is given a careful exposition in [TW].

A technical but important issue in electronic transactions is *failure mode*: what happens if an electronic transaction is interrupted before completion? Is money withdrawn from your bank, or not? Perhaps it is withdrawn from your account, but doesn't make it to your hands? Protocols, software and hardware ensuring *atomicity* of transactions are important.

6.5 More.... There are many other important ideas that can be realized via trapdoor mechanisms. **Bit commitment schemes** effectively allow Alice the electronic equivalent of putting either a 'yes' or a 'no' into a sealed envelope and giving the envelope to Bob to be opened later. **Coin flipping over the phone** allows two parties who don't trust each other to be confident that the other reports honestly the outcomes of certain events. Many questions about **electronic voting** remain open.

7 Certifiable Large Primes

For those who must have the traditional version of certainty, there *are* some reasonable algorithms for producing very large numbers together with additional data which makes possible a feasible computation whereby to prove primality. The additional data (and explanation of its role) is a **primality certificate**. At the very least, observe that for an integer $p \sim 2^{1024}$ it is ridiculously infeasible to pretend to list the failed trial divisions that would prove p prime. Yet to make the claim that one has done the trial divisions is not necessarily persuasive at all.

The oldest and very simple way to feasibly certify the primality of a large number is the **Lucas–Pocklington–Lehmer** criterion, originating in work of Edouard Lucas in 1876 and 1891. This is a technique especially useful to test primality of numbers N where the factorization of $N-1$ is known, most often applied to numbers of special forms, such as Fermat numbers $2^{2^n}+1$. A more sophisticated variant of it gives the Lucas-Lehmer test for primality of Mersenne numbers 2^n-1, among which are the largest explicitly known primes. We give a sufficiently simple version so that we can give the quick proof.

Theorem: Let $N-1 = p \cdot U$, where p is prime, $p > U$, and suppose that there is b such that $b^{N-1} = 1 \bmod N$ but $\gcd(b^U - 1, N) = 1$. Then N is prime.

To see this, we recall a fact observed by Fermat and Euler. Namely, for an integer N and integer b with $b^{N-1} = 1 \bmod N$ but $\gcd(b^{(N-1)/p} - 1, N) = 1$, we claim that any prime divisor q of N satisfies $q = 1 \bmod p$. To see this, as $b \cdot b^{N-2} = 1 \bmod N$ it must be that b is prime to N, so b is prime to q. Let t be the order of b in $\mathbb{Z}/q^\times$. By Fermat's Little Theorem $b^{q-1} = 1 \bmod q$, so $t|q-1$. But the *gcd* condition implies that

$$b^{(N-1)/p} \neq 1 \bmod q$$

Thus, t does not divide $(N-1)/p$. Yet, $t|N-1$. Thus, $p|t$. From $t|q-1$ and $p|t$ we get $p|q-1$, or $q = 1 \bmod p$. This proves the claim. Thus, if the conditions of the theorem are met, then all divisors of N are 1 modulo p. If N were not prime, it would have a prime divisor q in the range $1 < q \leq \sqrt{N}$. But $q = 1 \bmod p$ and $p > \sqrt{N}$ make this impossible. Thus, N is prime.

Let's construct a chain of every-larger certified primes. To get started, by trial division, $p = 1000003$ is prime. Testing by Miller–Rabin, the first strong pseudoprime above $1000 \cdot p$ of the form $p \cdot U + 1$ is $N = 1032003097 = 1032 \cdot p + 1$. By luck, with $b = 2$ $2^{N-1} = 1 \bmod N$ while (by Euclid) $\gcd(2^{(N-1)/p} - 1, N) = \gcd(2^{1032} - 1, N) = 1$ Therefore, N is *certified* prime.

Now let p be the certified prime 1032003097. The first strong pseudoprime above $10^9 \cdot p$ of the form $p \cdot U + 1$ is

$$N = 1032003247672452163 = p \cdot (10^9 + 146) + 1$$

By luck, with $b = 2$, $2^{N-1} = 1 \bmod N$, while $\gcd(2^{(N-1)/p} - 1, N) = 1$ Therefore, N is *certified* prime.

Now let p be the certified prime 1032003247672452163. The first strong pseudoprime N above $10^{17} \cdot p$ of the form $p \cdot U + 1$ is

$$N = p \cdot (10^{17} + 24) + 1 = 1032003247672452410680779441388851913$$

By luck, with $b = 2$, $2^{N-1} = 1 \bmod N$, while $\gcd(2^{(N-1)/p} - 1, N) = 1$. Therefore, N is *certified* prime.

Now let p be the prime just certified. The first strong pseudoprime N above $10^{34} \cdot p$ of the form $p \cdot U + 1$ is

$$p \cdot (10^{34} + 224) + 1$$

$$= 1032003247672452410680779441388542246872747862933999249459487102828513$$

Again, luckily, $b = 2$ provides a certificate that N is N is prime.

Let p be prime just certified. The first strong pseudoprime N above $10^{60} \cdot p$ of the form $p \cdot U + 1$ is (computing for about 5 seconds)

$$p \cdot (10^{60} + 1362) + 1$$

$$= \begin{array}{l} 103200324767245241068077944138854224687274786293399924946089269 12 \\ 518428801833472215991711945402406825893161069777638214340524347 07 \end{array}$$

By luck, $b = 2$ works again and N is *certified* prime.

Let p be the prime just certified. The first strong pseudoprime N above $10^{120} \cdot p$ of the form $p \cdot U + 1$ is (computing a few seconds)

$$p \cdot (10^{120} + 796) + 1 =$$

1032003247672452410680779441388542246872747862933999249460892691251 8
4288018334722159917119454024068258931610697776382225552701985427211 8
9019004353452796285107072988954634025708705822364669326259443883929 4
027085403158334109562115430000186150573802677 3

$b = 2$ works again and N is *certified* prime.

Listing the primes p and the values of b in the last few small paragraphs gives a *certification* that the last N is prime, since anyone who cares to do so can (in easy polynomial time, of course with the help of a machine) reproduce the (quick) computations reported above. That is, that relatively small amount of auxiliary information reduces the proof/testing of primality of N to an easy (machine-assisted) computation. It is only mildly ironic that we use a probabilistic algorithm (Miller-Rabin) to make a good first guess at candidates for (deterministic) certification.

8 Factorization Algorithms

The claim that factorization is harder than primality testing (or certification of primality) cannot be rigorously substantiated currently. Indeed, there are few natural algorithms which can be *proven* strictly more difficult than others. And it appears to be difficult to give interesting lower bounds on the computational complexity (in the sense of run-time per input size) of factoring, despite beliefs concerning its difficulty. [Shp] illustrates some recent work in the direction of lower bounds.

As some sort of backward evidence that factoring is hard, we give a brief introduction to factoring methods.

In extreme contrast to trial division, these methods have various peculiar failure modes, as well as demanding discretion in setting parameters. Thus, if there were any doubt: *one should not use these factorization methods on an integer n without having first used Fermat or Miller-Rabin to be sure that n is definitely composite.*

8.1 Euler-Fermat trick. This observation applies only to numbers of special forms. For example, for the special form $N = b^n - 1$, a prime p divisor of N *either* divides $b^d - 1$ for some proper divisor d of n, *or* $p = 1 \bmod n$. This follows immediately from the fact that if p divides N then b is an nth root of unity in the finite field $\mathbb{Z}/p$. This reduces the amount of required trial division by a significant constant factor, making feasible or palatable certain historic hand calculations. Similarly, if the Fermat number $N = 2^{2^q} + 1$ were divisible by a prime p, then 2 would be a 2^q-th root of -1 modulo p, from which it would follow that

$p = 1 \bmod 2^{q+1}$. This observation allowed Euler to find the factorization

$$2^{2^5} + 1 = 641 \cdot 6700417$$

with only $(641-1)/2^{5+1} = 10$ trial divisions rather than $(641-1)/2 = 320$, disproving the primality of this number as conjectured by Fermat. Indeed, this constant-factor speed-up finds a six-digit factor of $2^{2^7}+1$ in 150 trial divisions rather than 300000. (Still, the Lucas-Lehmer tests for primality of Mersenne numbers $2^p - 1$ and Fermat numbers $2^{2^p} + 1$ are much more efficient, though they test primality without attempting to find a factor.)

8.2 Pollard's rho method. This method [Po1] quickly finds relatively small factors p of composite numbers in perhaps $\sqrt{p}$ steps, and uses very little memory. (An algorithm [Po2] similar in spirit computes discrete logarithms.) It is very simple to implement, and illustrates the surprising power of algorithms which are irremediably probabilistic. Finally, though an obvious heuristic suggests the reasonableness of Pollard's rho, it is difficult to *prove* that it works as well as it does. See [B] for a rare result in this direction.

The description (hence, implementation) is indeed simple: Given an integer n, define a function f by $f(x) = x^2 + 2 \,\%\, n$, and initialize by setting $x = 2$, $y = f(x)$.

Compute $g = \gcd(x - y, n)$
If $1 < g < n$, stop: g is a proper factor of n
If $g = 1$, replace x by $f(x)$ and y by $f(f(y))$ and repeat.

(If $g = n$, we have *failure*, and the algorithm needs to be reinitialized.)

Why does this work? Indeed, the additional point that it hardly matters what function f is used may be disconcerting. The most compelling heuristic explanation is not rigorous, and attempts to be more rigorous do not easily succeed. The probabilistic idea involved is the so-called *birthday paradox*, that with n draws (with replacement) from a set of N things, if $n >> \sqrt{N}$ then the probability is greater than 1/2 that there will be a duplication. Perhaps less well-known is the other critical component, the Floyd cycle-detection method, used to make exploitation of the birthday-paradox idea practical.

The Birthday Paradox computation is easy: the probability that n things drawn (with replacement) from among N will be distinct is

$$p = \left(1 - \frac{1}{N}\right)\left(1 - \frac{2}{N}\right)\cdots\left(1 - \frac{n-1}{N}\right)$$

Taking logarithms and using $\log(1-x) \le -x$,

$$\log p \le \sum 1 \le i \le n-1 \; - \frac{i}{N} = \frac{-n(n-1)}{N} \sim \frac{-n^2}{N}$$

Thus, $p \le e^{-n^2/N}$, and $e^{-n^2/N} \le 1/2$ for

$$n \ge \sqrt{N \ln 2}$$

The heuristic for Pollard's rho is as follows. Suppose that n has a proper divisor p, much smaller than n. From the birthday paradox, if we have more than $\sqrt{p}$ integers $x_1, x_2, \ldots, x_t$, then the probability is greater than 1/2 that two of these will be the same modulo p. The idea of Pollard's rho method is that $\sqrt{p}$ is much smaller than $\sqrt{n}$, so we should expect that if we choose a 'random sequence' of integers $x_1, x_2, \ldots$, there will be two the same modulo p long before there are two the same modulo n. Thus, supposing that $x_i = x_k \bmod p$, compute $g = \gcd(x_i - x_j, n)$. This *gcd* will be a multiple of p, and will be a divisor of n *probably* strictly smaller than n itself.

It is too naive to compute the greatest common divisors $\gcd(x_i - x_j, n)$ as we go along, for *all* $i < j$, since this might take about $\sqrt{p} \cdot \sqrt{p} \sim \sqrt{n}$ comparisons, as bad as trial division.

We need a clever way to exploit the birthday paradox. Let's pretend that the function $f(x) = x^2 + 2 \,\%\, n$ used in the algorithm is a 'random map' from $\mathbb{Z}/n$ to itself, and we make the random x_i's by

$$x_0 = 2 \qquad\qquad x_i = f(x_{i-1}) \quad (\text{for } i > 0)$$

Note that if ever $x_j = x_i \bmod p$ with $i < j$, then $x_{j+\ell} = x_{i+\ell} \bmod p$ for all $\ell \geq 0$. Thus,

$$x_t = x_{t-(j-i)} = x_{t-2(j-i)} = x_{t-3(j-i)} = \ldots = x_{t-\ell(j-i)} \bmod p$$

Floyd's cycle-detection method is the following efficient way of looking for matches. Do not keep in memory the whole list of x_i's. Rather, just remember the last one computed, and separately compute $y_i = x_{2i}$. The efficient way to compute the sequence of y_i's is as

$$y_{i+1} = f(f(y_i))$$

At each step we only remember the last x_t and y_t computed, and consider $\gcd(x_t - y_t, n)$. Let j be the first index so that $x_j = x_i \bmod p$ for some $i < j$. Then

$$x_t = x_{t-\ell(j-i)} \bmod p$$

whenever $t - \ell(j-i) \geq i$. So, taking $t = 2s$:

$$y_s = x_{2s} = x_{2s-\ell(j-i)} \bmod p$$

for all s with $2s - \ell(j-i) \geq i$. So when $s = \ell(j-i)$ with $\ell(j-i) \geq i$

$$y_s = x_{2s} = x_{2s-\ell(j-i)} = x_{2s-s} = x_s \bmod p$$

for $s = 2s - \ell(j-i) \geq i$. This proves that we find x_i and x_j which are the same mod p.

Especially if one feels that Pollard's rho method is simply too wacky to work, some small examples are useful. Compare to the trial division examples above. In less than 10 seconds *total* (in C++ on a 2.4 G machine)

factor	10000103	of	100001220001957	(2661 steps)
factor	100000007	of	10000013000000861	(14073 steps)
factor	1000000103	of	100000110000000721	(9630 steps)
factor	10000000019	of	100000001220000001957	(129665 steps)
factor	100000000103	of	10000000010600000000309	(162944 steps)

Pollard's rho can easily factor integers which are well out of the range of trial division.

8.3 Pollard's $p - 1$ method.

This factorization method is specialized, finding prime factors p of given n with the property that $p - 1$ is divisible only by 'small' factors. It is easy to misunderstand this, so it bears reflection. Certainly trial division cannot make use of such a property. Integers n divisible only by primes q below a bound B are (B-) **smooth**. Primes p such that $p-1$ is relatively smooth are called *weak*, while primes

p such that $p-1$ has at least one large-ish prime factor p' are *strong*. Sometimes it is required that this prime factor p' of $p-1$ itself have the property that $p'-1$ has a large-ish prime factor p'', etc. (It should be said that such considerations seem to have been swamped by other issues.)

Fix an integer B. Given an integer n, Pollard's $p-1$ algorithm finds a prime factor p of n such that $p-1$ is B-smooth, using $O(B \ln n / \ln B)$ multiplications modulo n. Keeping B small is obviously desirable. On the other hand, a too-small value of B will cause the algorithm to fail to find factors. In practice, because the value of B must be kept too small to find all possible factors, the algorithm is used 'just a little' hoping for luck or negligence on the part of an adversary. The serious question of how large we should expect the prime factors of a randomly chosen number to be is not trivial and does not have a simple answer.

As usual, let floor(x) be the largest integer $\geq x$. Given an integer n known to be composite, but **not a prime power**, and given a smoothness bound B, choose a random integer b with $2 \leq b \leq n-1$. Compute $g = \gcd(b, n)$. If $g \geq 2$, then g is a proper factor, and stop. Otherwise, let $p_1, p_2, \ldots, p_t$ be the primes less than or equal B. For $i = 1, 2, 3, \ldots, t$: let $q = p_i$, and

Compute $\ell = \text{floor}(\ln n / \ln p_i)$.
Replace b by b^{q^ℓ}.
Compute $g = \gcd(b-1, n)$.
If $1 < g < n$: stop, g is a proper factor.
Else if $g = 1$: continue.
Else if $g = n$: stop, failure.

Why does this work? Let

$$p = 1 + p_1^{e_1} \ldots p_t^{e_t}$$

be a prime factor of n such that $p-1$ is B-smooth, with some integer exponents e_i. For any integer b prime to p by Fermat's Little Theorem $b^{p-1} = 1 \bmod p$, so

$$b^{p_1^{e_1} \ldots p_t^{e_t}} = 1 \bmod p$$

The quantity

$$\ell_i = \text{floor}(\ln n / \ln p_i)$$

is larger than or equal e_i. Let $T = p_1^{\ell_1} \ldots p_t^{\ell_t}$. Then $p_1^{e_1} \ldots p_t^{e_t}$ divides T, so certainly $b^T = 1 \bmod p$ for any integer b prime to p. That is,

$$p | \gcd(b^T - 1, n)$$

The actual algorithm given above computes *gcd*'s more often than indicated in the last paragraph, providing some opportunities to avoid $\gcd(b^T - 1, n) = n$.

Example: Factor 54541557732143. Initialize $b = 3$. The exponent for 2 is 45, the exponent for 3 is 28, and the exponent for 5 is 19. Replace b by

$$b^{2^{45}} \% 54541557732143 = 1333741139152$$

Since $\gcd(b-1, n) = 1$, continue. Replace b by

$$b^{3^{28}} \% 54541557732143 = 22167690980770$$

Since $\gcd(b-1, n) = 1$, continue. Replace b by

$$b^{5^{19}} \% 54541557732143 = 2268486536233$$

This time,

$$\gcd(n, b-1) = \gcd(54541557732143, 2268486536233 - 1) = 54001$$

Thus, we find the proper factor 54001 of 54541557732143. The prime 54001 is $\{2,3,5\}$-weak, meaning that $54001 - 1$ is $\{2,3,5\}$-smooth.

Incidentally, the format of the example shows how to use an indefinitely large bound B for the smoothness of $p-1$ for factors p of n. Then the issue becomes deciding when to quit in the case that one has found no weak prime factors.

There is an analogous $p+1$ method due to Williams [Wil]. In fact, for any cyclotomic polynomial

$$\varphi_n(x) = \frac{x^n - 1}{\prod_{d|n,\ d<n} \varphi_d(x)}$$

there is a $\varphi_n(p)$-method, with Pollard's being the case $n = 1$, and Williams' the case $n = 2$. However, for larger n these seem not to have immediate utility for factoring.

8.4 Toward the quadratic sieve.

We look first at a *generic random squares* algorithm, then the *continued fractions* refinement of this, and then a different refinement, the quadratic sieve. A *random squares* or *Fermat* factoring method earns the latter name since such factorization algorithms can be broadly viwed as a natural outgrowth of a more special method used by Fermat in case an integer n is a product $n = ab$ of two integers relatively close to $\sqrt{n}$. Such algorithms use much more memory than Pollard's algorithms, and, indeed, this is a chief bottleneck in scaling upward.

A **factor base** is a chosen initial set of primes

$$S = \{p_1, \ldots, p_t\}$$

(with $p_1 = 2$, $p_2 = 3$, etc.) Choose integers a_1, a_2, $\ldots$, and let $b_i = a_i^2 \,\%\, n$. We hope/require that every b_i be **smooth** with respect to the factor basis B (that is, all the prime factors of b_i are in B). Then find a subset of the b_is whose product is a perfect square in $\mathbb{Z}$, as follows. Write the factorizations

$$b_i = \prod_{j=1}^{t} p_j^{e_{ij}}$$

Suppose that we have $t+1$ of these a_i's with $b_i = a_i^2 \,\%\, n$ being B-smooth. Let v_i be the vector (in $\mathbb{F}_2^{t+1}$) of the exponents mod 2:

$$v_i = (e_{i1} \,\%\, 2, e_{i2} \,\%\, 2, e_{i3} \,\%\, 2, \ldots, e_{it} \,\%\, 2)$$

Since there are $t+1$ of these vectors in a t-dimensional vector space, they are linearly dependent over $\mathbb{F}_2$. That is, there are $c_1, \ldots, c_t$ in $\mathbb{F}_2$ such that

$$c_1 v_1 + \cdots + c_t v_t = (0, \ldots, 0) \in \mathbb{F}_2^{t+1}$$

Use *Gaussian elimination* to find such a relation. Then

$$\prod_{i=1}^{t+1} b_i^{c_i} = \prod_{i=1}^{t+1} (\prod_{j=1}^{t} p_j^{e_{ij}})^{c_i} = \prod_{j=1}^{t} \prod_{i=1}^{t+1} p_j^{c_i e_{ij}} = \prod_{j=1}^{t} p_j^{\sum_i c_i e_{ij}}$$

has *even* exponents $\sum_i c_i e_{ij}$, so is the square of an integer.

Take

$$x = \prod_{i=1}^{t+1} a_i^{c_i} \,\%\, n \qquad y = \prod_{j=1}^{t} p_j^{(\Sigma_i c_i e_{ij})/2} \,\%\, n$$

Then

$$x^2 = y^2 \bmod n$$

and a chance that

$$1 < \gcd(x - y, n) < n$$

thereby possibly obtaining a proper factor of n. If by mischance $x = \pm y \bmod n$, then we won't get a proper factor. In that case, compute one or more new values $b_i = a_i^2 \,\%\, n$ and repeat the Gaussian elimination step just above.

The merits of such a random squares algorithm hinge upon two things: adroit determination of the factor base $B = \{p_1, \ldots, p_t\}$, and choice of the a_i's so that $b_i = a_i^2 \,\%\, n$ factors into primes lying in the factor base. One approach, the basic **random squares** approach, also called **Dixon's algorithm**, chooses the a_i 'randomly', and uses **trial division** by primes in B to see whether or not $b_i = a_i^2 \,\%\, n$ is p_t-smooth. This requires $O(t)$ trial divisions. If b_i is not B-smooth, reject a_i and choose another. In practice, 'random' selection often means testing of successive a_i's in a specified interval.

Example: very small for the sake of human accessibility to details. Let $n = 10019$. We will try to select a_i's just above the square root of n, which has integer part $m = 101$. With any factor base smaller than $B = \{2, 3, 5, 7, 11, 13\}$ we do not find enough smooth $b_i = a_i^2 \,\%\, n$ below $2m$. This gives some idea of suitable choice of factor base, since it amounts to a failure to need to test more than a small fraction of the candidate a_i's between m and $2m$. We do find 6 B-smooth b_i's, whose vector of exponents for the primes $2, 3, 5, 7, 11, 13$ we display

$101^2 \,\%\, 10019 =$	182	with exponents	1	0	0	1	0	1
$102^2 \,\%\, 10019 =$	385	with exponents	0	0	1	1	1	0
$107^2 \,\%\, 10019 =$	1430	with exponents	1	0	1	0	1	1
$113^2 \,\%\, 10019 =$	2750	with exponents	1	0	3	0	1	0
$137^2 \,\%\, 10019 =$	8750	with exponents	1	0	4	1	0	0
$142^2 \,\%\, 10019 =$	126	with exponents	1	2	0	1	0	0

The first 3 rows sum to 0 mod 2, so we take

$$x = a_1 \cdot a_2 \cdot a_3 = 101 \cdot 102 \cdot 107 = 1102314$$

and

$$y = 2^{(1+1+0)/2} \cdot 3^{(0+0+0)/2} \cdot 5^{(0+1+1)/2} \cdot 7^{(1+1+0)/2} \cdot 11^{(0+1+1)/2} \cdot 13^{(1+0+1)/2}$$

$$= 10010$$

Then we find a proper factor of 10019 via Euclid

$$\gcd(10019, x - y) = 233$$

Improvement: If instead of reducing $b_i = a_i^2$ modulo n into the range $0 \leq b_i < n$ we reduce into the range $\frac{-n}{2} < b_i < \frac{-n}{2}$ (and add -1 to the factor base), then we obviously improve the chances that b_i is B-smooth. We will not use this for the moment, but will have an additional motivation to incorporate this improvement in the continued fractions algorithm (below).

Improvement: If we only choose the a_i's in the range $m < a_i < \sqrt{2}m$ then

$$b_i = a_i^2 \,\%\, n = a_i^2 - n$$

Then for a prime p dividing b_i, we have $n = a_i^2 \bmod p$, so n is a square modulo p. The point is that then we can drop primes p with quadratic symbol $(n/p)_2 = -1$ from our factor base. By quadratic reciprocity (and Dirichlet's theorem on primes in an arithmetic progression), this holds for roughly half the primes. That is, given n, after doing an easy preliminary computation of quadratic symbols, for the same computational load we have twice as large a factor basis. Of course, one would repeatedly discover that primes p for which $(n/p)_2 = -1$ do not appear *at all* in factorizations of $b_i = a_i^2 - n$.

Example: The integer $n = 1000001$ is a non-square modulo primes 3, 11, 13, 17, 19, 23. Thus, not surprisingly, only 2 a_i's in the range $m < a_i < \sqrt{2}m$ give $b_i = a_i^2 - n$ which are smooth with respect to the large-ish factor base $\{2, 3, 5, 7, 11, 13, 17, 19, 23\}$. That is, the most naive random square factorization seems to malfunction. But, in the improved form, taking into account the quadratic symbol condition, we realize that the first 4 primes we should include in a factor base are $\{2, 5, 7, 29\}$. And then, with *this* factor base rather than the full list of primes up to that point,

$$\begin{array}{rrlcccc}
1001^2 \,\%\, 1000001 = & 2000 & \text{with exponents} & 4 & 3 & 0 & 0 \\
1082^2 \,\%\, 1000001 = & 170723 & \text{with exponents} & 0 & 0 & 1 & 3 \\
1151^2 \,\%\, 1000001 = & 324800 & \text{with exponents} & 6 & 2 & 1 & 1 \\
1249^2 \,\%\, 1000001 = & 560000 & \text{with exponents} & 7 & 4 & 1 & 0
\end{array}$$

The second and third vectors sum to 0 modulo 2, so we take

$$x = a_2 \cdot a_3 = 1082 \cdot 1151 = 1245382$$

and

$$y = 2^{(0+6)/2} \cdot 5^{(0+2)/2} \cdot 7^{(1+1)/2} \cdot 29^{(3+1)/2} = 235480$$

and via Euclid we find the proper factor

$$\gcd(1000001, x - y) = 9901$$

The **quadratic sieve** of Pomerance [Pom] is the best current method to choose the a_i's in a classical random squares factoring algorithm, and for a while was the best factoring algorithm of any sort. It is apparently subexponential. (The number field sieve uses a more sophisticated mechanism than the random squares factoring discussed here, and is faster for sufficiently large inputs.) The quadratic sieve is the most clever known method to choose the a_i's in a random squares algorithm, and effectively entirely avoids *factoring*, but is still memory-intensive. This makes the operation of the algorithm even less human-accessible than the continued fraction algorithm.

Much as in our version of the basic random squares algorithm, given n to be factored, we will choose the a_i's in a particular range so that we have a fixed polynomial expression for the absolute reduction of a_i modulo n. For example, let $m = \text{floor}(\sqrt{n})$, and choose a_i's only in the range

$$m < a_i < m + L$$

with $L << (\sqrt{2}-1)m$, so that

$$b_i = a_i^2 \,\%\, n = a_i^2 - n$$

Thus, for a prime p dividing b_i, n is a square modulo p. As already exploited in the random squares case, this allows us to drop any prime p from the factor base if $(n/p)_2 = -1$, effectively doubling the size of the factor base for the same computational load.

Before explaining the actual sieving step, for given n one precomputes some square roots modulo prime powers p^e for the primes p in the factor base B, as follows. Using the square root algorithm modulo primes (4.17), together with Hensel's lemma (4.18), one computes the two square roots $\pm r_p$ of n modulo $p^{e(p)}$ for the largest exponent $e(p)$ (depending upon p) such that at least one of $\pm r_p$ falls in the range $m < a < m + L$.

Now the **sieving:** first observe the elementary fact that if $a = r_p \bmod p^f$ for some integer $f \leq e(p)$ then

$$a^2 - n = 0 \bmod p^f$$

For a in the chosen range, initialize a list A of values by

$$A(a) = \log(a^2 - n)$$

The sieving is the following. For each p in the factor base B,

For each p in the factor base B:
    For $i = e(p), e(p) - 1, \ldots, 1$:
        For $m < a < m + L$ with $a = \pm r_p \bmod p^i$,
            subtract $\log p$ from $A(a)$

After this take as a_i's the elements $a \in A$ with the (modified) value $L(a)$ suitably close to 0 or negative as the most likely to give B-smooth $b_i = a_i^2 - n$. Only *now* do we factor these b_i's and set up a matrix of exponents for the primes in B as before.

Remark: The point of this approach is to reduce the amount of factorization done, since for larger integers factorization is onerous, far more so than the algorithms to compute square roots, and to sieve, in that range. This sieving, much as Eratosthenes' sieve, is even more memory-intensive than the continued fractions algorithm, and manipulation of the large matrix of exponents is a bottleneck in scaling upward. On the other hand, in a certain range it appears that the trade-off of not needing to factor while keeping track of more partial results is advantageous.

Remark: In factoring genuinely large numbers n, it appears that the largest prime in a factor base should be on the order of

$$e^{\sqrt{\log n \, \log\log n}}$$

and the length L of the interval of candidates above m should be in the range

$$e^{\sqrt{\log n \, \log\log n}} < L < e^{2\sqrt{\log n \, \log\log n}}$$

We use an example to illustrate further details. Hoping to achieve a degree of human accessibility, nor surprisingly we are forced to use an unnaturally small n.

Example: To attempt to factor $n = 21311$, initially take a factor base $\{2, 3, 5, 7, 11, 13, 17, 19, 23, 29\}$. Dropping odd primes p with $(n/p)_2 = -1$ leaves us with $B = \{2, 5, 11, 13, 23, 29\}$. Compute

$$m = \text{floor}(\sqrt{n}) = 145$$

To be sure to have $a^2 \,\% = a^2 - n$, we only consider candidates below $\sqrt{2}m \sim 205$, for example

$$A = (146, 147, \ldots, 200)$$

Now we run through the generation of the data which would be used to sieve. Since $n = 3 \bmod 4$, the only power of 2 that can ever divide $a^2 - n$ is 2^1, for odd a. Powers of 5 are more interesting. Suppressing the computation of square roots, we find that $a = 169$ is the only integer in the indicated range satisfying

$$a^2 - n = 0 \bmod 5^3$$

Going up 5^2 from this, we see that 194 is a square root mod 5^2. The only other two square roots of n mod only 5^2 fitting into the range are 156 and 181, differing by multiples of 25 from the square root 81 of n modulo 5^2. The remaining square roots mod only 5^1 fall into two families mod 5

149	154	159	164	174	179	184	189	199	204
146	151	161	166	171	176	186	191	196	201

The square roots of n modulo 11^3 are 933 and 398, neither of which can be moved into the indicated range modulo 11^3. Modulo 11^2 the only square root is 156 in that range. Modulo only 11 we have two batches (distinguished mod 11), $167, 178, 189, 200$, and $152, 163, 174, 185, 196$. The only square roots modulo 13^2 are 37 and 132, neither of which can be adjusted by multiples of 169 to be in the indicated range, so we only have candidates which are square roots of n modulo 13 and no higher power of 13, namely $154, 158, 167, 171, 180, 184, 193, 197$. Modulo 23^2 there are again no square roots of n in the indicated range, but $155, 167, 178, 190, 201$ are the square roots modulo 23 in that range. Modulo 29 there are $150, 169, 179, 198$ and none modulo 29^2.

Since there are 6 primes in the factor base, we want at least 7 linear relations mod 2 among the exponents in factorizations. If any primes arise that are not already in the factor base, we'll need still more relations.

Of the candidates in the range $146 \leq a \leq 200$, we sieve out (to keep) those a such that

$$(a^2 - n)/(\text{powers of 2, 5, 11, 13, 23, 29}) < 50$$

setting the thresh-hold of 50 somewhat at random. (For readability, we don't take logarithms.) The following table lists the candidates $a = 146, \ldots, 200$ with prime powers from our factor base dividing $a^2 - n$, boxing the leftover if that leftover is under 50.

146	147	148	149	150	151	152	153	154	155	156
–	2	–	2	–	2	–	2	–	2	–
5	–	–	5	–	5	–	–	5	–	5^2
–	–	–	–	–	–	11	–	–	–	11^2
–	–	–	–	–	–	–	–	13	–	–
–	–	–	–	–	–	–	–	–	23	–
–	–	–	–	29	–	–	–	–	–	–
$\boxed{1}$	149	593	89	$\boxed{41}$	149	163	1049	$\boxed{37}$	59	$\boxed{1}$

157	158	159	160	161	162	163	164	165	166	167
2	–	2	–	2	–	2	–	2	–	2
–	–	5	–	5	–	–	5	–	5	–
–	–	–	–	–	–	11	–	–	–	11
–	13	–	–	–	–	–	–	–	–	13
–	–	–	–	–	–	–	–	–	–	23
–	–	–	–	–	–	–	–	–	–	–
1669	281	397	4289	461	4933	239	1117	2957	1249	$\boxed{1}$

168	169	170	171	172	173	174	175	176	177	178
–	2	–	2	–	2	–	2	–	2	–
–	5^3	–	5	–	–	5	–	5	–	–
–	–	–	–	–	–	11	–	–	–	11
–	–	–	13	–	–	–	–	–	–	–
–	–	–	–	–	–	–	–	–	–	23
–	29	–	–	–	–	–	–	–	–	–
6913	$\boxed{1}$	7589	61	8273	4309	163	4657	1933	5009	$\boxed{41}$

179	180	181	182	183	184	185	186	187	188	189
2	–	2	–	2	–	2	–	2	–	2
5	–	5^2	–	–	5	–	5	–	–	5
–	–	–	–	–	–	11	–	–	–	11
–	13	–	–	–	13	–	–	–	–	–
–	–	–	–	–	–	–	–	–	–	–
29	–	–	–	–	–	–	–	–	–	–
$\boxed{37}$	853	229	11813	6089	193	587	2657	6829	14033	131

190	191	192	193	194	195	196	197	198	199	200
–	2	–	2	–	2	–	2	–	2	–
–	5	–	–	5^2	–	5	–	–	5	–
–	–	–	–	–	–	11	–	–	–	11
–	–	–	13	–	–	–	13	–	–	–
23	–	–	–	–	–	–	–	–	–	–
–	–	–	–	–	–	–	–	29	–	–
643	1517	15553	613	653	8357	311	673	617	1829	1699

We have 8 outcomes below 50, but new primes 37 and 41 have appeared. Of some interest is the fact that the prime 31 did not appear at all. We can enlarge the factor base to include 37 and then discover that the candidate $a = 191$ gives a further relation $191^2 - n = 2 \cdot 5 \cdot 37 \cdot 41$. Thus, with 8 primes appearing, we have the requisite 9 relations

$$\begin{array}{rcc} 146^2 - n &=& 5 \\ 150^2 - n &=& 29 \cdot 41 \\ 154^2 - n &=& 5 \cdot 13 \cdot 37 \\ 156^2 - n &=& 5^2 \cdot 11^2 \\ 167^2 - n &=& 2 \cdot 11 \cdot 13 \cdot 23 \\ 169^2 - n &=& 2 \cdot 5^3 \cdot 29 \\ 178^2 - n &=& 11 \cdot 23 \cdot 41 \\ 179^2 - n &=& 2 \cdot 5 \cdot 29 \cdot 37 \\ 191^2 - n &=& 2 \cdot 5 \cdot 37 \cdot 41 \end{array}$$

Actually, by luck $156^2 - n$ is a square, and

$$\gcd(156 - 5 \cdot 11, n) = 101$$

so we have a proper factor without carrying out the Gaussian elimination. From this point, the algorithm proceeds exactly as the generic random squares and the continued fractions algorithms.

Elliptic curve algorithms and the **number field sieve** are more sophisticated, although implementation is possible without discussion of the underlying ideas. The elliptic curve algorithm is roughly a competitor for the quadratic sieve, while the number field sieve is faster at the top end of the range of integers factorable by any (generic) factoring method. The number field sieve has its origins in a *deterministic* (superpolynomial) algorithm of Adleman, Pomerance, and Rumely [APR] from 1983.

9 Randomness, Information, Entropy

While it is possible to formalize various statistical notions of 'randomness' of a string of 0's and 1's, the cryptographic sense is much stronger, specifically demanding *unpredictability* of the next bit given all the previous bits, by an adversary with substantial computing power. Statistical randomness merely means that the aggregate has properties within statistically plausible bounds of what one would obtain if the 0's and 1's had come from a genuinely random source. In effect, an allegedly random sequence might be *rejected* on statistical grounds due to presence of a simple pattern, but *absence* of a *simple* pattern does not usefully address predictability. Instead, the usual proof of unpredictability asserts something akin to 'if the adversary can *consistently* predict the next bit, then the adversary can factor large integers'. The Blum-Blum-Shub [BBS] and Naor-Reingold [NR] pseudo-random number generators both are of this sort.

Keys to both symmetric and asymmetric ciphers must be *random*, otherwise (in effect) the keyspace is greatly reduced in size, making brute force searches for the key feasible. Trying common words and variations as sources of keys is a **dictionary attack**. Reasonably good password checking programs carry out such attacks to test the quality of users' proposed passwords before accepting them. Several cautionary tales exist wherein the inadequacy of using process id's (PIDs) and current time as seeds for pseudo-random number generators (pRNGs). The SSL (Secure Sockets Layer) implementation in the Netscape browser at one point suffered from a fatally inadequate random number generator.

A naive notion of randomness, e.g, of a 1024-bit integer is that it be the result of choosing from among the first 2^{1024} integers with equal probabilities attached. However, this attempted answer begs the question, in practical terms, since it does not indicate how the 'choice' is to be made. Further, there is an intuitive inadequacy in this naive conception, since (as illustrated already in the discussion of Kolmogorov complexity) bit-strings

$$10101010101010101010$$

$$11100100011011111001$$

which are equally likely if we are choosing random 0's and 1's are not equally *random* to our eyes: the first is highly patterned, and the second seems not so. Again, see [LV] for an engaging dialectic developing the notion of *random*.

9.1 Entropy. The notion of **entropy** in this context was introduced decisively in Shannon's fundamental papers [Sh1], [Sh2] on *information theory.* These papers showed that, in analogy with the thermodynamical use of the term, in application to communication channels and abstractions thereof. (Hartley had used a similar idea earlier, but had been less persuasive in demonstrating its innate relevance to questions of communications.) Shannon's theorems bear upon data compression, information rate of channels and devices, and secrecy issues. The entropy $H(\Omega)$ of a finite probability space Ω is

$$H(\Omega) = \sum_{\omega \in \Omega} -P(\omega) \cdot \log_2 P(\omega)$$

where $P()$ is probability. Similarly, the entropy $H(X)$ of a random variable X with finitely-many values is

$$H(X) = \sum_{\text{values } x \text{ of } X} -P(X = x) \cdot \log_2 P(X = x)$$

The base-2 normalization of logarithms means that the entropy of a fair coin is 1, justifying taking *bits* as the unit of entropy. We are to think of *entropy* as a synonym for *uncertainty.* One may readily verify properties such as that $H(p_1, \ldots, p_n)$ is maximum when $p_1 = \ldots = p_n = \frac{1}{n}$: the most uncertainty is when all possibilities are equally likely. Also readily verifiable is

$$H(\underbrace{\frac{1}{n}, \ldots, \frac{1}{n}}_{n}) \le H(\underbrace{\frac{1}{n+1}, \ldots, \frac{1}{n+1}}_{n+1})$$

That is, a larger ensemble of equally likely possibilities is more uncertain than a smaller ensemble.

In this context, a **source** is a probability space whose elements are the (source) **alphabet**. The **entropy of a source** is the entropy of that probability space. For example, English may be naively modeled as the probability space

$$\Omega = \{e, t, o, a, n, i, r, s, \ldots\}$$

where $P(e) \approx 0.11$. $P(t) \approx .9$, etc., where the supposed probabilities are the approximate frequencies with which characters appear.

A naive but useful model of English makes the (naive) assumption that the next letter in a sequence is independent of the previous letter (and the probabilities do not change). This sort of hypothesis on the output of a source is the **i.i.d.** (independent, identically distributed) hypothesis. By contrast, a **Markov** source is one in which the next output of the source depends (in a uniform manner) on the previous output. A **hidden Markov** source is one in which the next output of the source depends (in a uniform manner) on not only the previous output, but on a *state* which may not be visible to an observer.

9.2 Shannon's Noiseless Coding. This is the basic result about **compression**. In a simple form, if the possible single outputs of an i.i.d. *source* are the elements of a finite probability space Ω, to be encoded as strings of 0's and 1's so as to minimize the expected length of the binary codewords,

$$H(\Omega) \leq (\text{expected word length with optimal encoding}) \leq H(\Omega) + 1$$

where $H(\Omega)$ is entropy, as above. (Analogues of this result hold for certain more complicated sources, as well.) This illustrates the aptness of the notion of entropy, since it is the answer to a fundamental question. Further, given a *fixed* source alphabet, construction of an optimal encoding is straightforward (Huffman encoding). Compression is also called *source coding*. See [G2] or [Ro], for example.

A far subtler aspect of serious compression schemes is, in effect, exactly the choice of an advantageous source alphabet, given a *real* source. E.g., see [Sn].

In this vein, we have a reasonable heuristic test of 'randomness' of a string of characters: if any one of the standard compression utilities (*gzip*, *zip*, *bzip2*, etc.) can compress the string, then the string is assuredly *not* random. Indeed, in successfully choosing a source alphabet with skewed probabilities, the algorithm has detected a pattern. Of course, the repertoire of patterns found in such a manner is limited.

Another basic communications notion is that of a **channel**, meant to mirror aspects of real-world communications channels, and also to abstract critical notions. The simplest interesting channel model is the **binary symmetric channel**, which accepts as inputs sequences of 0's and 1's, flipping each one to the other with a fixed (*bit error*) probability p, independent of previous flips-or-not. To successfully transmit information through such a channel the information must incorporate some sort of **redundancy**. The simplest version of redundancy is a *repetition code*: for example, to communicate a bit, one might send that bit through the channel 3 times, and have recipient take a *vote* of the 3 received bits: if a majority of the received bits are 1's, that is how the message is interpreted, while if a majority are 0's, it is inferred that the message was 0. It is a straightforward and elementary exercise to compute that the probability of *incorrectly* decoding a single bit is

$$\text{probability of incorrectible error} = 3p^2 + p^3$$

For n bits, the probability of correctly decoding *all* bits is $(1-p)^n$. Thus, using three-fold repetition, to have probability less than $\varepsilon > 0$ of incorrectly decoding any single bit of a message, we take

$$n < \frac{\log(1-\varepsilon)}{\log(1-p)}$$

Thus, for example, for p small, this allows us to send $n \sim \sqrt{p}$ bits correctly with probability about $1 - \sqrt{p}$.

But this three-fold repetition code uses (at least) 3 times the space and time of the original message itself. That is, the **information rate** of the three-fold repetition code is 1/3. It is not hard to imagine that repetition codes are not the most efficient choices available. Encodings with the intent to be robust against channel-induced errors are *error-correcting codes*, or *forward error-correction* schemes (as opposed to error *detection* schemes which must ask for retransmission upon detection of an error). See [Rn], [G2], for example, or the updated encyclopedic classic [MS]. Construction of error-correcting codes is much harder than construction of compression algorithms.

9.3 Shannon's Noisy Coding Theorem. This provides our second illustration of the aptness of the notion of entropy. This result is a surprisingly optimistic assertion about the creation of good error-correcting codes. (Roughly) define the **channel capacity** C of a binary symmetric channel (as above) with bit error rate p to be the upper bound information rates achievable by clever error correction encoding while simultaneously demanding that the probability of uncorrectible errors can be made as nearly 0 as one wishes. Surprisingly, Shannon's **Noisy Coding** theorem proves that

$$\begin{aligned}\text{capacity of channel with bit error rate } p &= 1 - H(\{p, 1-p\}) \\ &= 1 - \left(p \log_2 \frac{1}{p} + (1-p) \log_2 \frac{1}{(1-p)}\right)\end{aligned}$$

where $H(\{p, 1-p\})$ is the entropy of the two-element probability space with probabilities p and $1-p$. (The orthodox treatment of this would be to *define* the channel capacity to be the entropy, and then prove that this definition is 'correct'.) Shannon's proof in effect showed that the *average* code achieves that level of performance. Thus, one would tend to say that *random* codes are good. Paradoxically, it appears to be difficult to systematically choose these good random codes.

The fact that channel capacity is not zero while assuring nearly error-free transmission of information is striking. At the same time, the well-definedness of channel capacity as a definite limit on the transmission of correct information is almost equally striking. And, again, more than merely being a heuristic imitation of thermodynamical ideas, Shannon's two theorems show that entropy has a provable significance.

Information theory consists of issues surrounding compression and error correction. The Shannon theorems and successive developments are often implicitly understood as justification for thinking about cryptography in information-theoretic terms, at least as a heuristic, even though it appears to be difficult to give substance to the intuitively appealing notion that a cipher *increases entropy.* More plausible is the notion that limits on hiding information can be objectively measured.

9.4 Statistical randomness. This is quantifiable, although seems sharply insufficient to assure adequate cryptographic randomness. A statistically random sequence of 0's and 1's will pass various *low-level* tests. We will briefly survey *empirical* tests, meaning that one ignores the means of producing the pseudo-random bits, but simply measures various features of samples from the sequence.

First, Pearson's χ^2 test (e.g., see [Kn] section 3.3) gives potential quantitative sense to the intuitively plausible fact that sampling of the outcome of a genuinely random variable is skewed to various degrees. That is, in 100 flips of a fair coin one ought not rely upon an outcome of 50 heads and 50 tails, but, rather, an outcome merely *close* to that. The sense of *close* is quantified by the χ^2 test, though setting of thresh-holds still is a matter of subjective judgement. Again, see [Kn] for discussion of proper use of the χ^2 test in this context. Roughly, the χ^2 test reports the probability that a random variable with alleged probabilities would produce a given sample. Thus, apart from setting thresh-holds, all the following tests can be made quantitative via the χ^2 test, that is, the use of the term *roughly* below can be converted to something numerical, though we will not do so.

Samples of necessary but not sufficient statistical requirements on sequences of bits are: **Equidistribution:** The number of 0's should be roughly the number of 1's in a sample (but of course not *exactly*). **Serial test:** The four possible pairs of successive bits, 00, 01, 10, and 11, should be roughly equidistributed. **Poker test:** The various possibilities of (e.g.) 5 consecutive bits, namely, all the same, one 0 and four 1's, etc., with their respective probabilities, should appear roughly as expected. **Coupon collector's test:** This test chooses one or more unusual patterns (such as 11111) and looks at the length of subsequences necessary to see such a pattern. Failure of any of these tests is a fairly sharp denial of randomness.

In the same vein, there are heuristic methods to eliminate statistical biases from a given sequence of bits. Such procedures, or at least their intended effects, are known as **distillation** or **purification** of entropy or randomness. There is an obvious hazard in the very notion. For example, given a sequence of bits, to 'distill' a subsequence with roughly the same number of 0's and 1's, one might explicitly drop any 11's or 00's. But, of course, this produces the not-random ...101010.... As this trivial example illustrates, generally there is a tendency for too-naive distillation attempts to repair one bias at the expense of another. It seems fair to say that the problem of distillation of randomness or entropy is not simple, especially if the goal is the cryptographic one of unpredictability, since the distillation algorithm itself must be deterministic.

Again, statistical randomness is not cryptographic randomness, so the above samples of conditions are *necessary*, not *sufficient* conditions on a pRNG.

9.5 Deterministic pRNGs. As noted earlier, the existence of the Massey-Berlekamp decisively shows that LFSRs and LCGs are not useful as cryptographic pRNGs, even though such a pRNG can be arranged so it their state does not repeat for a very long time. A long period is a necessary, but not sufficient, condition for a good pRNG.

The **Blum-Blum-Shub** pRNG has provable properties, and is easy to describe, but is a bit inefficient, and still needs high quality random numbers to generate the data to construct the generator in the first place. The set-up is choice of large random primes p and q, and random seed s_o. Successive secret internal states are computed by

$$s_{n+1} = s_n^2 \,\%\, pq$$

and public output bits are produced by

$$b_n = s_n \,\%\, 2$$

One can prove (e.g., see also [St]) that being able to predict successive output bits consistently better than half the time allows one to factor pq. But note that perhaps 1000 genuinely random bits are needed to *set up* a secure BBS pRNG, so it would be silly to imagine using BBS to generate any smaller number of bits. Again, with insufficiently random set-up data, an attacker does not try to break the pRNG itself, but, instead, tries to guess the initial data (a dictionary attack). For example, with $p = 103$, $q = 211$, $s_0 = 13$, the first 120 bits generated are

1	1	0	1	1	1	1	1	1	0	0	1	1	1	1	0	0	1	1	0
0	1	0	0	1	1	0	1	1	1	1	1	1	0	0	1	1	1	1	0
0	1	1	0	0	1	0	0	1	1	0	1	1	1	1	1	1	0	0	1
1	1	1	0	0	1	1	0	0	1	0	0	1	1	0	1	1	1	1	1
1	0	0	1	1	1	1	0	0	1	1	0	0	1	0	0	1	1	0	1
1	1	1	1	1	0	0	1	1	1	1	0	0	1	1	0	0	1	0	0

As dubious as our powers of assessment of randomness may be, there seems to be no obvious elementary pattern. And, again, one should note the fact that the data p, q, and s_0 needed to be chosen.

The Naor-Reingold generator [NR] is of a similar nature, refining these ideas. As with the Blum–Blum–Shub algorithm, it is provably secure *assuming* the infeasibility of factoring integers $N = p \cdot q$, where p and q are large primes. Its set-up is a little more complicated. Fix a size n, and choose two random n-bit primes p and q, both equal to 3 mod 4, and put $N = pq$. Choose a random integer g which is a square mod N. Let

$$a = (a_{1,0}, a_{1,1}, a_{2,0}, a_{2,1}, \ldots, a_{n,0}, a_{n,1})$$

be a random sequence of $2n$ values in $\{1, 2, \ldots, N\}$. Let $r = (r_1, \ldots, r_n)$ be a random sequence of 0's and 1's. For an integer t of at most $2n$ bits, let $b_{2n}(t)$ be the vector of binary expansion coefficient of t, padded as necessary on the left to have length $2n$. For two such binary vectors

$$v = (v_1, \ldots, v_n), \qquad w = (w_1, \ldots, w_n)$$

with v_i's and w_i's all 0's or 1's, define

$$v \cdot w = (v_1, \ldots, v_n) \cdot (w_1, \ldots, w_n) = \Big(\sum_{1 \le i \le n} v_i w_i\Big) \% 2$$

Then for any n-tuple $x = (x_1, \ldots, x_n)$ of 0's and 1's, define a $\{0, 1\}$-valued function

$$f(x) = f_{N,g,a,r}(x) = r \cdot \underline{(}g^{a_{1,x_1} + a_{2,x_2} + a_{3,x_3} + \cdots + a_{n,x_n}} \% N)$$

Then, assuming that it is infeasible to factor N, the output of the function $f = f_{N,g,a,r}$ is indistinguishable from random bits.

9.6 Genuine randomness. Repeatedly flipping a (fair) coin to generate successive 0's and 1's yields (so far as we know) 'genuinely random' bits. The problem is that the process is slow. The decay of radioactive isotopes is genuinely random, so far as we know, but perhaps inconvenient, though see [Fo]. Atmospheric noise [RNG] and lava lamps are plausible generators.

Several commercial and open-source products exist which in conjunction with a desktop or laptop computer produce 'random' numbers by timing keyboard or mouse or other activities presumably influenced by irregular external events. For example, on most recent unix/linux systems the devices '/dev/random' and '/dev/urandom' (created by T. Ts'o) collect events, the former producing output whenever sufficient 'entropy' has been collected, while the latter produces output with whatever is available. The manpage for *urandom* contains platform-specific information about these parts of the kernel. For example, in Perl on a typical Linux platform,

```
#!/usr/bin/perl
open R, "/dev/random";
read R, $random, 1;
close R;
print unpack("H*", $random);
```

prints a plausibly random byte in hexadecimal. Typically, commercial products try to remove as many statistical biases as possible from bit streams produced by the environment, intending to leave us with 'genuinely random' bits.

Notes

Kahn [Ka] and Singh [Si] are historical discussions of cryptography. Grittier practical aspects with an exhaustive bibliography are in Schneier [Sch1]. To understand practical realities, one must also read Schneier's [Sch2]. A high-level engineering-oriented formal text paying attention to specifics of NIST standards is Stinson [St]. More mathematical is the Handbook [MOV] by Menezes, van Oorschot, and Vanstone, giving many algorithms in readable pseudo-code, with bibliographic commentaries, but not including more sophisticated items such as elliptic curve techniques. The *Handbook* provides no proofs, neither of underlying mathematical facts (some nonstandard), nor of correctness of algorithms, nor of runtime estimates. [Ga] is a representative of an older time. The discussion [DR] of the Advanced Encryption Standard, Rijndael, by its authors, Daemen and Rijmen, is informative about design issues. Despite being somewhat faster and more flexible than the other AES candidates, it was a surprise to this author that Rijndael, the most mathematically structured of the candidates, should have won. In this context, one should not overlook the new attack [FM] on Rijndael and similar ciphers. Koblitz' [Ko2] goes beyond elliptic curve methods to show how to use jacobians of certain hyperelliptic curves.

References

[A] L.M. Adleman, *The function field sieve*, Algorithmic Number Theory, Lecture Notes in Computer Science **877** (1994), 108–121.

[APR] L.M. Adleman, C. Pomerance, R. Rumely, *On distinguishing prime numbers from composite numbers*, Annals of Mathematics **117** (1983), 173-206.

[AES] *NIST AES homepage*, http://csrc.nist.gov/CryptoToolkit/aes/.

[AGP] W. Alford, A. Granville, C. Pomerance, *There are infinitely-many Carmichael numbers*, Annals of Mathematics **140** (1994), 703–722.

[AKS] M. Agrawal, N. Kayal, N. Saxena, *PRIMES is in P*, (preprint 2002) http://www.cse.iitk.ac.in/new/primality.html.

[AAG] I. Anshel, M. Anshel, D. Goldfeld, *An algebraic method for public-key cryptography*, Mathematics Research Letters **6** (1999), 1–5.

[B] E. Bach, *Toward a theory of Pollard's rho method*, Information and Computation **90** (1991), 139–155.

[BS] E. Bach, J. Shallit, *Algorithmic Number Theory*, MIT Press (1996).

[Ba] W.D. Banks, *Towards faster cryptosystems, II, (this volume).*

[Ba] F.L. Bauer, *Decrypted Secrets: Methods and Max-ims of Cryptology*, Springer-Verlag (2000).

[Be] J. Bell, *Speakable and Unspeakable in Quantum Mechanics*, Cambridge Univ. Press (1993).

[Ber] D. Bernstein, *http://www.cse.iitk.ac.in/new/primality.html.*

[BS1] E. Biham, A. Shamir, *Differential cryptanalysis of DES-like cryptosystems*, Journal of Cryptology **4** (1991), 3–72.

[BS2] E. Biham, A. Shamir, *Differential cryptanalysis of the Data Encryption Standard*, Springer-Verlag (1993).

[BS3] E. Biham, A. Shamir, *Differential cryptanalysis of the full 16-round DES*, Lecture Notes in Computer Science **740** (1993), 494–502.

[BKL] J. Birman, K. Ko, S. Lee, *A new approach to the word and conjugacy problems in the braid groups*, Advances in Mathematics **139** (1998), 322–353.

[BSS] I.F. Blake, G. Seroussi, N.P. Smart, *Elliptic curves in cryptography*, London Math. Soc. Lecture Note Series **265** (2000).

[BBS] L. Blum, M. Blum, M. Shub, *A simple unpredictable random number generator*, SIAM Journal on Computing **15** (1986), 364–383.

[Bo] D. Boneh, *Twenty years of attacks on the RSA cryptosystem*, Notices of the AMS **46** (1999), 203–213.

[BDF] D. Boneh, G. Durfee, Y. Frankel, *An attack on RSA given a fraction of the private key bits*, Advances in Cryptology, AsiaCrypt '98, Lecture Notes in Computer Science **1514** (1998), 25–34.

[Bor] F. Bornemann, *PRIMES is in P: a breakthrough for 'Everyman'*, Notices of the A.M.S. **50** (2003), 545–552.

[Br] S. Brands, *Untraceable off-line cash in wallets with observers.*, Advances in Cryptology, Crypto '93, Lecture Notes in Computer Science **773** (1994), 302-318.

[BLP] J. Buhler, H.W. Lenstra, C. Pomerance, *Factoring integers with the number fields sieve*, Development of the Number Field Sieve (ed. A.K. Lenstra and H.W. Lenstra), Lecture Notes in Mathematics **1554** (1993).

[CS] A.R. Calderbank, P. Shor, *Good quantum error-correcting codes exist*, Phys. Rev. A **54** (1996), 1098–1105.

[Ch] D. Chaum, *Security without identification: transactions systems to make Big Brother obsolete*, Communications of the ACM **28** (1985), 1030–1044.

[CFN] D. Chaum, A. Fiat, M. Naor, *Untraceable electronic cash*, Advances in Cryptology, Crypto '88, Springer-Verlag (1990), 319–327.

[C] H. Cohen, *A Course in Computational Number Theory*, Springer-Verlag (1993).

[Co1] D. Coppersmith, *Modifications to the number field sieve*, Journal of Cryptology **6** (1993), 169–180.

[Co2] D. Coppersmith, *Small solutions to polynomial equations, and low exponent RSA vulnerabilities*, J. Cryptology **10** (1997), 233–594.

[CLR] T.H. Cormen, C.E. Leiserson, R.L. Rivest, *Introduction to Algorithms*, MIT Press (1990).

[CP] R. Crandall, C. Pomerance, *Prime Numbers, a Computational Perspective*, Springer-Verlag (2001).

[DR] J. Daemen, V. Rijmen, *The design of Rijndael,. AES - The Advanced Encryption Standard*, Springer-Verlag (2002).

[DH] W. Diffie, M.E. Hellman, *New directions in cryptography*, IEEE Transactions on Information Theory **22** (1976), 644–654.

[EPR] A. Einstein, B. Podolsky, N. Rosen, *Can quantum-mechanical description of physical reality be considred complete?*, Phys. Rev. **47** (1935), 469-473.

[EFF] Electronic Frontier Foundation, *Cracking DES*, O'Reilly and Associates (1998).

[E] T. ElGamal, *A public key cryptosystem and signature scheme based on discrete logarithms*, IEEE Transactions on Information Theory **IT-31** (1985), 469–473.

[Fo] J. Walker, *http://www.fourmilab.ch/hotbits/*.

[FM] J. Fuller, William Millan, *On Linear Redundancy in the AES S-Box*, (preprint, 2002).

[Ga] H.F. Gaines, *Cryptanalysis, A Study of Ciphers and Their Solution*, Dover (1939, 1956).

[G] P.B. Garrett, *Making and Breaking Codes: An Introduction to Cryptography*, Prentice-Hall (2001).

[G2] P.B. Garrett, *The Mathematics of Coding Theory: Information, Compression, Error-Correction, and Finite Fields*, Prentice-Hall (2004).

[Gr1] O. Goldreich, *Modern Cryptography, Probabilistic Proofs, and Pseudorandomness*, Springer-Verlag (1999).

[Gr2] O. Goldreich, *Foundations of Cryptography: Basic Tools*, Cambridge University Press (2001).

[Go] S.W. Golomb, *Shift Register Sequences*, Holden-Day, San Francisco (1967).

[HPS] J. Hoffstein, J. Pipher, J. Silverman, *NTRU: A new high-speed public-key cryptosystem*, Crypto '96 rump session.

[HG] Nick Howgrave-Graham, *Public-key cryptology and proofs of security, (this volume).*

[HT] J. Hughes, A. Tannenbaum, *Length-based attacks for certain group-based encryption rewriting systems (preprint)* (2000).

[Ka] D. Kahn, *The Codebreakers*, Scribner (1996).

[KLMT]E. Knill, R. Laflamme, R. Martinez, C.-H. Tseng, *An algorithmic benchmark for quantum information processing*, Nature **404** (2000), 368–370.

[Kn] D. Knuth, *The Art of Computer Programming*, Addison-Wesley **2** (1989).

[Ko1] N. Koblitz, *A Course in Number Theory and Cryptography*, Springer-Verlag (1994).

[Ko2] N. Koblitz, *Algebraic Aspects of Cryptography*, Springer-Verlag (1998).

[Ko3] N. Koblitz, *Elliptic curve cryptosystems*, Mathematics of Computation **48** (1987), 203–209.

[KMV] N. Koblitz, A. Menezes, S. Vanstone, *The state of elliptic curve cryptography*, Designs, Codes, and Cryptography **19** (2000), 173–193.

[Ko] P.C. Kocher, *Timing attacks on implementations of Diffie-Hellman, RSA, DSS, and other systems*, Advances in Cryptology, Crytpo '96, Lecture Notes in Computer Science **1109** (1996), 104–113.

[L1] S. Landau, *Standing the test of time: the data encryption standard*, Notices of the AMS **47** (2000), 341–349.

[L2] S. Landau, *Communication security for the twenty-first century: the advanced encryption standard*, Notices of the AMS **47** (2000), 450–459.

[L3] S. Landau, *[review of ten books on crypto]*, Bulletin of the AMS **41** (2004), 357–367.

[LL] A.K. Lenstra, H.W. Lenstra, Jr. (eds.), *The Development of the Number Field Sieve*, Lecture Notes in Mathematics **1554** (1993).

[LLL] A.K. Lenstra, H.W. Lenstra, L. Lovasz, *Factoring polynomials with polynomial coefficients*, Math. Annalen **261** (1982), 515–534.

[Lie] D. Lieman, *Cryptography in the Real World Today, (this volume).*

[LV] M. Li, P. Vitányi, *An Introduction to Kolmogorov Complexity and Its Applications*, Springer-Verlag (1997).

[MS] F.J. MacWilliams, N.J.A. Sloane, *The Theory of Error-Correcting Codes*, North-Holland (1998).

[Ma] J.L. Massey, *Shift-Register Synthesis and BCH Decoding*, IEEE Trans. on Information Theory **IT-155** (1969), 122–127.

[Mat1] M. Matsui, *Linear cryptanalysis method for DES cipher*, Lecture Notes in Computer Science **765** (1994), 386–397.

[Mat2] M. Matsui, *The first experimental cryptanalysis of the data encryption standard*, Lecture Notes in Computer Science **839** (1994), 1–11.

[MOV] A.J. Menezes, P.C. van Oorschot, S.A. Vanstone, *Handbook of Applied Cryptography*, CRC Press (1997).

[MH] R. Merkle, M. Hellman, *Hiding information and signatures in trapdoor knapsacks*, IEEE Trans. on Information Theory **IT-24** (1978), 525–530.

[M] G.L. Miller, *Riemann's hypothesis and tests for primality*, Journal of Computer and Systems Science **13** (1976), 300–317.

[MB] M.A. Morrison , J. Brillhart, *A method of factoring and the factorization of F_7*, Math. Comp. **29** (1975), 183-205.

[NR] M. Naor, O. Reingold, *Synthesizers and their application to the parallel construction of pseudo-random functions*, Proceedings 36th IEEE Symposium on Foundations of COmputer Science (1995), 170–181.

[O] A.M. Odlyzko, *Discrete logarithms: the past and the future*, Designs, Codes, and Cryptography **19** (2000), 129–145.

[OO] T. Okamoto, K. Ohta, *Universal electronic cash*, Springer Lecture Notes in Computer Science **435** (1992), 324–337.

[PB] A. Pati, S. Braunstein, *Impossibility of deleting and unknown quantum state*, Nature **404** (2000), 164–165.

[P1] J.M. Pollard, *A Monte Carlo method for factorization*, BIT **15** (1975), 331–334.

[P2] J.M. Pollard, *Monte Carlo methods for index computation (mod p)*, Mathematics of Computation **32** (1978), 918–924.

[Pom] C. Pomerance, *Analysis and comparison of some integer factoring algorithms*, Computational Methods in Number Theory, ed. H.W. Lenstra, Jr., R. Tijdeman, Math. Centrum, Amsterdam (1982), 89–139.

[Ra] M.O. Rabin, *Probabilistic algorithms for testing primality*, Journal of Number Theory **12** (1980), 128–138.

[RNG] *http://www.random.org/*.

[RSA] R.L. Rivest, A. Shamir, L. Adleman, *A method for obtaining digital signatures and public key cryptosystems*, Communications of the ACM **21** (1978), 120–126.

[Ro] S. Roman, *Coding and information theory*, Springer-Verlag **GTM 134** (1992).

[Sa] A. Salomaa, *Public-Key Cryptography*, Springer-Verlag (1996).

[Sn] D. Salomon, *Data Compression: the Complete Reference*, Springer-Verlag (1997).

[Sch1] B. Schneier, *Applied Cryptography, Protocols, Algorithms, and Source Code in C*, John Wiley and Sons (1995).

[Sch2] B. Schneier, *Secrets and Lies*, John Wiley and Sons (2000).

[ST] B. Schneier, J. Kelsey, D. Whiting, D. Wagner, C. Hall, N. Ferguson, *The Twofish Encryption Algorithm*, John Wiley and Sons (1999).

[SE] C. Schnorr, M. Euchner, *Lattic basis reduction: improved practical algorithms and solving subset sum problems*, Mathematical Programming **66** (1994), 181–194.

[Sh] A. Shamir, *A polynomial-time algorithm for breaking the Merkle-Hellman cryptosystem*, Proc. 23d FOCS Symposium (1982), 145–152.

[Sh1] C.E. Shannon, *A mathematical theory of communication*, Bell Systems Technical Journal **27** (1948), 379–423, 623–656.

[Sh2] C.E. Shannon, *Communication theory of secrecy systems*, Bell Systems Technical Journal **28** (1949), 656–715.

[Sho1] P. Shor, *Algorithms for quantum computation: discrete logarithms and factoring*, Proceedings of the Thirty-Fifth Annual Symposium on the Foundations of Computer Science (1994), 124–134.

[Sho2] P. Shor, *Polynomial-time algorithms for prime factorization and discrete logarithms on a quantum computer*, SIAM Review **41** (1999), 303–332.

[Shou] V. Shoup, *Lower bounds for discrete logarithms and related problems*, Lecture Notes in Computer Science **1233** (1997), 256–266.

[Shp] I. Shparlinski, *Number Theoretic Methods in Cryptography, Complexity Lower Bounds*, Birkhauser-Verlag (1999).

[Shp2] I. Shparlinski, *Playing 'Hide-and-seek' with numbers: the hidden number problems, lattices, and exponential sums*, Birkhauser-Verlag (1999).

[Sil1] J.H. Silverman, *The arithmetic of elliptic curves*, Graduate Texts in Math., Springer-Verlag **106** (1986).

[Sil2] J.H. Silverman, *Advanced topics in the arithmetic of elliptic curves*, Graduate Texts in Math., Springer-Verlag **151** (1994).

[Sil3] J.H. Silverman, *Elliptic curves and cryptography, (this volume)*.

[Si] S. Singh, *The Code Book*, Doubleday (1999).

[So] R. Solovay, V. Strassen, *A fast Monte Carlo test for primality*, SIAM Journal on Computing **6** (1977), 84–85.

[St] D. Stinson, *Cryptography: Theory and Practice*, CRC Press (2002).

[TW] W. Trappe, L. Washington, *Introduction to Cryptography with Coding Theory*, Prentice-Hall (2002).

[WM] N. Wagner, M. Magyarik, *A public key cryptosystem based on the word problem*, Lecture Notes in Computer Science **196** (1985), 19–36.

[Wag] S.S. Wagstaff, *Cryptanalysis of Number Theoretic Ciphers*, Chapman-Hall/CRC (2003).

[Wash] L. Washington, *Elliptic Curves: Number Theory and Cryptography*, Chapman-Hall/CRC (2003).

[Wh] W. Whyte, *Towards faster cryptosystems, I, (this volume)*.

[Wie] M.J. Wiener, *Cryptanalysis of short RSA exponenets*, IEEE Trans. on Information Theory **36** (1990), 553–558.

[Wil] H.C. Williams, *A $p+1$ method of factoring*, Math. Comp. **39** (1982), 225-234.

School of Mathematics, University of Minnesota, Minneapolis, MN 55455
E-mail address: `garrett@math.umn.edu`

Proceedings of Symposia in Applied Mathematics
Volume **62**, 2005

Cryptography in the Real World Today

Daniel Lieman

ABSTRACT. The mathematics of cryptography is just the beginning of designing and deploying secure systems. Although mathematics can be used to construct cryptographic primitives, the process of incorporating these primitives into secure systems is a highly non-trivial one, involving issues such as performance constraints and key distribution.

This expository article focuses on why common cryptographic primitives are useful in building secure systems, on how typical secure systems are constructed, the security they actually provide, and their limitations. Its purpose is to introduce mathematicians to some of the real-world constraints and applications of mathematically-based cryptosystems.

Security Functionality

"Security" is a vague term. In different situations, the idea of "secure" communication means different things. For example, when sending a "secret" message to a coworker about my boss, I certainly want to enjoy **confidentiality**; it might be a disaster (for me) if my boss were to read the message. On the other hand, when getting a message from my wife, telling me that I need to come home right away, I need to verify the **authenticity** and **integrity** of the message. If it's authentic and if no mistakes were made when the mssage was passed on to me then I need to head home immediately. If I order an item from an "all sales are final" special in a catalog, that order needs to be protected with **non-repudiation** – I shouldn't be able to later claim that I didn't actually order the item in question. I'd also like, sometimes, to enjoy **privacy** or **anonymity**, the way I do if I purchase lottery tickets with cash at a gas station.

These assurances:

- Confidentiality
- Authenticity
- Non-repudiation
- Privacy

1991 *Mathematics Subject Classification.* Primary 54C40, 14E20; Secondary 46E25, 20C20.

Key words and phrases. Cryptography, Secure Systems Design.

The preparation of this article was supported in part by NSF Grant DMS-9700542. The author would like to thank the referee for many excellent suggestions.

are critical to how we process information, both personal and professional. We normally establish them by context, or by personal knowledge. For example, to pass a secret message to a coworker, we both might go out into a hallway, or leave the building, so we can't be overheard. I'm sure I'm talking to the correct coworker because I know this person to whom I wish to pass some gossip. To authenticate my wife's message, I might trust that I know her voice on the phone, or her tone when ordering me home. If the message comes through a coworker, I might trust that s/he knows my wife's voice, and is a reliable channel.

One goal of using cryptography is to gain a similar level of assurance without the context or personal knowledge we usually use to establish trust or identity. We want to establish that level of assurance even though we might be communicating over a public, easily intercepted or monitored, channel. When I order a book over the Internet from Amazon.com, I should be fairly sure I'm actually ordering from (and passing my credit card information to) Amazon.com, and Amazon.com should be fairly sure that I am the one who actually ordered the book. I may or may not require confidentiality (though I probably do if I'm sending my credit card number), but I certainly want to verify the authenticity of Amazon.com, and Amazon.com needs to verify my authenticity and, ideally, Amazon.com would get some assurance of non-repudiation.

Much of what we wish to authenticate is **identity.** The "authenticity" of Amazon.com that I'm verifying above is really the identity of the web server claiming to be Amazon.com. Identity management is one of the most important functions of cryptographic constructions. After all, we're trying to mimic the sorts of "trust" we have in real life and in real interactions, and those are usually based on the identities of the parties.

Although identity by itself isn't enough to determine whether you should trust someone (I know Paul Garrett personally, and I would recognize him handing me a check for $1,000,000, but that doesn't mean I'd think the check was valid), it's an important enough problem by itself that we will dedicate a large part of this article towards an understanding of how cryptographic primitives are used to establish identity in practice, and the transitive trust constructions that make this possible. What makes this problem interesting (besides its importance) is that most of the usual cues we use to establish identity and authentication (appearance, voice, physical context) are absent when we are performing a remote interaction (over the Internet or airwaves). In addition, the easily intercepted and modified nature of Internet and OTA (over the air) communications makes it easier for an adversary to carry out attacks (including "spoofing" - pretending to be a given party).

Finally, we should mention the need for a careful consideration of where trust resides in any allegedly secure system. If a protocol relies on a user's token, then all we really know upon completion of the protocol is that the token was present. True security might require multi-factor authentication (in addition to the token, some biometric or password input from the user) as well as users who deploy their various security tools only in appropriate environments. The classic examples of security failure are the bogus ATM machines. The users input their ATM cards and PIN codes, and left without complaining when the machines reported that access was temporarily disabled. Only when an alert user noticed that there were no cables to the machines, and that the machines were not in the usual locations did police realize a scam was operating. Even the most secure systems will require direct action and judgment on the part of the user. Such design considerations are obiously complicated, and well beyond the scope of this article.

Security Primitives

All of our systems will be built up from so-called "cryptographic primitives." Typical security primitives include:

- Public-key encryption/decryption;
- Symmetric-key encryption/decryption;
- Public-key signature/verification;
- Symmetric-key signature/verification;
- Hash functions.

There are others as well, both useful and "academic" constructions, but these will be the only ones used during this paper.

Public-key encryption/decryption.

In public-key encryption/decryption, a *public key* is used to encrypt messages, and a corresponding *private key* is used to decrypt them. Both the encryption and decryption algorithms are public. The picture is something like

$$\text{Original message} \longrightarrow \left\{\begin{array}{c}\text{Original message}\\ \text{Public key}\end{array}\right\} \stackrel{\text{Encryption}}{\longrightarrow} \underbrace{\text{Encrypted Message}}_{\text{transmitted, can be intercepted}}$$

$$\text{Encrypted Message} \longrightarrow \left\{\begin{array}{c}\text{Encrypted message}\\ \text{Private key}\end{array}\right\} \stackrel{\text{Decryption}}{\longrightarrow} \text{Original message}$$

It is obvious that in order for this to work, the public key must be distributed to the encrypting party, and the private key must be known only to the decrypting party. One of the greatest problems in using public-key encryption/decryption (which we will address below) is the problem of providing assurance that the encrypting party possesses the correct public key for his/her intended recipient.

Symmetric-key encryption/decryption.

In symmetric-key encryption/decryption, the same key is used for both encryption and decryption. Both the encryption and decryption algorithms are public. The picture is

$$\text{Original message} \longrightarrow \left\{\begin{array}{c}\text{Original message}\\ \text{Secret key}\end{array}\right\} \stackrel{\text{Encryption}}{\longrightarrow} \underbrace{\text{Encrypted Message}}_{\text{transmitted, can be intercepted}}$$

$$\text{Encrypted Message} \longrightarrow \left\{\begin{array}{c}\text{Encrypted message}\\ \text{Secret key}\end{array}\right\} \stackrel{\text{Decryption}}{\longrightarrow} \text{Original message}$$

It is clear that in order for this to work, the secret key must be kept, well, secret. The obvious problems with this particular model include secure distribution and storage of the (secret) keys.

Public-key signature/verification.

In public-key signature/verification, the *private key* is used to *sign* a document. Anyone can use the *public key* in order to verify that the proported signature was indeed generated by someone possessing the (secret) private key. The picture is

$$\text{Original message} \longrightarrow \left\{\begin{array}{c}\text{Original message}\\ \text{Private key}\end{array}\right\} \xrightarrow{\text{Signing}} \underbrace{\text{Signature}}_{\text{transmitted}}$$

$$\text{Signature} \longrightarrow \left\{\begin{array}{c}\text{Signature}\\ \text{Public key}\\ \text{Original message}\end{array}\right\} \xrightarrow{\text{Verification}} \left\{\begin{array}{c}\text{Yes/No, this was/wasn't}\\ \text{the valid signature}\end{array}\right\}$$

Note that in this model, in order to perform the verification, the verifying party needs a copy of the original message, as well. This isn't always the case - some signature/verification algorithms allow message recovery of (very) short messages.

As before, one of the key problems is the question of how the verifying party gains assurance that it is verifying with the correct public key.

Symmetric-key signature/verification.

In symmetric-key signature/verification, the (known to both parties) *secret key* is used both to sign and verify proported signatures.

$$\text{Original message} \longrightarrow \left\{\begin{array}{c}\text{Original message}\\ \text{Secret key}\end{array}\right\} \xrightarrow{\text{Signing}} \underbrace{\text{Signature}}_{\text{transmitted}}$$

$$\text{Signature} \longrightarrow \left\{\begin{array}{c}\text{Signature}\\ \text{Secret key}\\ \text{Original message}\end{array}\right\} \xrightarrow{\text{Verification}} \left\{\begin{array}{c}\text{Yes/No, this was/wasn't}\\ \text{the valid signature}\end{array}\right\}$$

Again, there are signature/verification algorithms which allow message recovery. It is also true in this setting that one of the most important problems is that of (secure) key distribution of the secret keys.

Hash functions.

In some sense, hash functions are the simplest to understand. A hash function is simply a collision-resistant one-way function that turns an arbitrary length message into a fixed digest. The picture is just

$$\text{Original message} \quad \xrightarrow{\text{Hash function}} \quad \text{Hash output}$$

Of course, many different messages hash to the same output (this follows from the usual requirement that the hash length be less than the original message lenth), but "collision-resistant" means that it should be difficult to find such a collision. One consequence of collision-resistance includes the requirement that changing a single bit of the hash input influences each bit of the output.

Hash functions are used in many different settings. For example, a hash function could be used to construct a signing algorithm, just by defining the signature of a *message* to be the

$$\mathcal{H}(\text{message}\|\text{secret key}).$$

Here, we have used $\mathcal{H}$ to denote the hash function, and we have introduced the notation $\|$ to denote concatenation. It is easy to see that anyone who possessed both the message and the secret key could easily verify a signature.

Symmetric-key vs. public-key cryptography

There are a number of different public-key and symmetric-key cryptosystems, but in general, symmetric-key cryptosystems are usually much faster and much smaller than public-key cryptosystems, and are thus usually cheaper to deploy.

There is another significant difference between public-key and symmetric-key cryptosystems. It is usually the case that the public keys are public information when using public-key cryptosystems. This means that an adversary can guess at the contents of a message. For example, if I know that you are encrypting either "yes" or "no," I can encrypt both of them, and compare the resulting ciphertexts to your encrypted message in order to determine your original plaintext. In order to avoid this "dictionary attack," public-key cryptosystems use techniques that add randomness to the message being encrypted (in a well-known way, in order that the randomness can be removed after decryption to recover the original message). Thus the ciphertext output of any public-key cryptosystem is usually longer than the plaintext intput. This is not the case for symmetric-key cryptosystems since they are not vulnerable to the same sort of dictionary attack, though other dictionary attacts may apply.

Public-key cryptosystems, however, do offer some advantages over symmetric key cryptosystems. The primary advantage is that there is no need to establish a shared secret before a secure communication occurs. This has important implications for the ease of adding new users to a secure system, and the complexity of key management. As we go through the examples below, keep in mind exactly which pieces of the system have to be compromised in order to compromise the entire system. With public-key techniques, it is usually easier to base the system security on a single, remote, easy-to-protect secret, instead of either having to distribute that root secret throughout the system or require constant "on-line" (as opposed to offline) access. As a result, many secure systems use a blend of public-key and symmetric-key techniques, leveraging the flexibility of public-key cryptography to distribute symmetric-key secrets.

For example, if one were going to encrypt a large piece of media (a song or a large document, say), one would usually encrypt that large piece of data using symmetric-key cryptography with a randomly chosen key, and then would encrypt that randomly chosen key using a public-key cryptosystem. Then both encrypted files (the encrypted symmetric key and then encrypted data) could be sent to a recipient. In practice, the large piece of media is often encrypted separately, once and for all, and then each download only requires one additional public-key encryption of that one symmetric key for the downloading party.

Typical public-key constructions

As a rule, public-key systems can be constructed in a "modular" function. The key to this flexibility is the concept of a certificate. For example, suppose I trust William's public key, of which I have a copy. Then William could sign a document saying "You should trust Nick's public key, and here's a copy of it: XXXX." Nick could show up at my door, present his (virtual) certificate, and I could verify William's signature, since I have a copy of William's public key. I'd then know to trust Nick's public key, and if Nick signed something, I could verify that it was indeed Nick who did the signing.

There are several key ideas illustrated in this example. One is the notion of the ability of "trust" to be transitive. This allows the construction and verification of "certificate chains." For example, my Internet browser trusts certain Verisign public keys, so if Macquarie University obtained a public/private keypair and a Verisign certificate of that public key, and then Igor Shparlinski obtained a public/private keypair and Macquarie signed his public key, Igor could present to me the "chain" of his certificate and Macquarie's certificate, and I would be able to verify that Verisign did sign the Macquarie certificate (and so I could verify Macquarie's public key) and that Macquarie did sign Igor's certificate (and so I could verify Igor's public key). I'd then be able to encrypt documents for Igor, or verify his signature of a document, and be certain that the public key I was using did in fact belong to Igor (as attested to by Macquarie, which in turn is attested to by Verisign, whom I trust).

Another key idea is the notion of binding an identity to a public/private keypair. This is critical in some applications, meaningless in others (especially when anonymity is a desired feature of the system).

So a typical public-key infrastructure (PKI) deployment includes some kind of registration authority (which can register users) and a certificate authority, as well as other functionality (an ability to tell if certificates have been revoked, or have expired, for example).

The good news is that the primitives of public-key cryptography allow these various pieces to be deployed in a modular fashion. There is often a single root of trust - a pair of keys on which all security is based. The public key in this pair is public (indeed, every party in the system could have a copy of it), but the security of that one private key is critical. Fortunately, it can be kept in a remote, secure facility. In the example above, that single root of trust is Verisign's private key. The Macquarie private key is also important, but not as much as Verisign's. In practice, that Verisign key is extremely highly protected, and the Macquarie key much less so. So the certificate Verisign would sign for Macquarie would usually be of a resonably short lifespan, and renewed as needed. In a truly secure system, the ability to check certificate revocation is critical.

It should be clear that a certificate can be a fairly long document; it includes identity information, public-key information, perhaps some attributes or authorizations. One aspect of current research is techniques to minimize certificate size. (Sometimes, this is fairly simple. For example, instead of providing the full certificate chain, a user could merely provide a link, or pointer, to the certificate chain. Since each piece of information in a certificate is verified before the recipient trusts it, it can be stored or transmitted somewhere else - the recipient (by checking the signature(s)) automatically verifies the integrity of each delivered certificate before trusting it.)

SSL: A public-key case study

SSL (or TLS, which is the name for SSL version 3.0) is the protocol used in a secure web browsing session - when that lock appears on your web browser window. (SSL stands for Secure Sockets Layer, and TLS for Transport Layer Security - these are general protocols that set up a secure link between two endpoints.) SSL/TLS establishes a confidential connection between two parties, after (optionally) verifying the identity of one or both of those parties.

In practice, SSL/TLS is used in two distinct flavors. In one, called *server-only authentication,* the identity of the *server* is verified, but that of the *client* is not. This is the typical model used on the Internet today. A user's web browser might verify that it is talking to Amazon.com (we discuss how this is accomplished, below). but Amazon.com gains its assurance not from a cryptographic construct, but from the credit card, name, address and other information that the user enters, once a secure connection has been established between Amazon.com and the user's browser.

In the other flavor, called mutual-authentication, both parties cryptographically (and transparently) prove their identities to each other. This is ideal when the client side device does not have a rich user interface - for example, when doing a bank transaction from a cell phone. It is (obviously) difficult to enter a name, account number, etc., using the screen and keyboard on a typical phone. More usually, the phone would have the ability to cryptographically establish its identity (once the user had entered a PIN to authorize the phone to proceed) using the mutual authentication feature of a protocol like SSL/TLS. The drawback of this second approach is that the phone must (quickly) perform private-key operations (decryptions or signings) to prove its identity. In practice, private-key operations are time-consuming; this has been the greatest single barrier to the widespread user adoption of secure systems.

We now explain (logically) how SSL/TLS server-only authentication is established. This is not the actual message flow between the server and the client. First, a certain amount of provisioning must already have taken place.

Client Has	Purpose
Root public-key	Used to verify server's certificate chain

Server Has	Purpose
Certificate	Used by client to verify server's credentials
Private key	Used by server to decrypt client's challenge

Client		Server
Hello message	$\longrightarrow$	
	$\longleftarrow$	Hello message, server's certificate
Verifies server's certificate and server's public key		
Generates random pre-secret		
Encrypts pre-secret using server's public key		
Encrypted Pre-secret	$\longrightarrow$	
		Decrypts pre-secret
Derive shared secret from pre-secret		Derive shared secret from pre-secret

The derived shared secret is used as a symmetric key for a symmetric encryption algorithm to ensure confidentiality and integrity for the rest of the communication. Note that the client is certain that it trusts a particular server because the client verifies the server's certificate, and the client verifies that this particular server is the one associated to that certificate by encrypting a challenge (the pre-secret) that only the trusted server could decrypt.

When client authentication is also required, the TLS protocol requires that the client provide its certificate to the server (which the server verifies). The server then issues a challenge to the client which the client signs, in order to prove it is the client associated with that (now trusted) public-key from the client's certificate.

Typical symmetric-key constructions

Symmetric-key cryptography is often used when a high-powered entity (typically a "server," or back-end operations center) wishes to establish some sort of secure or authenticated or verified communication with a constrained entity (which, for purposes of this section, we'll call the "client"). A classic example is that of using the Mobil Speedpass to pay for gas at a fuel pump. On one end, we have the Speedpass operations center, but on the other is the small speedpass token, which draws its power supply from the radio frequency field emitted by the pump (it doesn't even have a battery) and which doesn't have any central processor at all, just some hardwired logic.

In this case, even though a shared secret needs to be known to both the server and the client, we want to design a system where compromise of a single client does not lead to the failure of the entire system. There are many ways to do this, but one key differentiator among them is whether the servers are online or offline.

In the case of online servers, we can design a fairly secure system. A typical construction is that each client has an identification number, and one (or more) keys. These may be derived from the identification number, or assigned randomly. On the server side, each server is online – that is, it is connected to a central operations center, which maintains a list of each identification number, and the associated keys. Cryptographic operations can be securely performed in the operations center, and used to verify the identity of the clients. For example, once the client has broadcast its identification number, the operations center could issue a challenge to a client that could only be successfully answered by possession of the correct secret key. Compromise of a single client does not lead to the failure of the entire system, but the cost of adding additional servers is that each of them must be connected to that centeral operations center. In addition, at the time the clients are provisioned (i.e. loaded with their secret information) a copy of that secret information must be securely maintained and somehow transferred to the operations center.

In the case of offline servers, things get more complicated. Typically, now, each of the keys in the client is derived from a combination of the client identification number with a a master secret via some algorithm. Both the master secret and that algorithm are kept secret, and are embedded in each (offline) server. When an (allegedly valid) client is presented for authentication, the server can re-derive the keys (present in a valid client) and then challenge the client to prove it possesses the correct keys. The risk in this system is that if one could compromise a reader, one could forge an unlimited number of clients. In addition, that master secret and key derivation algorithm must be present not just in every server, but at the point of provisioning. In short, there are a number of points of attack, each of high vulnerability. The advantage is that one is able in return for this higher potential risk, one is able to employ symmetric-key algorithms, which are faster, smaller (and hence cheaper to implement) than public-key alternatives.

One particularly obvious example of offline authentication is that of vehicle immobilizers. Increasingly (in many cases, to comply with local law), auto manufacturers are embedding cryptographic technology into keys, so the car can determine whether the presented key is authentic. The car must authenticate the key without any access to any sort of infrastructure or database.

Note that in all of the above constructions, if the client will present its credentials to any requesting party then while identity might be preserved, privacy might simultaneously be compromised. There is a delicate balance in the design of systems to keep them lightweight, yet still provide the assurances we seek (confidentiality, authenticity, non-repudiation, privacy).

RFID security (through 2002): A symmetric-key case study

The Mobil Speedpass is a typical symmetric-key design. In this system, the server is a gas station pump or a point-of-sale device, and the client is a small RFID token, usually attached to a keychain. All Speedpass servers are connected to a central processing center. When a client is presented to a server, the server passes the client's ID back to the operations center, which generates a challenge. The client responds to the challenge, using its embedded secret key, and the operations center is able to verify that the client did indeed possess the correct secret key.

This sytem is fairly secure, but the cost of adding additional readers is great. Each reader needs to be connected to that online operations center, and it is impossible for a reader to authenticate a client if the reader cannot communicate with the operations center. In practice, Mobil has adopted a number of usage rules to determine when to trust, or not trust, a given client if communications are down. Gas stations often have fairly rich data connections, so this is not a common occurance. If one wanted to extend the use of Speedpass tokens to low-value, remote devices (soda machines, newspapers, readers in buses for city transportation), one would have to make a number of decisions about how to decide to trust a given token, based on the risks and value of fraud. The cost of connecting such devices to a central system is too great, in practice.

Conclusion

We have thought a bit about the idea of "security" and what it really means.

We have seen some of the trade-offs one must consider when deciding to use either public-key or symmetric-key cryptography, and some of the ways in which cryptographic techniques can be used to establish various types of "trust."

Problems in mathematical cryptography (e.g. *"how hard is factoring?"*) are only one small part of the design, deployment and user acceptance of secure cryptographic systems.

References

[AES] NIST, *Specification for the Advanced Encryption Standard (AES)*, which may be downloaded at http://csrc.nist.gov/publications/fips/fips197/fips-197.pdf (2001).

[KL] P. Karu and J. Loikkanen, *Practical Comparison of Fast Public-key Cryptosystems*, available at http://citeseer.nj.nec.com/karu01practical.html (2001).

[PRB] B. Preneel, V. Rijmen, and A. Bosselaers, *Recent Developments in the Design of Conventional Cryptographic Algorithms*, "State of the Art in Applied Cryptography," Lecture Notes in Computer Science 1528 (1998), 106–131.

[WS] D. Wagner and B. Schneier, *Analysis of the SSL 3.0 Protocol*, Proceedings of the Second USENIX Workshop on Electronic Commerce, Oakland, CA (1996).

Fidelity Investments, One Spartan Way TS2F, Merrimack, NH 03054

E-mail address: daniel.lieman@fmr.com

Proceedings of Symposia in Applied Mathematics
Volume **62**, 2005

Public key cryptology and proofs of security

Nick Howgrave-Graham

ABSTRACT. We explain how cryptographers attempt to justify the security of certain cryptological schemes, and discuss what it means to have a "proof of security". Concentrating mostly on encryption schemes, we introduce the notions of semantic security, bit security and security against chosen ciphertext attacks. We also briefly discuss the random oracle model, and consider the strength of results proved in this model. The report advocates the paradigm of *proving* security in a well-stated and believable model, via the use of efficient reduction algorithms.

1. The philosophy of cryptology

As humans, we live in the real world, but we have the power to imagine other worlds. We may let our imagination run wild, and dream up wonderful, exotic counter-existences, or we may imagine restricted versions of our normal world, e.g. a world in which all thought can be modeled by Turing machines (ordinary computers), or a world in which no-one lies[1].

Like most sciences, cryptology is of the latter type, and is involved in a world in which various parties want to execute a (multiparty) protocol to perform some task. However cryptology differs from standard information theory in the sense that there are adversarial parties at work who wish to make this protocol fail.

One can define these cryptological worlds by introducing the parties involved, the task that is to be accomplished, and the powers given to the various parties, whether they be legitimate, adversarial, or a mixture of both.

A very common world to imagine is one where there are three parties, say Alice, Bob and Eve. There is a *channel* by which Alice and Bob can send each other messages (for example they can each place an advertisement in the classified ads section of the local newspaper), but Eve can also see these messages (advertisements) and she can even place her own messages, purporting to be Alice or Bob. The task is for Alice to send Bob a message (say the code to a combination lock) without Eve being able to read it (and so go off and open the lock herself).

1991 *Mathematics Subject Classification.* Primary 54C40, 14E20; Secondary 46E25, 20C20.

[1]Such restrictions may prevent things from happening, which do happen in the real world. For example in the truthful world no-one would be able to say "I am lying".

In this world, as described so far, there is no way for Alice to distinguish between Bob and Eve (she knows nothing about either of them), and so she may well end up sending Eve the combination by mistake.

For this reason we change the world, so that *all* parties do know something about Bob, and Bob is free to choose what they know. Is it possible, in this altered world, for Alice to send a message to Bob, without Eve knowing it? It is one of the most wonderful conceptual achievements of the last century to both ask this question, and answer it with "yes!". See [**3, 4**].

1.1. A basic model of public key cryptography. The different worlds mentioned above are often called *models*, and a common assumption, not mentioned above, is that Alice, Bob and Eve are restricted to use efficient classical computer algorithms to reach their decisions. Indeed, when being strict, the parties are better stated purely by the algorithms and memory they have access to.

An algorithm $\mathcal{A}$ is considered *efficient* if (under some model of computation)

(1) it terminates in a relatively short amount of time, and
(2) it uses a relatively short number of logical gates.

We will write $\mathcal{A}_1 \sim \mathcal{A}_2$ to denote that two algorithms are semantically equivalent, i.e. they give the same output for the same input.

We now consider the algorithms needed in order for Alice to pass her secret to Bob. Let us consider a triple $(\mathcal{K}, \mathcal{E}, \mathcal{D})$ of efficient algorithms acting on the following spaces.

$$\begin{aligned} \mathcal{K} &: \mathcal{R}_{\mathcal{K}} \to \mathcal{PK} \times \mathcal{SK} \\ \mathcal{E} &: \mathcal{PK} \times \mathcal{M} \to \mathcal{C} \\ \mathcal{D} &: \mathcal{C} \times \mathcal{SK} \to \mathcal{M}. \end{aligned}$$

The algorithms $(\mathcal{K}, \mathcal{E}, \mathcal{D})$ are referred to as *key generation*, *encryption* and *decryption* algorithms respectively. The set $\mathcal{R}_{\mathcal{K}}$ is called the randomness used by key generation, the set $\mathcal{PK}$ is called the *public key space*, the set $\mathcal{SK}$ is called the *secret (or private) key space*, the set $\mathcal{M}$ is called the *message (or plaintext) space* and the set $\mathcal{C}$ is called the *ciphertext space*. Note that the efficiency of the algorithms implies that their input and output must be reasonably small, and such statement are made precise in cryptography by the standard computer science use of polynomial[2] time algorithms, and polynomial sized output (although we will keep this discussion fairly non-technical).

Let $(\mathsf{pk}_r, \mathsf{sk}_r)$ denote the output of $\mathcal{K}(r)$ for a given $r \in \mathcal{R}_{\mathcal{K}}$. If both of the following conditions are met:

- these algorithms satisfy $\mathcal{D}(\mathcal{E}(\mathsf{pk}_r, m), \mathsf{sk}_r) = m$ for each $m \in \mathcal{M}$, $r \in \mathcal{R}_{\mathcal{K}}$, and
- for all efficient probabilistic algorithms $\mathcal{D}'$ the probability that $\mathcal{D}'(\mathcal{E}(\mathsf{pk}_r, m), \mathsf{pk}_r) = m$ for randomly chosen $m \in \mathcal{M}$ and $r \in \mathcal{R}_{\mathcal{K}}$ is negligible,

then these algorithms may be used to allow Alice to transmit a (random) message securely to Bob, even in the presence of Eve. Bob simply picks $r \in \mathcal{R}_{\mathcal{K}}$ at random,

[2]Polynomial with respect to some global system parameter.

and makes public[3] (to Alice and Eve) the key pk_r, obtained from $\mathcal{K}(r)$. To send a message $m \in \mathcal{M}$ Alice sends $c = \mathcal{E}(\mathsf{pk}_r, m)$ from which Bob recovers $m = \mathcal{D}(c, \mathsf{sk}_r)$.

The second condition implies that there is no efficient algorithm $\mathcal{D}'$ which will help Eve recover m from c, without knowledge of sk_r.

Arguing about the non-existence of an efficient algorithm to solve a problem is a hard thing to do, and falls under the scope of the model. Why should we believe that there is not an efficient algorithm to solve a particular task? This is something we talk more about below.

Indeed the decryption algorithm is proof that there *is* an efficient algorithm, when this algorithm has sk_r as input. Turning the argument on its head it means that all inefficient adversarial algorithms $\mathcal{D}'' \sim \mathcal{D}(\mathsf{sk}_r, .)$ have a fantastic compression (namely $(\mathcal{D}, \mathsf{sk}_r)$), but there is no efficient way to find this compression from the public knowledge of $\mathcal{K}, \mathcal{E}, \mathcal{D}$ and pk_r.

Finally note that if no efficient algorithm $\mathcal{D}' \sim \mathcal{D}(\mathsf{sk}_r, .)$ exists, then it cannot be efficient to either search the space $\mathcal{R}_{\mathcal{K}}$, or search the space $\mathcal{SK}$.

1.2. Which problems have no efficient solution? What a question! For example, are all algorithms that can factor arbitrary length integers intrinsically inefficient!?

As with almost everything about the world we live in, we can not be sure. In the study of the physical world we come up with a hypothesis, and then go and measure the world to see if the hypothesis fits; if it does then we say the hypothesis might be true (if not we discard it immediately). If in addition it has a relatively nice mathematical structure we are more convinced (the principle of Occam's razor). If it predicts strange unexpected phenomenon which turn out to be true, we are even more convinced (a sign of human discovery, rather than human engineering).

The same is true of cryptography. We cannot be sure that there is no efficient algorithm to perform a particular task. The analogy with measuring the physical world is to give the problem to the world's cryptographers and mathematicians and see if they can find an efficient algorithm (if they can we discard the hypothesis immediately). If on top of this the task has a very natural mathematical formulation, then we may be more inclined to believe it is intrinsically hard. If the hardness of this task is a consequence of the hardness of another task (which we believe is hard for some reason), then we are even more convinced.

This last condition is a *reductionist* view and is highly regarded in cryptography. To show that the hardness of a task A is a consequence of the hardness of task B, it suffices to build an efficient algorithm $\mathcal{B}$ that achieves the task B, assuming that it has access to a subalgorithm $\mathcal{A}$ (called an *oracle*) that achieves the task A. Thus if B is truly hard, then $\mathcal{A}$ cannot exist, so A must be hard also.

In this paper we will attempt to build the "correct" notion of security, for encryption schemes, via a series of models and attacks. We shall try to make all the assumptions explicit, starting with one already discussed a little:

ASSUMPTION 1. *All parties must use classical efficient algorithms to reach their decisions.*

---

[3]We again stress the importance of Alice needing to be sure that this key is from Bob. In practice this is achieved by some initial trust, and the use of digital signatures, but we do not go in to the details here.

This is an assumption we shall stick to throughout this report. The assumption is common in cryptography, but not fundamental, e.g. there is a relatively small, but growing branch of cryptography related to when the parties have access to quantum particles and/or quantum computers.

In this exposition it will be helpful to have practical cryptosystems to discuss, and these bring their own assumptions. In section 2 we consider RSA based cryptography, and use this as an example to introduce the notions of semantic security and bit security. In section 3 we consider how to achieve semantic security using discrete logarithm based cryptography.

In section 4 we then give more power to the adversary by allowing them to have access to a decryption oracle. We show that it is still possible to achieve provable security in this setting.

In section 5 we introduce the random oracle model: a fundamental assumption placed on the model that allows us to prove security more easily. We also discuss the importance of a proof in the random oracle model.

In section 6 we talk briefly about the other security concerns, and discuss the line between what is considered the duty of an encryption scheme, or a higher level protocol. We conclude by summing up the most important points.

Note: We shall often use the constant 80 in reference to the security of cryptosystems. This is because, at the time of writing, 2^{80} machine operations is considered an infeasibly large number (and therefore good enough to base security on), and 2^{-k} for some $k \geq 80$ is usually considered an infeasibly small bias to be leaked by a cryptosystem.

1.3. Notation. We use the notation $s \in_R S$ to denote the process of picking an element s from a set S uniformly at random.

The cyclic group of order N will be represented $\mathbb{Z}_N$, and the multiplicative group of integers modulo N (of order $\phi(N)$) will be represented $\mathbb{Z}_N^*$. The set of bitstrings of length n will be represented by $\{0,1\}^n$, and the notation $b_1||b_2$ is used to represent the concatenation of two bitstrings.

Several abbreviations are used throughout the report; we sum up the main ones below:

OWF	one-way function
TDOWF	trapdoor one-way function
RSA	the RSA cryptosystem
DLOG	the discrete logarithm problem
DH	Diffie-Hellman (key exchange)
CDH	the computational Diffie-Hellman assumption
DDH	the decisional Diffie-Hellman assumption
RO & ROM	random oracle (model)

2. RSA based cryptography

The RSA cryptosystem was first given in [**17**].

ASSUMPTION 2. *The* RSA assumption *is, given an integer N (and knowing it is the product of two unknown equi-sized primes p and q), an integer e and $y = x^e \bmod N$ for some $x \in_R \mathbb{Z}_N^*$, there is no efficient algorithm to recover $x \bmod N$.*

The group $\mathbb{Z}_N^*$ is cyclic of order $\phi(N) = (p-1)(q-1)$ so with the factorization of N it is trivial to recover x. Thus implicit in the above assumption is that the following is also true.

ASSUMPTION 3. *The* (RSA) factoring assumption *is, given N and knowing it is the product of two unknown equi-sized primes p and q, it is hard to find p and q.*

It is not known if the factoring assumption is a consequence of the RSA assumption (in which case the two problems would be equivalent).

The raw RSA function to encrypt a message $m \in \mathbb{Z}_N^*$ to a ciphertext $c \in \mathbb{Z}_N^*$, is to apply $c = m^e \bmod N$. Decryption is then possible by forming $m' = c^d \bmod N$, where $ed = 1 \bmod \phi(N)$.

2.1. Dictionary attacks. In motivating public key encryption schemes in section 1, Alice sent Bob the combination to a lock. However this is not the only use of encryption schemes, e.g. one may wish to send a yes/no vote using an encryption scheme, or send the area code of your telephone number. In both of these last cases the actual message space $\mathcal{M}$ that is used is reasonably small.

When sending "yes" or "no" we must first encode these phrases to be elements of $\mathbb{Z}_N^*$. If this bijective[4] encoding is fixed so that "yes" maps to a constant $m_1 \in \mathbb{Z}_N^*$ and "no" maps to $m_2 \in \mathbb{Z}_N^*$, then it is trivial for Eve to know how Alice is voting, even assuming the RSA assumption is true. Eve simply encrypts "yes" and "no" herself, and sees which one agrees with Alice's ciphertext!

This attack is possible whenever the message space is small enough to be efficiently enumerated over, and such attacks are called *dictionary attacks*. The solution is to inject some randomness in to the encoding method, so that "yes" always encodes to different elements of $\mathbb{Z}_N^*$ (and at least enough randomness should be injected, so that one cannot efficiently enumerate over all the possible encodings of "yes"). When randomness is used with an encoding method, the combination is known as a *padding scheme.*

As a point of interest notice that in the example case given in section 1, where Alice sends Bob the combination to a lock, then the dictionary attack also applies. The security of a physical combination lock relies on the fact that it takes a long time to enter each combination and test if works (and this process is error prone). By sending an encryption of the combination, Alice has given Eve a way to do this search electronically. The lock would have to have a lot of combinations for it to be secure against such an algorithmic attack.

2.2. Padding schemes. A padding scheme must be carefully worked out, since placing even a substantial amount of randomness in the wrong place can be a weakness. The padding scheme must be tied closely with the underlying (one-way) encryption function.

EXAMPLE 1. *Let $\left(\frac{x}{N}\right)$ denote the Jacobi symbol of x and N, and consider the following padding scheme. To send "yes" Alice picks a completely random x such that $\left(\frac{x}{N}\right) = 1$, to send "no" she finds an x such that $\left(\frac{x}{N}\right) = -1$ (both of these may involve Alice testing a small number of Jacobi symbols, but this is efficient). Alice then uses the RSA encryption function and sends $y = x^e \bmod N$. Bob can decrypt to recover x, and then compute the Jacobi symbol to see how Alice voted.*

[4]To enable decryption.

All seems well: if N is large it would be impossible for Eve to guess Alice's x, and compare x^e to the ciphertext, so we have successfully combatted simple dictionary attacks, and moreover we are using the RSA function which is assumed to be hard to invert on random input.

Unfortunately this would not be the right conclusion; it is very simple (since e is odd) for Eve to compute

$$\left(\frac{x^e}{N}\right) = \left(\frac{x}{N}\right)^e = \left(\frac{x}{N}\right),$$

which gives Alice's vote!

What went wrong in the above example? Is this a contradiction to the fact that RSA is hard to invert in the average case? No, it is not: Eve managed to recover Alice's vote, not by recovering x, but due to the fact that the RSA function leaks some information about x.

The use of an underlying one-way function (OWF) which leaks some (but not all the) bits of information is not considered a serious weakness in cryptography, but this means the analysis of padding schemes is extremely important. This is what a cryptographic proof of security refers to; it does not prove that the underlying one-way function is secure (this is assumed by the model), but it should show that the placement of the randomness *with* this one-way function is a secure combination.

As another example consider the following scheme.

EXAMPLE 2. *Let $||$ denote bitwise concatenation. Alice sends a message x of bit length $\lfloor \log_2 N \rfloor - 80$ to Bob in the following way*

$$y \quad = \quad (b||x)^e \bmod N$$

where b is 80 bits of randomness. Bob decrypts to find $(b||x) \bmod N$ and reads x from the bottom bits.

Is this secure? For $\log_2 N \approx 1024$ this is an open question. One might ask that since we are already assuming that RSA is hard to invert, why don't we just *assume* this is secure too, i.e. add it to the list of assumptions in the model? There are two reasons:

- Such assumptions are often ugly, and often wrong. Even if an assumption has not been proved wrong, if it is ugly it often means it has received/will receive less scrutiny from the academic community[5], and is thus less trusted.
- It is very important and interesting to study the information leaked by underlying OWF's anyway. Once this has been done there are often good and provable strategies for padding schemes (albeit possibly at the cost of a slight loss in efficiency).

With respect to minimizing the assumptions in the model, the best we can hope for is to find a padding scheme that adds no new assumptions to the model. Below we will see cases when this can actually be achieved.

For now let us define precisely what we mean to be secure against dictionary attacks.

[5]Although this is not necessarily the case, if we define an ugly problem as not having a neat formulation or a wider-application then it is not likely to provoke much academic interest.

2.3. Semantic security. This definition was first given in [**9**].

DEFINITION 1. *Let δ be a non-negligible quantity, e.g. 2^{-k} for some $k \geq 80$. A randomized encryption scheme $\mathcal{E}(m,r) : \mathcal{M} \times \mathcal{R}_{\mathcal{E}} \to \mathcal{C}$ is called* semantically secure *if there is no pair of efficient algorithms $(\mathcal{A}_1, \mathcal{A}_2)$ with the following properties.*

The algorithms $\mathcal{A}_1, \mathcal{A}_2$ act on the sets

$$\begin{aligned} \mathcal{A}_1 &: \mathcal{PK} \to \mathcal{M} \times \mathcal{M} \times \mathcal{T} \\ \mathcal{A}_2 &: \mathcal{T} \times \mathcal{C} \to \{0,1\} \end{aligned}$$

with the property that, if $\mathcal{A}_1(\mathsf{pk}) = (m_0, m_1, t)$, and $c = \mathcal{E}(m_b, r)$, then

$$|Pr(\mathcal{A}_2(t,c) = b) - 1/2| \quad > \quad \delta$$

where this probability is defined over random instances of the encryption scheme (i.e. a random choices from $\mathcal{R}_{\mathcal{K}}$) and random choices of $b \in \{0,1\}$, $r \in \mathcal{R}_{\mathcal{E}}$.

The set $\mathcal{T}$ is just a technical means to convey information (such as the public parameters) from $\mathcal{A}_1$ to $\mathcal{A}_2$, and the quantity $|Pr(\mathcal{A}_2(t,c) = b) - 1/2|$ is known as the *advantage* of the algorithms $(\mathcal{A}_1, \mathcal{A}_2)$. The role of the algorithm $\mathcal{A}_1$ is, given the public parameters, to choose two "very different" messages from the message space. The role of the algorithm $\mathcal{A}_2$ is then, given a random encryption of one of the messages, to decide which one it is.

If no such algorithms exist, it means that Eve gets a negligible amount of information from each encryption (given the ciphertext she cannot discern the true message from any other possible one).

EXAMPLE 3. *We show the scheme in example 1 is* not *semantically secure. Since there the message space only consists of two messages, algorithm $\mathcal{A}_1$ is redundant in this case; it just returns "yes" and "no". Using randomness that it out of the control of Eve, we randomly pick elements of $\mathbb{Z}_N^*$ until an element x with a correctly signed Jacobi symbol is found; the encryption is then $y = x^e \bmod N$. If we let $\mathcal{A}_2(y) = \left(\frac{y}{N}\right)$ then this is both an efficient algorithm, and has significant advantage in guessing which message was encrypted (in fact this $\mathcal{A}_2$ never errs, so it has the maximal advantage of $1/2$).*

The standard way to show a randomized encryption scheme $\mathcal{E}(m,r)$ *is* semantically secure is to show that any pair of algorithms $(\mathcal{A}_1, \mathcal{A}_2)$ which break the semantic security of $\mathcal{E}(m,r)$ can be used to break another, supposedly hard, problem (i.e. using a standard reduction argument).

Conceptually it is attractive if the hard problem the algorithms $(\mathcal{A}_1, \mathcal{A}_2)$ can be used to break is inverting the underlying TDOWF. One way to do is via the concept of *bit security* and *hard-core bits.*

2.4. Bit security. Bit security is just concerned with one-way functions, so we can temporarily forget all about the padding issues with encryption schemes, and the existence of trapdoors to enable efficient decryption algorithms. The following definition was first given in [**2**].

DEFINITION 2. *Let δ be a non-negligible quantity, e.g. 2^{-k} for some $k \geq 80$. Given a one-way function $f : \{0,1\}^n \to \{0,1\}^n$ we say that $\pi : \{0,1\}^n \to \{0,1\}$ is a* hard-core predicate for f *if, given $y = f(x)$, but not x, there is no efficient algorithm $\mathcal{A}$ such that*

$$|Pr[\mathcal{A}(x) = \pi(x)] - 1/2| \quad > \quad \delta$$

where this probability is defined over random choices of $x \in \{0,1\}^n$.

As before, the quantity $|Pr[\mathcal{A}(x) = \pi(x)] - 1/2|$ is known as the *advantage* of the algorithm $\mathcal{A}$. The above definition means that if we are given the output of a one-way function, a predicate (e.g. the least significant bit of the input) is called hard-core if there is no algorithm to guess it with significant advantage.

With respect to the RSA function $\mathsf{RSA}_{N,e}(x) = x^e \bmod N$, the following result was shown in [**10**].

THEOREM 1. *Every individual bit of* x *is a hard-core bit of* $\mathsf{RSA}_{N,e}$.

The common way to prove a statement like this is to build an efficient algorithm that can invert the whole one way function, assuming it has access to an oracle for a particular bit (if so that bit is hard-core). In the case of RSA it was shown that if one has an oracle for any individual bit, then by manipulating the calls to the oracle, one can actually find all the values of all the bits of x, i.e. invert $\mathsf{RSA}_{N,e}$.

We may now use Theorem 1 to show that one can use RSA to semantically securely encrypt 1 bit of data (e.g. a vote). This is our first proof of security!

THEOREM 2. *Assuming the RSA assumption, the following is a secure randomized encryption scheme of* $m \in \mathcal{M} = \{0,1\}$ *when* r *is chosen uniformly at random from* $\mathcal{R}_{\mathcal{E}} = \{0, \ldots, (N-3)/2\}$*:*

$$\mathcal{E}(m,r) \quad = \quad (2r+m)^e \bmod N.$$

Proof: (sketch) Since the message space is just 2 messages, the algorithm $\mathcal{A}_1$ is redundant. If an algorithm $\mathcal{A}_2$ exists which breaks the semantic security of the above encryption scheme then, given $y = x^e \bmod N$, it has non-negligible advantage in guessing the bottom bit of x. By Theorem 1 if such an algorithm exists, then so does an algorithm $\mathcal{B}$ which can recover the whole of $x \in \mathbb{Z}_N^*$. By assumption 2 algorithm $\mathcal{B}$ does not exist, so the above scheme must be semantically secure. □

A paradox with this way of proving schemes, is that the types of function that are proved secure are invariably ones with good bit security properties, which in turn are ones with good algebraic properties[6].

It means that using such techniques we cannot prove the security of complex functions, which don't possess nice algebraic properties, even though these may very well be hard to invert when used with a reasonable amount of randomness.

For this reason, one place in cryptography where proofs of security are often foregone for the sake of efficiency, is in the design of fast hash functions, e.g. `SHA-1`. In these cases one should take the necessary assumption (e.g. 2nd preimage resistance) as part of the model, and believe in its validity because of the (hopefully) well documented design of the function, and the (hopefully) large amount of it attention it has received.

Unfortunately showing that k bits are individually hard-core does not allow us to encrypt k bits semantically securely, e.g. the inability to guess individual bits, does not imply that it is hard to distinguish between encryption when $00\ldots0_2$ and $11\ldots1_2$ are placed in the hard-core bits.

If one wants to encrypt more than one bit in a semantically secure fashion, then obviously one may use the above algorithm a number of times, using different

[6]The algebraic properties allow us to glean useful information from manipulations of the input to the hard-core bit oracle.

randomness each time. However one can save in both bandwidth and on the amount of randomness needed, by considering the following notion (first introduced in [**14**]).

DEFINITION 3. *We say that k predicates $\pi_1, \ldots, \pi_k$ are* simultaneously *hard-core for f if given $f(x)$ there is no efficient algorithm $\mathcal{A}$ which can distinguish (with non-negligible advantage) between the k-tuple $\{\pi_1(x), \ldots, \pi_k(x)\}$ and a totally random k-tuple drawn from $\{0,1\}^k$, when x is randomly distributed over the input space of f.*

Equivalent to saying that there is no algorithm to distinguish the predicates from random, is that there is no algorithm $\mathcal{A}$ that is given $f(x)$ and $\pi_1(x), \ldots, \pi_{i-1}(x)$, and is able to distinguish $\pi_i(x)$ from a bit $b \in_R \{0,1\}$, for all $i = 1, \ldots, k$.

If one can show that a trapdoor one-way function has m simultaneously hard-core bits, then this enables us to encrypt m bits semantically securely by placing the message in to the hard-core bits, and putting randomness elsewhere (the security holds since one cannot distinguish a message from random bits, then one cannot distinguish two messages m_0, m_1).

A simultaneous hard-core bit oracle requires $f(x), \pi_1(x), \ldots, \pi_{k-1}(x)$ as input, in order to guess $\pi_k(x)$. The need for more (correct) input makes it harder to use this oracle in reduction algorithms. However if k is small then often these bits can just be guessed, and if a reduction algorithm allows them to guessed once at the start of the algorithm (after which the input to the (many) oracle calls can be worked out), then we can often modify a reduction algorithm needing access to a hard-core bit oracle, to a reduction algorithm just needing access to a simultaneous hard-core bit oracle (of a small number of bits). The modification normally implies a slight loss in advantage/efficiency.

Using such techniques, it was shown in [**10**] that the RSA function has $\log\log N$ simultaneous hard-core bits, so it can be used to semantically securely encrypt up to $\log\log N$ bits per invocation of RSA. However these techniques are still not strong enough to prove that the scheme proposed in example 2 is semantically secure.

2.5. Paillier's scheme. If one wants to encrypt up to $O(\log N)$ bits, then there are many other ways to adapt RSA to be semantically secure. If one doesn't mind adding an extra assumption to the model, then a particularly attractive one was proposed by Paillier in [**15**]. The assumption is as follows:

ASSUMPTION 4. *Given an RSA modulus N and $x \in_R \mathbb{Z}_{N^2}^*$, there is no efficient algorithm $\mathcal{A}$ that can decide if x is an N'th power, i.e. if there exists $y \in \mathbb{Z}_{N^2}^*$ such that $y^N = x \bmod N^2$.*

Paillier's scheme is based on working in the multiplicative group $\mathbb{Z}_{N^2}^* \simeq \mathbb{Z}_N^* \times \mathbb{Z}_N$. Since $(1+t_1N)(1+t_2N) \equiv 1 + (t_1+t_2)N \bmod N^2$, we have that the set $H = \{1 + tN \mid 0 \le t \le N-1\}$ is a subgroup of $\mathbb{Z}_{N^2}^*$ which is isomorphic to $\mathbb{Z}_N$. From the fact that the cosets of H partition $\mathbb{Z}_{N^2}^*$ we also know that every element $x \in \mathbb{Z}_{N^2}^*$ can be uniquely written as $s(1+tN)$ for some unique $(s,t) \in \mathbb{Z}_N^* \times \mathbb{Z}_N$. Alternatively, since $\gcd(N, \phi(N)) = 1$, we know that every element $x \in \mathbb{Z}_{N^2}^*$ can be uniquely written as $s^N(1+tN)$ for some unique $(s,t) \in \mathbb{Z}_N^* \times \mathbb{Z}_N$. The Paillier assumption clearly requires that assumption 3 (the hardness of factoring) is true.

DEFINITION 4. *Paillier's randomized encryption function is defined as*

$$\mathcal{E}(m,r) \quad = \quad r^N(1+mN) \bmod N^2.$$

Given $y = r^N(1+mN) \bmod N^2$ one can efficiently recover m by either removing r or m from the equation, and solving for the other. To remove r one can form $y^{\phi(N)} \equiv (1+mN)^{\phi(N)} \equiv (1+m\phi(N)N) \bmod N^2$, from which one can easily solve for m. Alternatively to remove m from the equation one can consider $y \equiv r^N \bmod N$, and solve for r using the standard RSA decryption procedure.

THEOREM 3. *Assuming assumption 4, then Paillier's encryption function is semantically secure.*

Proof: We describe an efficient algorithm $\mathcal{B} : \mathbb{Z}_{N^2}^* \to \{0,1\}$ that, given $x \in \mathbb{Z}_{N^2}^*$, identifies if x is an N'th power with non-negligible advantage (let us assume if $\mathcal{B}$ thinks x is an N'th power it will return 1, otherwise it will return 0). This algorithm uses the algorithms $(\mathcal{A}_1, \mathcal{A}_2)$ which break the semantic security of Paillier's scheme. Assuming $\mathcal{B}$ does not exist, then $(\mathcal{A}_1, \mathcal{A}_2)$ cannot exist, i.e. Paillier's scheme is semantically secure.

If we wish to decide whether $x \in \mathbb{Z}_{N^2}^*$ is an N'th power or not we first run $\mathcal{A}_1(N)$ to obtain two messages m_0, m_1 which $\mathcal{A}_2$ can distinguish between. We then choose $b \in \{0,1\}$ at random, and we define $\mathcal{B}(x) = 1$ if and only if $\mathcal{A}_2(x(1 + m_bN) \bmod N^2) = b$.

The reason that $\mathcal{B}$ has non-negligible advantage in identifying N'th powers is because if x is an N'th power, then $y = x(1 + m_bN) \bmod N^2$ is a valid encryption of m_b, and so with non-negligible advantage the output of $\mathcal{A}_2$ should be b. On the other hand if x is a random element of $\mathbb{Z}_{N^2}^*$, then $x = s^N(1+tN) \bmod N^2$ for some unique random $(s,t) \in \mathbb{Z}_N^* \times \mathbb{Z}_N$, in which case

$$\begin{aligned} y &\equiv s^N(1+tN)(1+m_bN) \bmod N^2 \\ &\equiv s^N(1+(t+m_b)N) \bmod N^2, \end{aligned}$$

i.e. y is an encryption of $t + m_b \bmod N$. When $t \in \mathbb{Z}_N$ is randomly distributed over $\mathbb{Z}_N$, the distributions of $t + m_0 \bmod N$ and $t + m_1 \bmod N$ look identical, so the output of $\mathcal{A}_2$ is independent of m_b. □

3. Discrete logarithm based cryptography

The notions of padding schemes, semantic security, proofs of security etc., are independent of the underlying trapdoor one-way functions. In this section we show how to obtain similar results to the above, in the field of discrete logarithm cryptography.

ASSUMPTION 5. *The* discrete logarithm (DLOG) assumption *is, given a generator g of an arbitrary group G of order m, and an element $g^a \in G$ there is no efficient algorithm to recover $a \in \mathbb{Z}_m$.*

The most common groups for which DLOG is considered in cryptography are the multiplicative groups $\mathbb{Z}_p^*$ for prime integers p, and the group of elliptic curve points $E_{a,b}(\mathbb{F})$ over some field $\mathbb{F}$, or explicit subgroups of these groups.

THEOREM 4. *If we consider the case of $G = \mathbb{Z}_p^*$ for some prime p, and examine the one-way function $\mathsf{exp}_g : \mathbb{Z}_{p-1} \to \mathbb{Z}_p^*$ defined by $\mathsf{exp}_g(x) = g^x \bmod p$, then the following statements are true.*

(1) *The least significant bit of x* is not *a hard-core bit of exp_g.*

(2) *Almost every other block of* $\log \log p$ *bits of* x *are simultaneously hard-core bits of* exp_g.

The first of these follows from the fact that $\left(\frac{g^x}{p}\right) = 1$ if and only if $x \equiv 0 \bmod 2$. The next was firstly proved for the least significant bits (not including the bottom one) in [**14**], and then it was somewhat generalized by results in [**20**].

Another related assumption common in cryptography is the following:

ASSUMPTION 6. *The* computational Diffie-Hellman (CDH) assumption *is, given a generator* g *of an arbitrary group* G *of order* m*, and two elements* $g^a, g^b \in G$*, there is no efficient algorithm to recover* $g^{ab} \in G$*. Alternatively it is sometimes stated, given* g_1, g_2, g_1^a *one cannot calculate* g_2^a.

Clearly the DLOG assumption is implicit in the CDH assumption. The CDH assumption is useful to make because it comes naturally out of the following key exchange protocol due to Diffie and Hellman (DH), see [**4**]:

(1) Alice and Bob agree on a cyclic group G of order m, and a generator g of G (all of this is public information).
(2) Alice chooses $a \in \mathbb{Z}_m$ and sends Bob g^a.
(3) Bob chooses $b \in \mathbb{Z}_m$ sends Alice g^b.
(4) Alice and Bob compute the shared secret g^{ab} as $(g^b)^a$ and $(g^a)^b$ respectively.

In such a protocol a passive attacker knows g and sees g^a, g^b whereupon the shared secret is g^{ab}. If CDH is true, then a passive attacker cannot recover this shared secret from the information they know.

An even stronger assumption is given below.

ASSUMPTION 7. *The* decisional Diffie-Hellman (DDH) assumption *is that there is no efficient algorithm which has non-negligible advantage, given a* 4*-tuple* $(g_1, g_2, u_1, u_2) \in G^4$*, in deciding if it was either randomly selected from* G^4 *or randomly selected subject to the constraint* $u_1 = g_1^a, u_2 = g_2^a$.

Under this assumption a passive attacker, given g^{ab} and a random $g' \in G$, cannot even tell with non-negligible advantage, which is the correct shared key.

3.1. El Gamal. The term *hybrid encryption* is used by cryptographers when public key encryption is used to achieve key exchange, and then a symmetric key algorithm is used to share data with the shared secret.

Any two round key exchange protocol can be made in to an encryption protocol in exactly the same way as hybrid encryption, using a one time pad as the symmetric key algorithm. For example in the case of DH if Bob has $\mathsf{pk} = g^a$ and $\mathsf{sk} = a$ and Alice wishes to send a secret $g' \in G$ to Bob, he can send the pair $(g^b, g^{ab}g')$. The first entry establishes g^{ab} as their shared secret, and then multiplying the second entry by g^{-ab} reveals g'. This was first noticed in [**7**].

THEOREM 5. *Let* $h = g^x$ *be Bob's public key. Assuming assumption 7, then the following (El Gamal) encryption is semantically secure:*

$$\mathcal{E}(m, r) \quad = \quad (g^r, mh^r)$$

Proof: Suppose $(\mathcal{A}_1, \mathcal{A}_2)$ breaks the semantic security of El-Gamal encryption; we will build an algorithm $\mathcal{B}$ which can distinguish (with non-negligible advantage) between a DH-tuple or a random group 4-tuple (let us say $\mathcal{B}$ outputs 1 if and only if it think the input is a DH tuple). By assumption 7 the algorithm $\mathcal{B}$ cannot exist, so El-Gamal encryption is secure.

To form $\mathcal{B}$, given $(g_1, g_2, u_1, u_2) \in G^4$ as input, we first run $\mathcal{A}_1(g_1, u_1)$ to find two messages m_0, m_1 the algorithm $\mathcal{A}_2$ can distinguish between. We then pick $b \in_R \{0,1\}$, and define $\mathcal{B}(g_1, g_2, u_1, u_2) = 1$ if and only if $\mathcal{A}_2((g_2, m_b u_2)) = b$.

The reason this function has a non-negligible advantage in correctly guessing DH-tuples, is that if its input is a DH-tuple then the input to $\mathcal{A}_1$ is valid El Gamal public information, and the input to $\mathcal{A}_2$ is a correctly formed El Gamal encryption (with $u_1 = g_1^r$ and $u_2 = u_1^r$), so $(\mathcal{A}_1, \mathcal{A}_2)$ have non-negligible advantage in recovering b correctly. On the other hand, if the input to $\mathcal{B}$ is a random 4-tuple, then $u_2 m_b$ is completely independent of b (and hence the output of $\mathcal{A}_2$ must be independent of b in this case). $\square$

4. Chosen ciphertext security

Up to now we have only considered a passive attacker Eve, who has just observed the protocol. However often a more realistic model in which to prove security is assuming an attacker can actually influence the information on the channel as well (e.g. delete it, or modify it). We will refer to an active attacker by the name of Mallory, and in this section we try to estimate how much information he can learn by modifying data during a protocol, and observing the outcome.

If Alice encrypts a message m to Bob using say, RSA, and Bob accepts whatever is sent to him, then clearly Mallory can learn nothing. The issue of Mallory learning something only arises when Bob tries to *use* the information. If Mallory can change the ciphertext c so that the resulting message m' is sometimes satisfactory, and sometimes unsatisfactory (and neither happens with negligible probability), then it is possible that Mallory may learn something about m from Bob's action.

EXAMPLE 4. *For example suppose Alice sends information to Bob using RSA. If Bob is always expecting an odd x, and he returns a complaint email if Alice sends him an even one, then Bob is acting exactly like a hard-core bit oracle. Mallory can use Bob to recover the whole of any message sent to him!*

In many applications we cannot stop Mallory from learning whether the protocol has been successful or not, so instead we must limit the information which Mallory learns from this. If it were the case that every time (or very close to every time) Mallory fiddled with the input the protocol failed, then Mallory would learn nothing.

A consequence of this is that only a negligible proportion of the ciphertexts should be valid (of course the output of the encryption algorithm should always be valid). Another consequence is that it ought to be impossible for Mallory to transform a valid ciphertext in to another ciphertext which has a non-negligible probability of being valid (this is referred to an *non-malleability*).

The notion of non-malleability is equivalent to the following notion. These ideas and equivalences were first introduced in [**5, 12, 16**].

DEFINITION 5. *A randomized encryption scheme $\mathcal{E}(m, r)$ is called* secure against chosen-ciphertext attacks *(CCA2-secure) if the scheme remains semantically secure, even when the algorithms $(\mathcal{A}_1, \mathcal{A}_2)$ have access to a decryption oracle, which can be called on all but the challenge ciphertext c.*

The reason that it is called CCA2 rather than just CCA, is that there is a slightly relaxed definition of chosen ciphertext security (CCA1) where only $\mathcal{A}_1$ has access to the decryption oracle. However the fact that a cryptosystem is CCA1-secure does not mean that there is no attack against it: Mallory may break the semantic security of the cryptosystem by asking Bob to decrypt messages related to the challenge ciphertext c, for example $c + 1$. At present the ultimate notion of security for an encryption scheme is considered to be CCA2-security (i.e. we are aware of no attacks against a CCA2-secure cryptosystem, which we consider the responsibility of the encryption scheme to be secure against[7]).

In the odd/even example above, Bob thought he was just leaking one bit of information, but in fact, by submitting multiple ciphertexts to him, he leaked a whole lot more. If Bob were using a CCA2-secure cryptosystem this could not happen: to show that Mallory learns nothing more than Bob leaks we assume Bob leaks everything about other ciphertexts (i.e. we give Mallory a decryption oracle). If Mallory still cannot break the semantic security of the cryptosystem on a challenge ciphertext, then he knows nothing about the plaintext (so if Bob does actually leak one bit then this is *all* that Mallory knows).

This is a strong model in which to prove security, which is independent of the amount of information that Bob leaks (as long as it is significantly less than all of it). However, it is very attractive if we can prove security in this setting, since inventors of cryptosystems cannot know in advance all the situations their scheme will be used in (e.g. some protocols might leak no bits, while others might leak 10 etc.). A proof of CCA2-security means that the encryption scheme can be used in almost any higher protocols.

The standard way to prove CCA2-security is once again to use reduction algorithms, however the major obstacle to proofs is that reduction algorithms cannot "be aware" of the private key (otherwise we will reach no contradiction in inverting the underlying TDOWF). In the next sections we will introduce some ways of coping with this.

4.1. The Cramer-Shoup CCA2-secure encryption scheme. Most strategies for creating CCA2-secure cryptosystems involve hash functions:

DEFINITION 6. *A* hash function *is just an efficient algorithm $H : \{0,1\}^n \to \{0,1\}^m$ where $m < n$. Often there are explicit restrictions put on the hash function, e.g. a* 2nd preimage resistant hash function *is one where there is no efficient algorithm $\mathcal{A}$, given $x_1 \in \{0,1\}^n$, to find $x_2 \in \{0,1\}^n$ such that $H(x_1) = H(x_2)$.*

Hash functions are used a lot in cryptography; the most commonly used being the NSA-invented, and NIST-standardized function `SHA-1`.

The following was first given in [**6**] and is based in a cyclic group G of order m. The scheme uses a 2nd preimage resistant hash function $H : G^3 \to \mathbb{Z}_m$, so G, m and H are all part of the public information.

Secret key: $x_1, x_2, y_1, y_2, z \in_R \mathbb{Z}_m$

[7]e.g. the various side channel attacks only apply in specific settings.

Public key: $g_1, g_2 \in G$, $c = g_1^{x_1} g_2^{x_2}$, $d = g_1^{y_1} g_2^{y_2}$, and $h = g_1^z$

Encryption:

$$\begin{aligned} \mathcal{E} : G \times \mathbb{Z}_m &\rightarrow G^4 \\ \mathcal{E}(m, r) &= (g_1^r, g_2^r, h^r m, c^r d^{r\alpha}) \end{aligned}$$

where $\alpha = H(g_1^r, g_2^r, h^r m)$.

Decryption:

$$\begin{aligned} \mathcal{D} : G^4 &\rightarrow G \\ \mathcal{D}(u_1, u_2, e, v) &= e u_1^{-z} \text{ or “fail”} \end{aligned}$$

where the output is “fail” if and only if

$$v \neq u_1^{x_1 + \alpha y_1} u_2^{x_2 + \alpha y_2},$$

where $\alpha = H(u_1, u_2, e)$.

The scheme is an extension of El Gamal encryption, and so is dependent on assumption 7. A particularly nice thing about this scheme is that it does not add any extra assumptions to the model[8].

A full proof of security of this scheme is given in [**6**]. We omit the details here, but note that the check and possible output of “fail” prevent Mallory from learning anything by manipulating ciphertexts.

5. The random oracle model

Although the scheme proposed in [**6**] is CCA2-secure, it has proved quite hard for cryptographers to find many other such systems, and provably secure CCA2-secure systems (under standard assumptions) are often a little less efficient.

Another strategy used by cryptographers is to forego a standard proof of security, and instead change the model somewhat. A model proposed in [**1**] is the *random oracle model*, in which security is proved assuming that the adversarial algorithms must work for every instance of possible hash functions used by the encryption/decryption algorithms. This is formalized by removing the hash functions descriptions from the public information of the encryption scheme, and instead insisting that the adversarial algorithms make explicit calls to the (random) oracles.

ASSUMPTION 8. *An oracle $\mathcal{O} : X \rightarrow Y$ is called a* random oracle *(RO) if for all $x \in X$ there is no algorithm $\mathcal{A}_x : Y \rightarrow \{0,1\}$ which has* any *advantage is distinguishing between input $y = \mathcal{O}(x)$ and $y \in_R Y$, without querying the oracle $\mathcal{O}$ at x.*

This enables a reduction algorithm to look at the input to the hash function calls, and even dictate their output (as long as it is indistinguishable from random). One can try to prove basic semantic security, CCA1-security or CCA2-security in the random oracle model.

In practical terms a proof in the random oracle model means that Mallory cannot attack the cryptosystem until he knows what hash function is being used.

When the cryptosystem is instantiated with `SHA-1` say, then we cannot say the cryptosystem remains secure, especially if the proof of security has relied on the

[8]Cynics may say that this is at the cost of assuming such a strong assumption as DDH. The hash function 2nd preimage resistance might be considered an extra assumption, though this depends on the hash function used (there do exist 2nd preimage resistant hash functions just dependent on DDH).

fact that the output of the oracles is dictated by the reduction algorithm (which invariably would disagree with the output of `SHA-1`).

For this reason the *computational random oracle model* was proposed in [**13**], which removes the power to dictate the output of the random oracles from the reduction algorithm.

This still does not mean that we can argue that the cryptosystem is secure when instantiated with `SHA-1`, but it does mean that if we find code, on the Internet say, that breaks our cryptosystem, but does so by making *explicit* calls to `SHA-1`, then we can reverse engineer the code and use the input to `SHA-1`, together with the reduction algorithm, to solve some supposedly hard problem.

CCA2-proofs of security in the random oracle model are certainly not ideal, but they are far better than no proof at all. They do imply that the combination of padding scheme and TDOWF is not so bad as to be weak for every instantiation of hash functions. For this reason if one cannot obtain a standard proof of security, then it is common practice to give a proof of security in the random oracle model.

Such proofs are normally fairly easy to obtain, and often have a standard form (searching the hash function calls to help the simulated decryption oracle). There are generic constructions to transform any trapdoor one-way permutation to a CCA2-secure encryption scheme in the ROM (see [**19**]), and also generic constructions to transform any semantically secure randomized encryption schemes to a CCA2-secure encryption scheme (see [**8**]).

6. Is this the end of the story?

We have built up a picture of what it means to be a secure encryption scheme, via a series of attacks, and fixes, and at each stage we have been careful to define exactly what we mean to be secure against a particular type of attack. We ended up with the ultimate notion of CCA2-secure encryption schemes.

Although this is certainly not the end of the *security* story, it *is* the end of the encryption story in the sense that this is all that is (presently) required of an encryption scheme.

Creators of encryption schemes are expected to meet this bar, but since the encryption scheme may be used for a whole host of applications, this is all that is normally required of, say, an academic paper.

Some other common security issues that must be considered in the real world applications are discussed briefly below:

Public key infrastructure: We have not discussed anything about how Bob shares his secret key with Alice, and why Alice believes it is from Bob, and not some malicious party. There is a whole area of cryptography concerned with how to do this efficiently and securely.

Even if the public information is correct, there may be parameters involved with the padding scheme, and if these can be adversarially manipulated then the consequences of this should be thoroughly examined.

Side channel attacks: Depending on where the encryption scheme is going to be used there may be many more feasible attacks than the notion of CCA2-security allows for. For example if the decryption algorithm is in software on a machine it may be possible to get very accurate timing results on how long the algorithm takes, and this information may leak something about the ciphertext or worse still, the private key. If the algorithms are in hardware on a smart-card say, then power analysis and probing may be realistic attacks. Also bombarding the card with radiation to induce faults may leak significant information.

Exploiting pseudorandomness: The use of provably semantically secure cryptosystems place us on a knife edge. The proofs of security are often extremely dependent on the fact that variables are uniformly distributed over some set. If this is not the case either by engineering carelessness, or by induced physical means, then this may significantly alter the proof of security.

7. Summary

It is hoped that this report has shown that cryptography can be treated in a formal way. Just as mathematicians say "let G be a group ...", it is possible for computer scientists to say "let $\mathcal{E}$ be a CCA2 secure encryption scheme ...", and go on to use this fact usefully. The definition of an encryption scheme is purely algorithmic, and it is arguable that even the properties, such as always decrypting a validly encrypted message correctly, should be written as a (polynomial time[9]) algorithm `isValid`, even though such an algorithm is never actually run by one party. The "adversary to hard-problem" reduction algorithm should certainly be stated algorithmically, and proved to be polynomial time, even though this too will probably never actually be run (assuming the hard problem is indeed hard, it just serves to point out the non-existence of an adversary).

To highlight the computational aspect of cryptography, it is suggested that the reader writes (or at least thinks about!) a `C++` (signature) template showing the form of (and interaction between) all the relevant functions, e.g. `keygen`, `encrypt`, `decrypt`, `isValid`, `reductionAlgorithm`, etc. The functions (including reduction algorithms) could then be implemented with a couple of existing schemes, e.g. RSA with OAEP padding and Cramer-Shoup. It is interesting to observe how different models of security, e.g. the ROM, change the signatures of the functions.

For would-be discovers of new cryptosystems, the general recipe for making a secure cryptosystem is:

(1) Find a good TDOWF.
(2) Explore the properties (e.g. hard-core bits) of this OWF.
(3) Find a good padding scheme for the OWF.
(4) Prove this combination is CCA2-secure (stating all the necessary assumptions).
(5) If application necessitates, then consider security in stronger models (e.g. side channel attacks).

The model in which the proof of security works should be examined with extreme care, to see if it closely resembles the real life situation the algorithm is being used in. It is relatively unlikely the standard mathematical assumptions (such as CDH, DDH, etc.) will be broken, but even these should be treated with some care.

Lastly it is stressed that while a proof of security is only valid in a certain model, it is a far better to have even a limited proof of security (with clearly stated assumptions), rather than no security proof at all.

---

[9] In a security parameter k.

References

[1] M. Bellare and P. Rogaway. Random Oracles are Practical: A Paradigm for Designing Efficient Protocols. In *ACM Conference on Computer and Communications Security*, pp. 62–73, 1993.

[2] M. Blum and S. Micali. How to generate cryptographically strong sequences of pseudorandom bits. In *SIAM Journal on Computing*, Vol. 13, No. 4, pp. 850–864, 1984.

[3] CESG. The history of non-secret encryption. Available at `http://www.cesg.gov.uk/about/nsecret.htm`

[4] W. Diffie, M. Hellman. New Directions in Cryptography. In *IEEE Transactions on Information Theory*, Vol. 22, pp. 644–654, 1976.

[5] D. Dolev, C. Dwork and M. Naor. Non-malleable cryptography. In *23rd Annual ACM Symposium of Theory of Computing*, pp. 542–552, 1991.

[6] R. Cramer, V. Shoup. A Practical Public Key Cryptosystem Provably Secure against Adaptive Chosen Ciphertext Attack. *Advances in Cryptology - CRYPTO '98 Proceedings*, pp. 13–25, Springer-Verlag, 1998.

[7] T. El Gamal. A Public Key Cryptosystem and a Signature Scheme Based on Discrete Logarithms. In *Proc. of CRYPTO '84*, Vol. 196 of LNCS, pp. 10–18. IACR, Springer-Verlag, 1984.

[8] E. Fujisaki and T. Okamoto. How to enhance the security of public-key encryption at minimum cost. In Proc. of PKC '99. LNCS, Volume 1560, pp. 53–68, 1999.

[9] S. Goldwasser and S. Micali. Probabalistic encryption. In *Journal of computer and system sciences*, Vol 28, pp. 270–299, 1984.

[10] J. Håstad and M. Näslund. The Security of Individual RSA Bits. In *IEEE Symposium on Foundations of Computer Science*, pp. 510–519, 1998.

[11] `www.ntru.com`

[12] M. Naor and M. Yung. Public-key cryptosystems provably secure against chosen ciphertext attacks. In *22nd Annual ACM Symposium on Foundations of Computer Science*, 1997.

[13] J. B. Nielsen. Separating random oracle proofs from complexity theoretic proofs: The non-committing encryption case. *Proc. of CRYPTO '02*, Vol. 2442 of LNCS, pp. 111–126. IACR, Springer-Verlag, 2002.

[14] R. Peralta. Simultaneous security of Bits in the Discrete Log. In *Proc. of Eurocrypt '85*. Springer, LNCS, Vol. 219, pp. 62–72, 1986.

[15] P. Paillier. Public key cryptosystems based on composite degree residuosity classes. In *Proc. of Eurocrypt '99*, volume 1592 of LNCS, pp. 223–238. IACR, Springer-Verlag, 1999.

[16] C. Rackoff and D. Simon. Noninteractive zero-knowledge proof of knowledge and chosen ciphertext attack. In *Advances in Cryptology - Crypto '91*, pp. 433-444, 1991.

[17] R. Rivest, A. Shamir, L. Adleman. A method for obtaining digital signatures and public-key cryptosystems. In *Communications of the ACM*, Vol. 21, pp. 120–126, 1978.

[18] V. Shoup. Why chosen security matters. *IBM Research report*, RZ 3076 (#93122), 1998.

[19] V. Shoup. OAEP Reconsidered. In *Proc. of Crypto '01*. Springer, LNCS, Vol. 2139, pp. 239–253, 2001.

[20] C. Schnorr. Security of Almost ALL Discrete Log Bits. In *Electronic Colloquium on Computational Complexity (ECCC)*, Vol. 5, No. 33, 1998.

NTRU Cryptosystems, 5 Burlington Woods, MA 01803

Proceedings of Symposia in Applied Mathematics
Volume **62**, 2005

Elliptic Curves and Cryptography

Joseph H. Silverman

ABSTRACT. We give a brief introduction, without proofs, to the theory of elliptic curves, with an emphasis on those aspects that are most relevant to cryptography.

Introduction

Modern cryptography depends for its security on the difficulty of solving certain mathematical problems. An important example of such a problem is the *Discrete Logarithm Problem*, which asks for the exponent m such that $h = g^m$ for two given elements g and h in a group G. If $G = \mathbb{F}_p^*$ is the multiplicative group of a finite field, this is a difficult problem and has been used as the basis for a variety of cryptographic constructions. Typically, the group $G = \mathbb{F}_p^*$ is chosen to have approximately 2^{1000} elements.

In order to make discrete logarithm cryptography more efficient, one can try to find groups in which the discrete logarithm problem is even harder to solve than it is for $\mathbb{F}_p^*$. This led Neal Koblitz and Victor Miller to (independently) suggest using the group of points on an elliptic curve modulo p. Typically one uses elliptic curve groups with approximately 2^{160} elements, which despite the more complicated nature of the group law on elliptic curves, makes them more efficient than the multiplicative group $\mathbb{F}_p^*$.

The theory of elliptic curves is vast and rich, and the application of elliptic curves to cryptography is an historically recent development. In this article we give a brief introduction to the theory of elliptic curves, with an emphasis on those aspects that are most applicable to cryptography. However, the reader should be aware that even in the cryptographic arena, our coverage is by no means complete, and in particular we have made no effort to present the most efficient methods or results. The interested reader will find additional details and sources for further study in the annotated bibliography.

2000 *Mathematics Subject Classification.* Primary: 14G50; Secondary: 11G05, 11G20, 11T71, 94A60.

Key words and phrases. elliptic curve, elliptic curve cryptography.

This article is an expanded version of a presentation at the MAA MathFest Minicourse on Cryptography, Burlington, VT, July 30–31, 2002.

Bob's Tasks		**Alice's Tasks**
Choose secret $0 < b < n$		Choose secret $0 < a < n$
Compute $B = g^b$		Compute $A = g^a$
Send B	$\longrightarrow$	to Alice
to Bob	$\longleftarrow$	Send A
Compute A^b		Compute B^a
Bob and Alice have the shared value $A^b = g^{ab} = B^a$		

TABLE 1. Diffie-Hellman key exchange

1. The Discrete Logarithm Problem

We begin with a brief discussion of the Discrete Logarithm Problem in an arbitrary group.

1.1. The Discrete Logarithm Problem. Fix a group G and an element $g \in G$. The *Discrete Lograrithm Problem* (DLP) for G is the following:

> Given an element h in the subgroup of G generated by g, find an integer m satisfying
> $$h = g^m$$
> **The Discrete Logarithm Problem**

The smallest positive integer m satisfying $h = g^m$ is called the *logarithm* (or *index*) of h with respect to g and is denoted

$$m = \log_g(h) \qquad \text{or} \qquad m = \text{ind}_g(h).$$

The Discrete Logarithm Problem is used as the underlying hard problem in many cryptographic constructions, including key exchange, encryption, digital signing, and hashing.

1.2. The Diffie-Hellman Key Exchange Protocol. Originally proposed for the multiplicative group of a finite field, the Diffie-Hellman key exchange protocol can be applied to any group. In this protocol, Bob and Alice want to create a shared secret quantity while communicating over an insecure channel.

The first step is to agree on a group G and an element g of G of some order n. The group G and the element g are assumed to be public knowledge, and in particular to be known to an eavesdropper who we shall call Eve. Bob and Alice now perform the steps described in Table 1.

At the end of Diffie-Hellman Key Exchange, Bob and Alice share the value $A^b = B^a$, since the law of exponents (and commutativity of multiplication of integers!) gives

$$A^b = (g^a)^b = g^{ab} = (g^b)^a = B^a.$$

The eavesdropper Eve sees the values of $A = g^a$ and $B = g^b$. If she can solve the DLP, then she can solve for a and b and compute Bob and Alice's shared secret g^{ab}. One hopes that this is the only way in which Eve can find Bob and Alice's shared secret. The security of Diffie-Hellman key exchange thus relies on the difficulty of the following problem, which may or may not be easier than the DLP:

> Given g and two elements g^a and g^b in the subgroup of G generated by g, find the element g^{ab} in G.
>
> **The Diffie-Hellman Problem**

1.3. How Hard is the Discrete Logarithm Problem. For some groups, the DLP is very easy:

- In $\mathbb{Z}/m\mathbb{Z}$ under addition, the Euclidean algorithm solves the DLP.
- In $\mathbb{R}^*$ under multiplication, the usual analytic logarithm solves the DLP.

For some groups, the DLP is quite difficult. The classical example, and the case cited in Diffie and Hellman's original paper, is the multiplicative group $\mathbb{F}_p^*$ of a finite field under multiplication. Indeed, when someone refers to the DLP with no further adjectives, it generally indicates this case.

The best known algorithm to solve the DLP in $\mathbb{F}_p^*$ is based on the index calculus and uses the number field sieve to achieve a running time of

$$O\left(e^{c\sqrt[3]{(\log p)(\log\log p)^2}}\right),$$

where c is a constant. This is a *subexponential* time algorithm, since it is faster than exponential (in $\log p$), although it is not as fast as polynomial time.

For cryptographic purposes, it would be better to use a group G in which it takes fully exponential time to solve the DLP. This led Neal Koblitz [**6**] and Victor Miller [**12**] to independently suggest the use of elliptic curves for Diffie-Hellman and other discrete logarithm based cryptographic constructions.

2. Elliptic Curves

2.1. What is an Elliptic Curve?

- An *elliptic curve* is a curve (a geometric object) that is also a group (an algebraic object).
- The group law on an elliptic curve is constructed using the geometry of the curve.
- Elliptic curves have (almost) nothing to do with ellipses, so it is wise to put ellipses and conic sections out of your thoughts!
- Elliptic curves appear in many diverse areas of mathematics, ranging from number theory to complex analysis, from cryptography to mathematical physics, and on and on.[1]

2.2. Points on Elliptic Curves.

- An elliptic curve may have points whose coordinates lie in any field, for example in $\mathbb{R}$ or $\mathbb{C}$ or $\mathbb{Q}$ or even a finite field $\mathbb{F}_p$.
- An elliptic curve with points in a finite field is a finite group, and thus is a natural candidate for studying the DLP.

---

[1]It has been opined [**10**, page iv] that "it is possible to write endlessly on elliptic curves." We have tried to avoid this temptation by including only the basic properties needed to understand how elliptic curves are used in cryptography. But the reader should be aware that the theory of elliptic curves is vast, and we will not even touch on all of the aspects used by cryptographers.

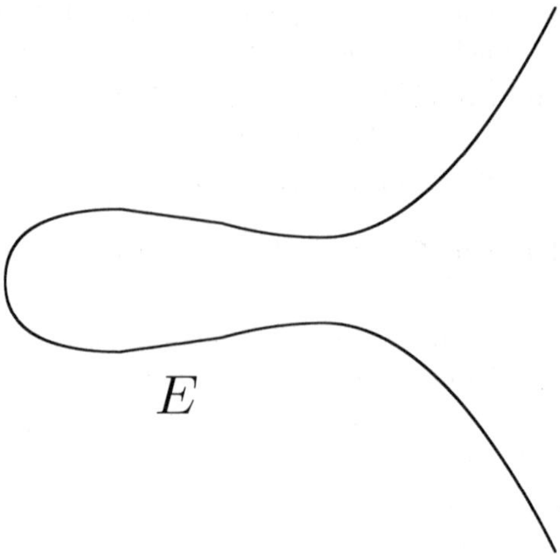

FIGURE 1. The elliptic curve $E : y^2 = x^3 - 5x + 8$

- The *Elliptic Curve Discrete Logarithm Problem* (ECDLP) is the discrete logarithm problem for the group of points on an elliptic curve whose coordinates lie in a finite field $\mathbb{F}_p$.
- Currently, the best algorithms for solving the ECDLP have running time that is fully exponential, which makes elliptic curve groups a natural choice for cryptography.
- More precisely, the best known method to solve the ECDLP on an elliptic curve over the finite field $\mathbb{F}_p$ has running time $O(\sqrt{p})$.

2.3. The Equation of an Elliptic Curve. The most prosaic definition of an *Elliptic Curve* is that it is a curve in the plane given by an equation of the form

$$\textbf{Elliptic Curve} \qquad \boxed{E : y^2 = x^3 + Ax + B}$$

(An example is given in Figure 1.) There is also the requirement that the *discriminant* Δ not vanish, where Δ is the quantity

$$\Delta = 4A^3 + 27B^2 \neq 0.$$

This condition on the discriminant is equivalent to the condition that the cubic polynomial $x^3 + Ax + B$ has no repeated roots, and is also equivalent to the condition that the curve E is nonsingular.

For reasons that will become apparent later, we also include an extra point $\mathcal{O}$, which we call the "point at infinity," so E is really the set

$$\boxed{E = \{(x, y) : y^2 = x^3 + Ax + B\} \cup \{\mathcal{O}\}}$$

Formally, we treat $\mathcal{O}$ as an extra point lying on every vertical line. The reader who is familiar with the construction of the projective plane will realize that we have added one of the points that is needed to form the projective plane from the affine plane. In general, the projective plane has one extra point for every line (or direction) through the origin, but for elliptic cruves we need only the one extra point corresponding to the vertical direction.

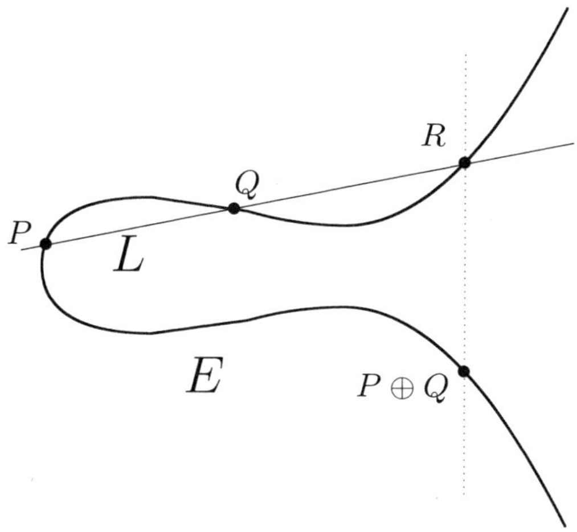

FIGURE 2. Adding points on an elliptic curve

3. The Group Law on an Elliptic Curve

3.1. A Geometric Description of the Group Law. The geometric description of the group law on an elliptic curve is best illustrated with pictures, as shown in Figures 2, 3, and 4. Here are verbal descriptions to accompany the pictures. (N.B. We will be cheating a little bit in places, and then we fix things as we move along.)

3.1.1. *Adding Distinct Points.* See Figure 2.

- Let P and Q be distinct points on the curve E.
- Draw the line L connecting P and Q.
- The line L intersects E in exactly three points, two of which are obviously P and Q. Let R be the third point in $L \cap E$. (It's possible that R equals P or Q, since if the line L is tangent to E, we count the intersection with its multiplicity.)
- Reflect the point R across the x-axis and call the resulting point "$P + Q$", i.e., if $R = (x, y)$, then $P + Q = (x, -y)$.

3.1.2. *Adding a Point to Itself.* If $P = Q$, then the prescription for adding $P + P$ begins by taking "the" line L connecting P to P. There are many lines through P. However, suppose that we fix P and take nearby points Q. Let L_Q be the line connecting P to Q. Then as $Q \to P$, the limiting line L_P is the tangent line to E at P. Hence in order to add a point P to itself, we use the tangent line to E at P. This line intersects E at the point P with multiplicity two, so it intersects E in exactly one additional point. The reflection of that point is $P + P$, which we also denote by $2P$. See Figure 3.

- Let P be a point on the curve E.
- Draw the tangent line L to E at P.
- The line L intersects E in exactly two points, one of which is P (with multiplicity two). Let R be the other point in $L \cap E$. (It's possible that R equals P, if L has a triple order contact with E.)

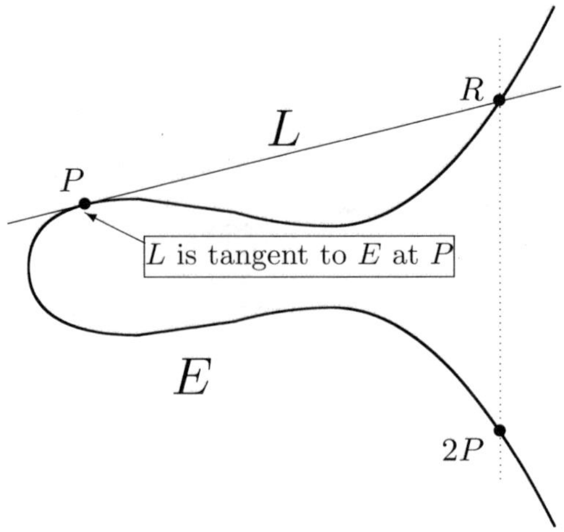

FIGURE 3. Adding a point to itself on an elliptic curve

- Reflect the point R across the x-axis and call the resulting point "$P + P$" or "$2P$".

3.1.3. *Vertical Lines and the Point at Infinity.* There is a serious difficulty with the addition law. If P and Q lie on a vertical line L, then $L \cap E$ only contains the two points P and Q. For notational convenience, we denote the reflection of a point P by $-P$, i.e.,

$$-(x, y) = (x, -y).$$

How should we deal with the $Q = -P$ problem? Since there is no third intersection point in the plane, we simply create a new point $\mathcal{O}$ which is "at infinity" and we impose by fiat the property that $\mathcal{O}$ lies on every vertical line, but on no other lines. We also specify that the tangent line to E at the point $\mathcal{O}$ has a triple order intersection with E at $\mathcal{O}$. With these defining properties, we immediately find that $P+(-P) = \mathcal{O}$, which solves the problem of adding points that lie on vertical lines.[2] See Figure 4.

- Let $P = (x, y)$ be a point on E.
- The reflection of P is the point $-P = (x, -y)$.
- The sum of P and $-P$ is the point $P + (-P) = \mathcal{O}$.
- The point $\mathcal{O}$ lies on every vertical line. This leads to the rule $P + \mathcal{O} = P$ for every point P of E.

3.2. Properties of Addition on E. The following theorem summarizes the properties of the addition law on E.

---

[2]The reader who has seen the construction of the projective plane $\mathbb{P}^2$ will realize that we have started this construction by using the one point in $\mathbb{P}^2$ corresponding to the vertical direction. The full projective plane consists of the affine plane together with one point for every direction. In terms of projective coordinates, the elliptic curve E is given by the equation $E : Y^2Z = X^3 + AXZ^2 + BZ^3$. The point at infinity on E is the point $\mathcal{O} = [0, 1, 0]$, and the tangent line to E at $\mathcal{O}$ is the line $Z = 0$ at infinity.

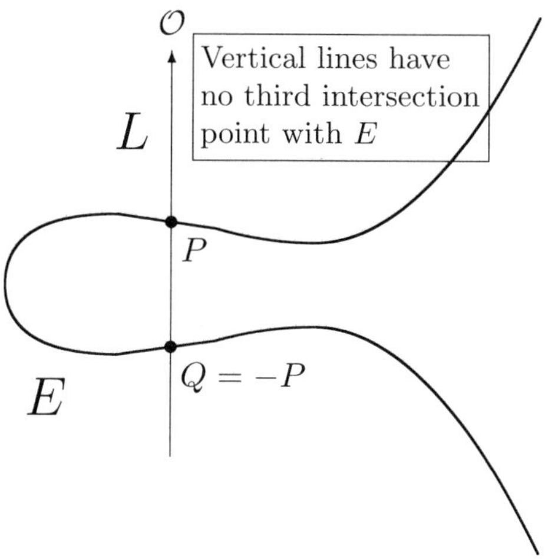

FIGURE 4. Vertical lines and the extra point "at infinity"

THEOREM 1. *The addition law on an elliptic curve E has the following properties:*

(a)	$P + \mathcal{O} = \mathcal{O} + P = P$	*for all* $P \in E$.
(b)	$P + (-P) = \mathcal{O}$	*for all* $P \in E$.
(c)	$(P+Q)+R = P+(Q+R)$	*for all* $P, Q, R \in E$.
(d)	$P + Q = Q + P$	*for all* $P, Q \in E$.

In other words, the addition law described above makes the points of E into a commutative group.

All of the group properties are trivial to check *except* for the associative law (c). The associative law can be verified by a lengthy computation using explicit formulas, or by using more advanced algebraic or analytic methods.

3.3. Explicit Formulas for the Group Law on E. Suppose that we want to add the points

$$P_1 = (x_1, y_1) \qquad \text{and} \qquad P_2 = (x_2, y_2)$$

on the elliptic curve

$$E : y^2 = x^3 + Ax + B.$$

Let the line connecting P_1 and P_2 be

$$L : y = \lambda x + \nu.$$

Explicitly, the slope and y-intercept of L are given by

$$\lambda = \begin{cases} \dfrac{y_2 - y_1}{x_2 - x_1} & \text{if } P_1 \neq P_2 \\ \dfrac{3x_1^2 + A}{2y_1} & \text{if } P_1 = P_2 \end{cases} \qquad \text{and} \qquad \nu = y_1 - \lambda x_1.$$

We find the intersection of

$$E : y^2 = x^3 + Ax + B \qquad \text{and} \qquad L : y = \lambda x + \nu$$

• If $P_1 \neq P_2$ and $x_1 = x_2$, then $P_1 + P_2 = \mathcal{O}$.
• If $P_1 = P_2$ and $y_1 = 0$, then $P_1 + P_2 = 2P_1 = \mathcal{O}$.
• If $P_1 \neq P_2$ (and $x_1 \neq x_2$), let $\lambda = \dfrac{y_2 - y_1}{x_2 - x_1}$ and $\nu = \dfrac{y_1 x_2 - y_2 x_1}{x_2 - x_1}$.
• If $P_1 = P_2$ (and $y_1 \neq 0$), let $\lambda = \dfrac{3x_1^2 + A}{2y_1}$ and $\nu = \dfrac{-x^3 + Ax + 2B}{2y}$.
• Then $P_1 + P_2 = (\lambda^2 - x_1 - x_2, -\lambda^3 + \lambda(x_1 + x_2) - \nu)$.

TABLE 2. Addition algorithm for $P_1 = (x_1, y_1)$ and $P_2 = (x_2, y_2)$ on the elliptic curve $E : y^2 = x^3 + Ax + B$

by solving

$$(\lambda x + \nu)^2 = x^3 + Ax + B.$$

We already know that x_1 and x_2 are solutions, so we can find the third solution x_3 by comparing the two sides of the polynomial identity

$$\begin{aligned} x^3 + Ax + B - (\lambda x + \nu)^2 \\ &= (x - x_1)(x - x_2)(x - x_3) \\ &= x^3 - (x_1 + x_2 + x_3)x^2 + (x_1 x_2 + x_1 x_3 + x_2 x_3)x - x_1 x_2 x_3. \end{aligned}$$

Equating the coefficients of x^2, for example, gives

$$-\lambda^2 = -x_1 - x_2 - x_3, \qquad \text{and hence} \quad x_3 = \lambda^2 - x_1 - x_2.$$

Then we compute y_3 using $y_3 = \lambda x_3 + \nu$, and finally

$$P_1 + P_2 = (x_3, -y_3).$$

Putting all of this together gives the algorithm described in Table 3.3.

3.4. The Group of Points with Coordinates in a Field. Notice that the coordinates of $P_1 + P_2$ are rational expressions involving only the quantities x_1, y_1, x_2, y_2, A, B. For example, the x-coordinate of $2P_1$ expands out to

$$x(2P_1) = \frac{x_1^4 - 2Ax_1^2 - 8Bx_1 + A^2}{4y_1^2}.$$

This leads to the following fundamental observation.

THEOREM 2 (Poincaré, ≈ 1900). *Let K be a field and suppose that an elliptic curve E is given by an equation of the form*

$$E : y^2 = x^3 + Ax + B \qquad \textit{with} \quad A, B \in K.$$

Let $E(K)$ denote the set of points of E with coordinates in K, i.e.,

$$E(K) = \{(x, y) \in E : x, y \in K\} \cup \{\mathcal{O}\}.$$

Then $E(K)$ is a subgroup *of the group $E(\bar{K})$ of all points of E.*

3.5. A Numerical Example Over $\mathbb{Q}$. The elliptic curve (see Figure 1)

$$E : y^2 = x^3 - 5x + 8$$

contains the point $P = (1,2) \in E$. Using the tangent line construction or the explicit formula for adding a point to itself, we find that

$$2P = P + P = \left(-\frac{7}{4}, -\frac{27}{8}\right).$$

Let $Q = \left(-\frac{7}{4}, -\frac{27}{8}\right)$. Using the secant line construction or the explicit formula for adding distinct points, we find that

$$3P = P + Q = \left(\frac{553}{121}, -\frac{11950}{1331}\right) \quad \text{and} \quad 4P = \left(\frac{45313}{11664}, \frac{8655103}{1259712}\right).$$

As is readily apparent, the numerators and the denominators get quite large very rapidly.[3] On the other hand, we see that the multiples $2P, 3P, 4P, \ldots$ of P are in $E(\mathbb{Q})$, in accordance with the statement of Theorem 2. It is actually possible to say something quite precise about the size of the numerators and denominators of the multiples of a point in $E(\mathbb{Q})$, see Section 5.4

3.6. A Finite Field Numerical Example. The formulas giving the group law on E are valid if the points have coordinates in any field, even if the geometric pictures may not make sense. Poincaré's Theorem 2 tells us that the points form a group.

For example, we may take points with coordinates in a finite field $\mathbb{F}_p$. There are only finitely many such points, since there are only p choices for each coordinate. Hence $E(\mathbb{F}_p)$ is a finite group.

For example, consider the elliptic curve

$$E : y^2 = x^3 - 5x + 8 \pmod{37}.$$

It is easy to check that

$$P = (6,3) \in E(\mathbb{F}_{37}) \qquad \text{and} \qquad Q = (9,10) \in E(\mathbb{F}_{37}).$$

Using the addition formulas, we can compute in $E(\mathbb{F}_{37})$:

$$2P = (35,11), \quad 3P = (34,25), \quad 4P = (8,6), \quad 5P = (16,19), \ldots$$
$$P + Q = (11,10), \quad 3P + 4Q = (31,28), \ldots$$

Substituting in each possible value $x = 0, 1, 2, \ldots, 36$ and checking if $x^3 - 5x + 8$ is a square modulo 37, we find that $E(\mathbb{F}_{37})$ consists of the following 45 points modulo 37:

$$(1, \pm 2), (5, \pm 21), (6, \pm 3), (8, \pm 6), (9, \pm 27), (10, \pm 25), (11, \pm 27),$$
$$(12, \pm 23), (16, \pm 19), (17, \pm 27), (19, \pm 1), (20, \pm 8), (21, \pm 5), (22, \pm 1), (26, \pm 8),$$
$$(28, \pm 8), (30, \pm 25), (31, \pm 9), (33, \pm 1), (34, \pm 25), (35, \pm 26), (36, \pm 7), \mathcal{O}.$$

Further, there are eight points of exact order three, so as an abstract group,

$$E(\mathbb{F}_{37}) \cong \mathbb{Z}/3\mathbb{Z} \times \mathbb{Z}/15\mathbb{Z}.$$

---

[3] The astute reader may have observed that the denominators of the x and y coordinates are closely related. For example, $11664 = 108^2$ and $1259712 = 108^3$. It is a nice exercise to prove that if $A, B \in \mathbb{Z}$ and if the coordinates of $P \in E(\mathbb{Q})$ are written in lowest terms, then $P = (a/d^2, b/d^3)$ for some $a, b, d \in \mathbb{Z}$.

4. Computing Large Multiples of a Point

In order to use the finite group $E(\mathbb{F}_p)$ for Diffie-Hellman key exchange or other cryptographic constructions, we need p to be quite large, generally at least $p > 2^{160}$. This means we need to compute multiples

$$mP = \underbrace{P + P + \cdots + P}_{m \text{ times}} \in E(\mathbb{F}_p)$$

for very large values of m.

The classical double-and-add method allows us to compute mP in $O(\log m)$ steps. First expand the multiplier m into binary,

$$m = m_0 + m_1 * 2 + m_2 * 2^2 + \cdots + m_r * 2^r \qquad \text{with } m_0, \ldots, m_r \in \{0, 1\}.$$

Then mP can be computed as

$$mP = m_0 P + m_1 * 2P + m_2 * 2^2 P + \cdots + m_r * 2^r P,$$

where $2^k P = 2 * 2 * \cdots * 2P$ requires only k doublings. Thus on average, it takes approximately $\log_2(m)$ doublings and $\frac{1}{2}\log_2(m)$ additions to compute mP.

There is a simple way to reduce the computation time even further. Since it takes the same amount of time to subtract two point as it does to add two points, we can instead look at a "trinary" expansion of m, which means writing

$$m = m_0 + m_1 * 2 + m_2 * 2^2 + \cdots + m_r * 2^r \qquad \text{with } m_0, \ldots, m_r \in \{-1, 0, 1\}.$$

On average, this can be done with approximately $\frac{2}{3}$ of the m_i's equal to 0, which reduces the number of necessary additions to approximately $\frac{1}{3}\log_2(m)$.

5. The Structure of the Group $E(K)$

The structure of $E(K)$, the group of points on E having coordinates in the field K, depends on the structure of the field K itself. In this section we take a brief tour of some of the possibilities.

5.1. What does $E(K)$ look like for $K = \mathbb{R}$? We have already seen an example of $E(\mathbb{R})$ as illustrated in Figure 1. In that example, $E(\mathbb{R})$ consists of one connected component. It is also possible for $E(\mathbb{R})$ to have two components,[4] as shown in Figure 5. Analytically, $E(\mathbb{R})$ is isomorphic to the circle group $S^1 = \mathbb{R}/\mathbb{Z}$ or to two copies of the circle group $S^1 \times (\mathbb{Z}/2\mathbb{Z})$. (Remember that $E(\mathbb{R})$ includes that extra point $\mathcal{O}$ at infinity.)

5.2. What does $E(K)$ look like for $K = \mathbb{C}$? The points of an elliptic curve with coordinates in the complex numbers $\mathbb{C}$ form a *torus*, that is, the surface of a donut. There are complex numbers $\omega_1, \omega_2 \in \mathbb{C}$, called periods for E, and a complex analytic isomorphism from the parallelogram spanned by the periods with opposite sides identified to the complex points of E.

In order to make this more precise, let

$$L = \{n_1\omega_1 + n_2\omega_2 : n_1, n_2 \in \mathbb{Z}\} \subset \mathbb{C}$$

[4]Exercise: Prove that $E(\mathbb{R})$ has one component if $\Delta < 0$ and two components if $\Delta > 0$, where recall that the discrimiant Δ of $E : y^2 = x^3 + Ax + B$ is $\Delta = 4A^3 + 27B^2$.

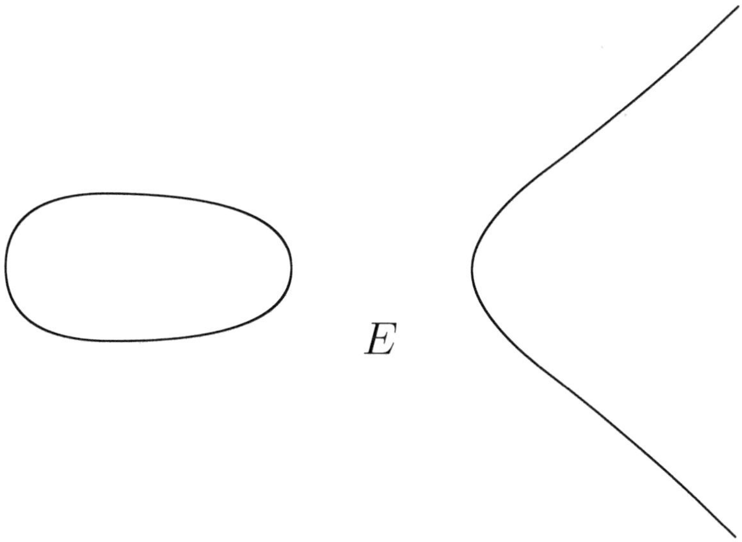

FIGURE 5. An elliptic curve with two real components

be the lattice spanned by ω_1 and ω_2 (see Figure 6). Then there is a complex analytic isomorphism

$$\frac{\mathbb{C}}{L} \xrightarrow{(\wp(z), \frac{1}{2}\wp'(z))} E(\mathbb{C}),$$

where the *Weierstrass* $\wp$*-function* is defined by the Laurent series

$$\wp(z) = \frac{1}{z^2} + \sum_{\substack{\omega \in L \\ \omega \neq 0}} \left(\frac{1}{(z-\omega)^2} - \frac{1}{\omega^2} \right)$$

and satisfies

$$\wp(z+\omega) = \wp(z) \qquad \text{for all } \omega \in L.$$

Thus $\wp(z)$ is a *doubly periodic function*, since it has two independent periods ω_1 and ω_2. It generalizes the classical function e^z that has the single period $2\pi i$.

5.3. What does $E(K)$ look like for $K = \mathbb{Q}$? The group of rational points $E(\mathbb{Q})$ is a subgroup of the group of real points $E(\mathbb{R})$, but we can no more draw a nice picture of $E(\mathbb{Q})$ sitting inside $E(\mathbb{R})$ than we can draw a nice picture of the rational numbers $\mathbb{Q}$ sitting inside the real numbers $\mathbb{R}$. However, the group $E(\mathbb{Q})$ has played an important role in the development of many areas of number theory, and the following description of $E(\mathbb{Q})$ is a landmark in the modern study of Diophantine equations.[5]

THEOREM 3 (Mordell, 1922). *Let E be an elliptic curve given by an equation*

$$E : y^2 = x^3 + Ax + B \qquad \textit{with } A, B \in \mathbb{Q}.$$

[5]A *Diophantine equation* is a system of one or more polynomials equations that are to be solved using only integers or rational numbers. They are named after Diophantus of Alexandria, who lived in Egypt in the 3rd century and wrote a book containing equations of this type.

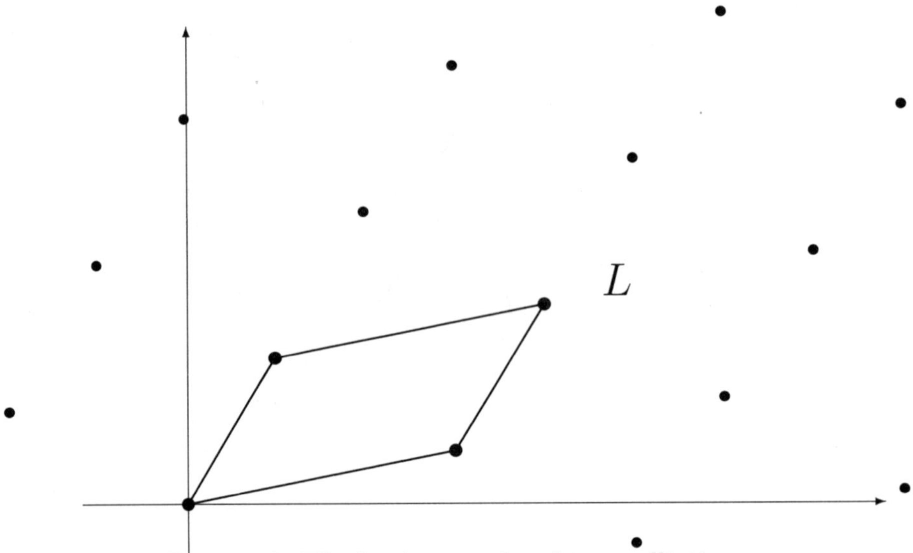

FIGURE 6. The lattice associated to an elliptic curve

Then the group of rational points $E(\mathbb{Q})$ *is a* finitely generated *abelian group. In other words, there is a finite set of points* $P_1, \ldots, P_t \in E(\mathbb{Q})$ *so that every point* $P \in E(\mathbb{Q})$ *can be written in the form*

$$P = n_1 P_1 + n_2 P_2 + \cdots + n_t P_t \qquad \text{for some } n_1, n_2, \ldots, n_t \in \mathbb{Z}.$$

A standard result on finitely generated abelian groups says that $E(\mathbb{Q})$ is isomorphic to

$$E(\mathbb{Q}) \cong \Phi \times \mathbb{Z}^r$$

for a finite group Φ and an integer $r \geq 0$. The finite group Φ is called the *torsion subgroup* of $E(\mathbb{Q})$ and the integer r is called the *rank* of $E(\mathbb{Q})$.

It is easy to state a complete characterization for torsion subgroups, although the proof is quite deep.

THEOREM 4 (Mazur, 1977). *The torsion subgroup* Φ *of the group of rational points* $E(\mathbb{Q})$ *on an elliptic curve must be one of the following 15 groups:*

$$\Phi \cong \frac{\mathbb{Z}}{N\mathbb{Z}} \quad \text{with } 1 \leq N \leq 10 \text{ or } N = 12, \text{ or} \qquad \Phi \cong \frac{\mathbb{Z}}{2N\mathbb{Z}} \times \frac{\mathbb{Z}}{2\mathbb{Z}} \quad \text{with } 1 \leq N \leq 4.$$

In particular, Φ *has order at most 16.*

The rank is a far more mysterious quantity, although there is a folklore conjecture.

CONJECTURE 5. *There exist elliptic curve groups* $E(\mathbb{Q})$ *of arbitrarily large rank.*

The best evidence for this conjecture comes from the analogous statement with $\mathbb{Q}$ replaced by the field of rational functions $\mathbb{F}_p(T)$, where it is known to be true. For $E(\mathbb{Q})$, there is currently one example known of rank 24, and none of higher rank.

5.4. The Canonical Height. We digress briefly to discuss height functions. These are an important tool used to study the points in $E(\mathbb{Q})$, but they also have profound implications for cryptography. Indeed, Neal Koblitz calls height functions the "golden shield protecting elliptic curve cryptography" from subexponential attacks [**9**].

For any rational number $\alpha = a/b \in \mathbb{Q}$ written in lowest terms, we define the *height* of α to be

$$h(\alpha) = h\left(\frac{a}{b}\right) = \log \max\{|a|, |b|\}.$$

For a number theorist, the height of α measures how complicated the number α is. For a computer scientist, the same is true, since it takes $O(h(\alpha))$ bits to exactly specify the number α.

THEOREM 6 (Néron-Tate). *Let $P \in E(\mathbb{Q})$ be an elliptic curve, and for each integer $n \geq 1$, write*

$$nP = (x_n, y_n).$$

Then the following limit exists:

$$\hat{h}(P) = \lim_{n\to\infty} \frac{1}{n^2} h(x_n).$$

The quantity $\hat{h}(P)$ is called the canonical height *of P. It has the following properties:*

(a) $\hat{h}(P) \geq 0$, *and $\hat{h}(P) = 0$ if and only if P has finite order in the group $E(\mathbb{Q})$.*

(b) *There are positive constants $c_1(E)$ and $c_2(E)$, depending only on E, so that for any point $P \in E(\mathbb{Q})$ and any integer $n \geq 1$,*

$$n^2\hat{h}(P) - c_1(E) \leq h(x_n) \leq n^2\hat{h}(P) + c_2(E).$$

(c) *For any constant C, the set*

$$\{P \in E(\mathbb{Q}) : \hat{h}(P) \leq C\} \quad \text{is finite.}$$

(d) *For any points $P, Q \in E(\mathbb{Q})$ and any integer $n \geq 1$,*

$$\hat{h}(nP) = n^2\hat{h}(P) \qquad \text{and} \qquad \hat{h}(P+Q) + \hat{h}(P-Q) = 2\hat{h}(P) + 2\hat{h}(Q).$$

A less formal, but more striking, way to state property (b) is that if $P \in E(\mathbb{Q})$ has infinite order, then for large values of n, either (or both) the numerator or the denominator of the x-coordinate of nP has $O(n^2)$ digits. In fact, a deep result of Siegel says that the numerator and denominator have approximately the same number of digits (see Section 5.5), so both actually have $O(n^2)$ digits.

5.5. What does $E(K)$ look like for $K = \mathbb{Z}$? The ring $\mathbb{Z}$ is not a field, so the set

$$E(\mathbb{Z}) = \{(x, y) \in E(\mathbb{Q}) : x, y \in \mathbb{Z}\} \cup \{\mathcal{O}\}$$

is not necessarily a subgroup of $E(\mathbb{Q})$. If P_1 and P_2 are points on E having integer coordinates, then $P_1 + P_2$ has rational coordinates, but there is no reason for it to have integer coordinates.

Indeed, the formulas for $P_1 + P_2$ are so complicated, it seems unlikely that the point $P_1 + P_2$ will have integer coordinates. Complementing Mordell's finite generation theorem for rational points is a famous finiteness result for integer points.

THEOREM 7 (Siegel, 1928). *Let E be an elliptic curve given by an equation*

$$E : y^2 = x^3 + Ax + B \qquad \text{with } A, B \in \mathbb{Z}.$$

Then E has only finitely many points $P = (x, y)$ with integer coordinates $x, y \in \mathbb{Z}$, i.e., $E(\mathbb{Z})$ is a finite set.

Siegel actually proves something much stronger. For each point $P \in E(\mathbb{Q})$, write the x-coordinate of P in lowest terms as $x(P) = a(P)/b(P)$. Then Siegel proves that

$$\lim_{\substack{P\in E(\mathbb{Q}) \\ \max\{|a(P)|,|b(P)|\}\to\infty}} \frac{\log |a(P)|}{\log |b(P)|} = 1.$$

Roughly speaking, Siegel's result says that the numerator and the denominator of $x(P)$ tend to have approximately the same number of digits.

5.6. What does $E(K)$ look like for $K = \mathbb{F}_p$? The group $E(\mathbb{F}_p)$ is obviously a finite group, since there are only finitely many possibilities for the x and y coordinates of each point. These finite groups are used extensively for cryptographic purposes and thus will be our main object of study in the remainder of this article.

6. The Group of Points $E(\mathbb{F}_p)$ on an Elliptic Curve over a Finite Field

6.1. The Order of the Group $E(\mathbb{F}_p)$. It is clear that $E(\mathbb{F}_p)$ has at most $2p + 1$ points, since there are only p choices for $x \in \mathbb{F}_p$, and for each x, there are at most two values of y satisfying

$$y^2 = x^3 + Ax + B.$$

(That point $\mathcal{O}$ accounts for the extra $+1$.)

However, it seems very unlikely that we actually get $2p + 1$ points. Indeed, as we take different $x \in \mathbb{F}_p$, the value of $x^3 + Ax + B$ ranges over some random-looking subset of $\mathbb{F}_p$, so for any given x we expect a 50% chance that $x^3 + Ax + B$ is a square in $\mathbb{F}_p$, in which case it has two square roots. Thus we expect that half the values of x give two points in $E(\mathbb{F}_p)$ and the other half give no points. Adding in the point $\mathcal{O}$, this leads us to expect that

$$\#E(\mathbb{F}_p) \approx \frac{1}{2} \cdot 2 \cdot p + 1 = p + 1 \text{ points.}$$

Of course, this rough heuristic approximation is unlikely to be entirely accurate. A famous theorem of Hasse gives a precise estimate for the error.

THEOREM 8 (Hasse, 1922). *Let E be an elliptic curve given by an equation*

$$E : y^2 = x^3 + Ax + B \qquad \text{with } A, B \in \mathbb{F}_p.$$

Then

$$\#E(\mathbb{F}_p) = p + 1 - a_p(E) \qquad \text{with } \left|a_p(E)\right| \le 2\sqrt{p}.$$

Thus Hasse's theorem says that the error in approximating $\#E(\mathbb{F}_p)$ by $p + 1$ is $O(\sqrt{p})$. For technical reasons that we do not discuss, the error

$$a_p(E) = p + 1 - \#E(\mathbb{F}_p)$$

is called the *trace of Frobenius*.[6] Hasse's theorem says that the trace of Frobenius is small, and hence that the order of $E(\mathbb{F}_p)$ is large if p is large.

6.2. The Distribution of the Trace of Frobenius. For cryptographic purposes, we want $E(\mathbb{F}_p)$ to contain a subgroup of large *prime* order. So it is useful to know the distribution of $\#E(\mathbb{F}_p)$, or equivalently, the distribution of $a_p(E)$, as E varies.

There are approximately $2p$ different elliptic curves[7] defined over $\mathbb{F}_p$, where we consider two elliptic curves to be equivalent (or isomorphic) if they differ by a change of coordinates $(x, y) \mapsto (u^2x, u^3y)$ for some $u \in \mathbb{F}_p^*$. If the $a_p(E)$ values were uniformly distributed in the interval from $-2\sqrt{p}$ to $2\sqrt{p}$, then we would expect each value to appear approximately $\frac{1}{2}\sqrt{p}$ times.

This is not quite true, but it is true that the values of $a_p(E)$ between $-\sqrt{p}$ and $\sqrt{p}$ appear quite frequently. The precise statement says that the $a_p(E)$ values follow a Sato-Tate distribution, see [**1**]. We are content to state the following approximation formula, where now note that we are counting isomorphism classes of elliptic curves, not points:

$$\#\{E/\mathbb{F}_p : \alpha \le a_p(E) \le \beta\} \approx \frac{1}{\pi}\int_\alpha^\beta \sqrt{4p - t^2}\, dt.$$

6.3. Computing the Order of $E(\mathbb{F}_p)$.

- If p is small, then we can simply compute $x^3 + Ax + B$ for each value $x = 0, 1, 2, \ldots, p-1$ and check if it is a square modulo p. This is not recommended unless p is very small, since the running time is $O(p \log p)$.
- Schoof devised a deterministic polynomial time algorithm to compute $\#E(\mathbb{F}_p)$ in time $O(\log^6 p)$, although the big-O constant is quite large.
- Elkies and Atkin turned Schoof's algorithm into an efficient probabilistic algorithm, which is now called the SEA-algrorithm for computing $E(\mathbb{F}_p)$.
- The details of SEA are somewhat complicated, but roughly, one studies the collection of all maps of a fixed degree from E to other elliptic curves. These correspond to quotients E/F for finite subgroups F of E, which in turn give information about $a_p(E)$ modulo ℓ for various primes ℓ. Fitting together this information for many values of ℓ gives $a_p(E)$, and thence $\#E(\mathbb{F}_p) = p + 1 - a_p(E)$. See [**14, 15**].

7. Elliptic Curves in Characteristic 2

As a practical matter, computers tend to work more efficiently with fields of characteristic 2 than they do with fields of (large) prime characterstic. For this reason, cryptographers often use elliptic curves defined over a field $\mathbb{F}_q$ with $q = 2^k$ elements. Generally k is taken to be prime, or at least to have no very small prime factors. The reason for this choice is the fact that if d divides k, then $\mathbb{F}_{2^k}$ contains

---

[6] The Frobenius map on E is the map $(x, y) \mapsto (x^p, y^p)$. The Frobenius maps acts as a linear transformation on a certain space $V_\ell(E)$ associated to E, and then one proves that the trace of this linear map is the quantity $a_p(E)$.

[7] Let $p \ge 5$ and let $n \in \mathbb{F}_p$ be a quadratic nonresidue modulo p. Then every elliptic curve $y^2 = x^3 + Ax + B$ with $AB \ne 0$ is isomorphic to a unique elliptic curve $cy^2 = x^3 - 3tx - 2t$ with $c \in \{1, n\}$ and with $t \in \mathbb{F}_p$ satisfying $t \ne 0$ and $t \ne 1$. This gives $2(p-1)$ isomorphism classes, and then the curves with $A = 0$ or $B = 0$ add a few more.

the subfield $\mathbb{F}_{2^d}$, and in some cases the existence of these intermediate fields can be exploited to help solve the ECDLP.

7.1. Equations for Elliptic Curves in Characteristic 2. In characteristic 2, the curve $y^2 = x^3 + Ax + B$ is always singular. Thus we need to use a more general elliptic curve equation:

$$E : y^2 + a_1xy + a_3y = x^3 + a_2x^2 + a_4x + a_6 \qquad \text{with } a_1, \ldots, a_6 \in \mathbb{F}_q.$$

There is also a discriminant nonvanishing condition, where the discriminant Δ is a somewhat complicated polynomial[8] in the coefficients $a_1, \ldots, a_6$.

The group law on E is defined in the same way, since every line still intersects E in exactly three points (counted with appropriate multiplicities). The explicit formulas for the group law are more complicated, but have the same general form as before. Satoh [**13**] has described a fast way to compute the number of points in $E(\mathbb{F}_q)$ when q is a large power of a small prime, so it is even easier to compute $\#E(\mathbb{F}_{2^k})$ than it is to compute $\#E(\mathbb{F}_p)$ when $p \approx 2^k$.

7.2. Koblitz Curves. For maximum efficiency over the field $\mathbb{F}_{2^k}$, one can use a *Koblitz curve*

$$E : y^2 + xy = x^3 + ax^2 + 1 \qquad \text{with } a = 0 \text{ or } 1.$$

The Koblitz curves have coefficients in $\mathbb{F}_2$, but for cryptography we take points in $E(\mathbb{F}_q)$ with $q = 2^k$ and $k \approx 160$ (or larger for even higher security).

Computing the number of points on a Koblitz curve is amazingly easy due to the following closed formula.

PROPOSITION 9. *Let E be a Koblitz curve. Then*

$$\#E\left(\mathbb{F}_{2^k}\right) = 2^k - \left(\frac{-1+\sqrt{-7}}{2}\right)^k - \left(\frac{-1-\sqrt{-7}}{2}\right)^k + 1.$$

This formula may look strange at first, since the lefthand side is an integer, while the righthand side appears to involve $\sqrt{-7}$. However, when it is all multiplied out using the binomial formula, one sees that the irrational quantities cancel out, leaving

$$\#E\left(\mathbb{F}_{2^k}\right) = 2^k - \frac{1}{(-2)^{k-1}} \sum_{0 \le i \le k/2} \binom{k}{2i} (-7)^i + 1.$$

The principal reason to use a Koblitz curve is due to the existence of the map

$$\tau : E\left(\mathbb{F}_{2^k}\right) \longrightarrow E\left(\mathbb{F}_{2^k}\right), \qquad \tau(x, y) = (x^2, y^2).$$

Using the fact that $x \to x^2$ is a field automorphism of $\mathbb{F}_{2^k}$, it is not hard to check that τ is actually a homomorphism of $E\left(\mathbb{F}_{2^k}\right)$ to itself, i.e.,

$$\tau(P + Q) = \tau(P) + \tau(Q) \qquad \text{for all } P, Q \in E\left(\mathbb{F}_{2^k}\right).$$

It is also true, but not as easy to prove, that the map τ satisfies the quadratic equation $T^2 + T + 2 = 0$. In other words,

$$\tau^2(P) + \tau(P) + 2P = \mathcal{O} \qquad \text{for all } P \in E\left(\mathbb{F}_{2^k}\right).$$

[8]In characteristic 2, the discriminant is given by the formula $\Delta = a_6a_1^6 + a_4a_3a_1^5 + a_3^2a_2a_1^4 + a_4^2a_1^4 + a_3^3a_1^3 + a_3^4$

(Here $\tau^2(P)$ means the composition $\tau(\tau(P))$.) Using this relation, every integer m has a "τ-adic" expansion, similar to its binary expansion, of the form

$$m = m_0 + m_1\tau + m_2\tau^2 + \cdots + m_r\tau^r \qquad \text{with } m_0, m_1, \ldots, m_r \in \{0, 1\}.$$

Then the multiple mP can be computed, without using doubling maps, as

$$mP = m_0P + m_1\tau(P) + m_2\tau^2(P) + \cdots + m_r\tau^r(P).$$

Since the map τ takes virtually no time to compute, this means that on average, the computation of mP requires $\frac{1}{2}\log_2(m)$ additions.[9]

8. The Elliptic Curve Discrete Logarithm Problem (ECLDP)

The *Elliptic Curve Discrete Logarithm Problem* (ECLDP) for the elliptic curve

$$E : y^2 = x^3 + Ax + B \qquad \text{with } A, B \in \mathbb{F}_p$$

and the points $S, T \in E(\mathbb{F}_p)$ is to find an integer m (assuming that such an integer exists) with the property that

$$T = mS = \underbrace{S + S + \cdots + S}_{m \text{ terms}}.$$

The smallest integer $m \geq 1$ with this property is called the *discrete logarithm* (or *index*) *of* T *with respect to* S and is denoted

$$m = \log_S(T) \qquad \text{or} \qquad m = \operatorname{ind}_S(T).$$

In order to use the ECDLP as the underlying hard problem for cryptographic constructions, it is important to evaluate the difficulty of solving the ECDLP.

9. General Methods for Solving ECDLP

We begin by describing some general methods for solving the ECDLP. All of these methods actually can used to solve the DLP in arbitrary groups.

9.1. Solving ECDLP via Exhaustive Search. Exhaustive search is the trivial algorithm in which one computes multiples $m_1S, m_2S, m_3S, \ldots$ for randomly chosen values $m_1, m_2, m_3, \ldots$ until finding a multiple of S that satisfies $mS = T$. The expected running time of this naive algorithm is $O(p)$, since $\#E(\mathbb{F}_p) = O(p)$.

9.2. Solving ECDLP via Collision Search. Compute two lists for randomly chosen values of $m_1, m_2, m_3, \ldots$:

List 1: $m_1S,\ m_2S,\ m_3S, \ldots$
List 2: $T - m_1S,\ T - m_2S,\ T - m_3S, \ldots$

The well-known "Birthday Principle"[10] predicts that if the two lists have $O(\sqrt{p})$ elements, then there is a high probability that they share a common element, i.e., there is a collision between the two lists. That collisions leads to an equation

$$m_iS = T - m_jS,$$

which solves the ECDLP. The running time of this algorithm is $O(\sqrt{p})$ However, note that the method also requires storing $O(\sqrt{p})$ numbers.

---

[9] If we allow $m_0, \ldots, m_r$ to be drawn from the set $\{-1, 0, 1\}$, then the average computation time is reduced to approximately $\frac{1}{3}\log_2(m)$ additions.

[10] In this context, the *Birthday Principle* says that if a large set S contains N elements and if two subsets S_1 and S_2 of S of size $\sqrt{N}$ are chosen at random from S, then the probability that S_1 and S_2 have an element in common is approximately $1 - e^{-1} \approx 63.2\%$.

9.3. Solving ECDLP via Pollard's ρ Method. Pollard's ρ method for discrete logarithms achieves the same $O(\sqrt{p})$ running time as the collision method, but it only requires negligible amount of storage. The basic idea is to traverse a "random" path through the multiples $n_1S + n_2T$. Eventually this path loops back onto itself, forming a loop with a tail attached (just like the letter ρ, whence the name of the algorithm!).

Once we arrrive on the loop part of the path, we can detect a collision by storing a small proportion of the visited points, where the stored points are chosen according to a criterion that is reasonably independent of the underlying group law. One can prove that for a sufficintly randomly chosen path, both the tail and the loop portions of the path have length $O(\sqrt{p})$, and hence the running time of the algorithm is $O(\sqrt{p})$.

10. Better Methods for Solving the DLP in Certain Groups

The collision method is a general method that solves the DLP in any group G in $O(\sqrt{\#G})$ steps, and a variation of Pollard's method virtually always does the same with minimal storage requirements.

Suppose now that you are presented with a group G that is completely abstract, in the sense that the group law is a black box. You can give the black box two elements $x, y \in G$ and it will tell you their product xy, and you an give the black box an element $x \in G$ and an integer $n \in \mathbb{Z}$ and it will tell you its power x^n. But you're not allowed to peer into the black box and see how it performs the computation. In this abstract setting, it is possible to prove that there are no algorithms that solve the DLP for G in fewer than $O(\sqrt{\#G})$ steps. In other words, for an abstract group, the elementary collision method and its variants, such as Pollard's ρ method, are provably the fastest possible algorithms for solving the DLP.

Of course, if one knows more about the structure of the group law for G, then often there are much faster ways to solve the DLP. We have already seen some examples, but it is worth recalling them here:

- In the additive group $\mathbb{Z}/N\mathbb{Z}$ of integers modulo N, the Euclidean algorithm solves the DLP in essentially $O(\log N)$ steps.
- In the multiplicative group $\mathbb{R}^*$ of real numbers, the DLP can be solved using the standard logarithm, i.e., if $\alpha, \beta \in \mathbb{R}^*$ and β is in the cyclic group generated by α, then $\beta = \alpha^m$ with $m = \log(\beta)/\log(\alpha)$.
- In the multiplicative group $\mathbb{F}_p^*$ of a finite field, the DLP is more difficult, but there are a number of algorithms that are qualitatively much faster than the collision algorithms. The best current algorithm for solving the DLP in $\mathbb{F}_p^*$ is called the *index calculus* (and uses ideas from the number field sieve) to achieve a running time of

  $$O\left(e^{c\sqrt[3]{(\log p)(\log\log p)^2}}\right),$$

  where c is a constant. This is a *subexponential* time algorithm, since it is faster than exponential (in $\log p$), although it is not as fast as polynomial time.

The principal reason that elliptic curves and the ECDLP are so important for cryptography can be summed up in one sentence:

> **For general elliptic curves, the fastest *known* algorithms to solve the ECDLP are collision methods such as Pollard's ρ!!**

In other words, the fastest known method to solve the ECDLP in $E(\mathbb{F}_p)$ has running time $O(\sqrt{p}\,)$, which is no better than the running time for an abstract group in which nothing is known about the group law.

This means that it is currently infeasible to solve the ECLDP in $E(\mathbb{F}_p)$ when $p > 2^{160}$. In order to achieve an equivalent level of difficulty for the DLP in $\mathbb{F}_p^*$, for which there exists a subexponential algorithm, it is necessary to take $p > 2^{1000}$. Similarly, the existence of a subexponential integer factorization algorithm means that equivalent security for RSA also requires using 1000 bit numbers. Hence cryptographic constructions based on ECDLP have smaller keys and smaller message blocks, and they may also be faster (although it should be noted that adding two points on an elliptic curve is considerably more complicated than multiplying two numbers modulo p).

11. Methods for Solving ECDLP in Special Cases

Although the best known general method for solving the ECDLP is via collisions, which has exponential running time, there are some special cases of ECDLP that are known to have faster solutions. When using elliptic curves and ECDLP for cryptographic purposes, it is important to understand and avoid these easier special cases.

11.1. Elliptic Curves with Exactly p Points. If $E(\mathbb{F}_p)$ has exactly p points, then there is a sort of p-adic logarithm map

$$\log_{p\text{-adic}} : E(\mathbb{F}_p) \longrightarrow \mathbb{F}_p^+$$

which is an easly computed homomorphism from the group $E(\mathbb{F}_p)$ to the additive group mod p. It is easy to solve the DLP in $\mathbb{F}_p^+$, indeed it is a simple application of the Euclidean algorithm. Thus if $\#E(\mathbb{F}_p) = p$, then the ECDLP can be solved in linear time $O(\log p)$.

11.2. The Tate Pairing. Before describing the next ECDLP method, we digress to discuss an important tool used in studying elliptic curves. For any integer N that is not divisible by p, let

$$\boldsymbol{\mu}_N = \{\zeta \in \bar{\mathbb{F}}_p : \zeta^N = 1\}$$

be the group of Nth roots of unity contained in an algebraic closure $\bar{\mathbb{F}}_p$ of $\mathbb{F}_p$.

THEOREM 10 (Tate Pairing). *Let $N = \#E(\mathbb{F}_p)$. There exists a nondegenerate symmetric bilinear form*

$$\langle\,\cdot\,,\,\cdot\,\rangle : E(\mathbb{F}_p) \times E(\mathbb{F}_p) \longrightarrow \boldsymbol{\mu}_N.$$

Further, if $t \geq 1$ is chosen so that $\boldsymbol{\mu}_N \subset \mathbb{F}_{p^t}$, then it is possible to compute the value $\langle P, Q\rangle$ in time that is more-or-less linear in $\log(p^t)$.

Notice in particular that if $p \equiv 1 \pmod{N}$, then computing the Tate pairing $\langle P, Q\rangle$ of two points $P, Q \in E(\mathbb{F}_p)$ requires approximately the same amount of work as does computing the multiple mP of a point.

11.3. Reduction of ECDLP in $E(\mathbb{F}_p)$ to DLP in $\mathbb{F}_q^*$. The Tate pairing can be used to reduce the ECDLP in $E(\mathbb{F}_p)$ to the DLP in $\mathbb{F}_q^*$ for a certain power $q = p^t$. Let $N = \#E(\mathbb{F}_p)$, where for simplicity we assume that N is prime. Let $t \geq 1$ be the smallest integer such that[11]

$$p^t \equiv 1 \pmod{N}.$$

Then the following procedure, called the MOV method, reduces the ECDLP in $E(\mathbb{F}_p)$ to the DLP in $\mathbb{F}_q^*$ with $q = p^t$:

- Let $S, T \in E(\mathbb{F}_p)$ satisfy $T = mS$ for an unknown m.
- Compute the Tate pairing values $\langle S, S\rangle$ and $\langle S, T\rangle$ as elements of $\mathbb{F}_q^*$.
- Solve the DLP in $\mathbb{F}_q^*$ to find an exponent $n \geq 1$ so that $\langle S, S\rangle^n = \langle S, T\rangle$.
- By linearity, we have $\langle S, S\rangle^n = \langle S, T\rangle = \langle S, mS\rangle = \langle S, S\rangle^m$, and then by nondegeneracy, we deduce that $n = m$.
- Hence solving the DLP in $\mathbb{F}_q^*$ reveals m and solves the ECDLP in $E(\mathbb{F}_p)$.

As we have seen, there is a subexponential algorithm to solve the DLP in $\mathbb{F}_q^*$. The moral is that for cryptographic purposes, one should only use elliptic curves for which p^t is large, say $p^t > 2^{1000}$. Fortunately, for most fields and curves, the quantity p^t is enormous; and in any case, it is easy enough to check the size of t before actually using any particular curve.

12. Elliptic Curves and Tripartite Diffie-Hellman Key Exchange

Earlier we discussed Diffie-Hellman key exchange, in which Bob and Alice were able to exchange a piece of secret information over an insecure communication channel. Classical Diffie-Hellman key exchange can be performed using any group G, and the security depends (at least) on the difficulty of solving the DLP in G.

It was a longstanding problem to find a way in which three people could exchange a key. This tripartite Diffie-Hellman problem was recently solved by Antoine Joux [**5**] by using the Tate pairing to combine the ECDLP in $E(\mathbb{F}_p)$ and the DLP in $\mathbb{F}_p^*$. In the last section we saw that it is a bad idea to use the ECDLP when $p \equiv 1 \pmod{N}$, since that allows an attacker to reduce the ECDLP in $E(\mathbb{F}_p)$ to the simpler DLP in $\mathbb{F}_p^*$. Joux turns this attack on its head by exploiting the reduction to $\mathbb{F}_p^*$ and relying on the fact that although easier than ECDLP, the DLP in $\mathbb{F}_p^*$ is still quite difficult if p is reasonably large.

Joux's Tripartite Diffie-Hellman Key Exchange Algorithm is described in Table 3. At the end of the algorithm, Alice, Bob, and Carl compute the respective quantities

$$\begin{aligned} \text{Alice:} &\quad \langle B, C\rangle^a = \langle bS, cS\rangle^a = \langle S, S\rangle^{abc}, \\ \text{Bob:} &\quad \langle A, C\rangle^b = \langle aS, cS\rangle^b = \langle S, S\rangle^{abc}, \\ \text{Carl:} &\quad \langle A, B\rangle^c = \langle aS, bS\rangle^c = \langle S, S\rangle^{abc}. \end{aligned}$$

Note that the last step on each line follows from the bilinearity of the Tate pairing. They thus all end up with the same shared value. And one hopes that the only way to compute the shared quantity $\langle S, S\rangle^{abc}$ is by one of the following methods:

- Compute the three quantities a, b, c, which means solving the ECDLP in $E(\mathbb{F}_p)$ for the points $A, B, C \in E(\mathbb{F}_p)$ with respect to the generating point S.

[11]Exercise: Prove that this t is also the smallest integer such that $\boldsymbol{\mu}_N \subset \mathbb{F}_{p^t}$.

Three Person Diffie-Hellman Key Exchange		
Initial Setup: • Fix a prime p so that DLP in $\mathbb{F}_p^*$ is hard (say $p > 2^{1000}$). • Fix an elliptic curve E over $\mathbb{F}_p$ • Fix a point $S \in E(\mathbb{F}_p)$ of order N with $p \equiv 1 \pmod{N}$.		
Alice	**Bob**	**Carl**
Choose secret a	Choose secret b	Choose secret c
Publish $A = aS$	Publish $B = bS$	Publish $C = cS$
Compute $\langle B, C\rangle^a$	Compute $\langle A, C\rangle^b$	Compute $\langle A, B\rangle^c$
Alice, Bob and Carl share the value $\langle S, S\rangle^{abc}$		

TABLE 3. Tripartite Diffie-Hellman key exchange

- Compute the three quantities ab, ac, bc, which means solving the DLP in $\mathbb{F}_p^*$ for the quantities $\langle A, B\rangle$, $\langle A, C\rangle$, and $\langle B, C\rangle$ with respect to the generating value $\langle S, S\rangle$.
- Compute the three quantities a^2, b^2, c^2, which means solving the DLP in $\mathbb{F}_p^*$ for the quantities $\langle A, A\rangle$, $\langle B, B\rangle$, and $\langle C, C\rangle$ with respect to the generating value $\langle S, S\rangle$. (It is comparatively easy to compute square roots modulo N, so the values of a^2, b^2, c^2 allow easy computation of a, b, c.)

This combination of ECDLP and DLP via the Tate pairing has had many other cryptographic applications in the past few years. However, there is still no method known to do "Four-Way Diffie-Hellman Key Exchange" via an underlying hard discrete logarithm problem.

13. Epilog

This brief survey article has only touched on the vast and rich mathematical theory of elliptic curves. And even within the small stream of cryptography, we have merely skimmed the surface of the subject.

In the vaster ocean of mathematics, the theory of elliptic curves appears and reappears in contexts too numerous to even begin to list here, ranging from Wiles' proof of Fermat's Last Theorem to elliptic genera in topology to noncommutative quantum algebras to string theory and beyond. The annotated bibliography to this article includes a few references to assist you in learning more about the number theory and the cryptographic applications of elliptic curves. Happy Sailing!

References

[1] B.J. Birch, How the number of points of an elliptic curve over a fixed prime field varies, *J. London Math. Soc.*, **43**, (1969), 57–60.

[2] I.F. Blake, G. Seroussi, N.P. Smart, *Elliptic curves in cryptography*, London Mathematical Society Lecture Note Series, 265, Cambridge University Press, Cambridge, 2000. [A good introduction to the subject.]

[3] Certicom tutorials and white papers <www.certicom.com>. [Certicom markets products that employ elliptic curve cryptography.]

[4] J.E. Cremona, *Algorithms for modular elliptic curves*, Cambridge University Press, Cambridge, 1997. [Extensive coverage of mathematical algorithms for elliptic curves, although not specifically for cryptography.]

[5] A. Joux, A one round protocol for tripartite Diffie-Hellman, *Algorithmic number theory* (Leiden, 2000), Lecture Notes in Comput. Sci., 1838, Springer, Berlin, 2000, 385–393. [How to use the Tate pairing to perform a three-person Diffie-Hellman key exchange.]

[6] N. Koblitz, Elliptic curve cryptosystems, *Mathematics of Computation* **48** (1987), 203-209. [One of the original articles that proposed the use of elliptic curves for cryptography. The other is by Victor Miller.]

[7] ______ *A course in number theory and cryptography*, Graduate Texts in Mathematics, 114, Springer-Verlag, New York, 1994. [A course in basic cryptography.]

[8] ______ *Algebraic aspects of cryptography*, Algorithms and Computation in Mathematics 3, Springer-Verlag, Berlin, 1998. [Cryptography from an algebraic viewpoint.]

[9] ______ Miracles of the height function—a golden shield protecting ECC, 4th Workshop on Elliptic Curve Cryptography (ECC 2000), University of Essen, Essen, Germany, October 4–6, 2000, `http://www.cacr.math.uwaterloo.ca/conferences/2000/ecc2000/koblitz.ps`. [An enlightening discussion of heights and ECC.]

[10] S. Lang, *Elliptic Curves: Diophantine Analysis*, Grundlehren der math. Wissenschaften 231, Springer-Verlag, Berlin, 1978. [An introduction to advanced number theoretic properties of elliptic curves.]

[11] A. Menezes, *Elliptic curve public key cryptosystems*, The Kluwer International Series in Engineering and Computer Science, 234, Communications and Information Theory, Kluwer Academic Publishers, Boston, MA, 1993. [An early description of ECC with implementation methods.]

[12] V. Miller, Use of elliptic curves in cryptography. Advances in cryptology-CRYPTO '85 (Santa Barbara, CA, 1985), 417–426, Lecture Notes in Comput. Sci., 218, Springer, Berlin, 1986. [One of the original articles that proposed the use of elliptic curves for cryptography. The other is by Neal Koblitz.]

[13] T. Satoh, The canonical lift of an ordinary elliptic curve over a finite field and its point counting, *J. Ramanujan Math. Soc.* **15** (2000), 247–270. [Algorithm to count number of points in $E(\mathbb{F}_p^k)$ for small p and large k.]

[14] R. Schoof, Elliptic curves over finite fields and the computation of square roots mod p, *Math. Comp.* **44** (1985), 483–494. [First polynomial time algorithm to count number of points in $E(\mathbb{F}_p)$.]

[15] R. Schoof, Counting points on elliptic curves over finite fields, *J. Théor. Nombres Bordeaux* **7** (1995), 219–254. [More efficient algorithm to count number of points in $E(\mathbb{F}_p)$.]

[16] J.H. Silverman, *The Arithmetic of Elliptic Curves*, Graduate Texts in Mathematics 106, Springer-Verlag, New York, 1986. [The number theory of elliptic curves at a level suitable for advanced graduate students.]

[17] ______ *Advanced Topics in the Arithmetic of Elliptic Curves*, Graduate Texts in Mathematics 151, Springer-Verlag, New York, 1994. [Additional topics in the number theory of elliptic curves at an advanced graduate level.]

[18] J.H. Silverman, J. Tate, *Rational points on elliptic curves*, Undergraduate Texts in Mathematics, Springer-Verlag, New York, 1992. [An introduction to the number theoretic properties of elliptic curves at an advanced undergraduate level.]

[19] D. Stinson, *Cryptography: Theory and Practice*, 2nd ed., CRC Press, 2002. [An excellent introduction to modern cryptography, with a chapter on elliptic curves and their use in cryptography.]

Mathematics Department, Box 1917, Brown University, Providence, RI 02912 USA
E-mail address: `jhs@math.brown.edu`

Proceedings of Symposia in Applied Mathematics
Volume **62**, 2005

Towards faster cryptosystems I

William Whyte

ABSTRACT. We outline the discrete logarithm problem and describe some popular cryptosystems based on this problems and some central issues in these systems. Performance and bandwidth improvements can be obtained by using the discrete log problem defined over groups other than the multiplicative group $\mathbb{Z}_p^*$; we outline the EC Discrete Log problem and discuss key points in Elliptic Curve Cryptography, and finally discuss the use of techniques such as Optimal Extension fields to speed up ECC operations.

1. The Discrete Logarithm Problem

1.1. Basic Concepts.

1.1.1. *Group Theory: Review.* In lecture 1, we introduced public-key cryptosystems, with an emphasis on those built on factoring products of large integers. In this lecture, we look at another difficult mathematical problem which is often used as a basis for cryptosystems, the *Discrete Logarithm Problem.*

First, we review some fundamental concepts in group theory.

A *group* G is a set of elements $\{\alpha_i\}$ and an operation $\odot$ such that:

(1) *Closure*: If $\alpha_i, \alpha_j \in G$, then $\alpha_i \odot \alpha_j \in G$.
(2) *Associativity*: The operation $\odot$ is associative, i.e. $\alpha_i \odot (\alpha_j \odot \alpha_k) = (\alpha_i \odot \alpha_j) \odot \alpha_k \, \forall \, \alpha_i, \alpha_j, \alpha_k \in G$.
(3) *Identity*: There is an *identity element* I such that $\alpha_i \odot I = I \odot \alpha_i = \alpha_i \, \forall \, \alpha_i, \in G$.
(4) *Inverse*: For every element α_i there is an *inverse element* α_i^{-1} such that $\alpha_i \odot \alpha_i^{-1} = \alpha_i^{-1} \odot \alpha_i = I \, \forall \, \alpha_i, \in G$.

A *generator of a group* is any element α_i such that successively $\odot$'ing α_i, first with I, then with the result of the previous operation, returns all the elements of the group. Not all groups can be generated by a single element, but the groups used in cryptography often have this property. Groups with this property are called *cyclic groups*.

The *order of a group* is the number of elements $\#E(G)$.

If n is any integer, and $\odot$ is defined as "Addition modulo n", then the integers $\{0, 1, \ldots, n-1\}$ form a group under $\odot$.

1991 *Mathematics Subject Classification.* Primary 54C40, 14E20; Secondary 46E25, 20C20.

Power	Value
α	2
α^2	4
α^3	8
α^4	5
α^5	10
α^6	9
α^7	7
α^8	3
α^9	6
α^{10}	1

TABLE 1. The multiplicative group $\mathbb{Z}_{11}^*$, as generated by $\alpha = 2$.

If p is a prime, and $\odot$ is defined as "multiplication modulo p", then the integers $\{1, 2, \ldots, p-1\}$ form a group under $\odot$. More generally, if n is any integer, the integers which are relatively prime to n form a group under multiplication mod n.

As an example, look at table 1. This shows the multiplicative group $\mathbb{Z}_{11}^*$, as generated by the integer $\alpha = 2$.

1.1.2. *The Discrete Logarithm Problem.* Having reviewed these basic concepts, we can return to the *discrete logarithm problem*, introduced in Lecture 1.

Definition: Let p be a prime number, and g, x be integers in the range $[2, p-1]$. The *discrete logarithm problem over* $\mathbb{Z}_p^*$ is the problem, given p, g, and $y = g^x \bmod p$, of recovering x.

The best known algorithms for solving the discrete logarithm problem over $\mathbb{Z}_p^*$ are subexponential (but superpolynomial) in p. It has therefore been used as the underlying problem in many different cryptosystems. The most important of these are Diffie-Hellman key exchange [**8**], ElGamal encryption [**9**], and the DSA and related signature algorithms [**9, 31, 10**].

Good reviews of the discrete logarithm problem can be found in [**24, 28**].

1.2. Cryptosystems based on the Discrete Log Problem.

1.2.1. *Diffie-Hellman.* Diffie-Hellman key exchange was the first public-key cryptography algorithm to be made known in the scientific literature, in 1976 [**8**]. It has been standardized in [**39, 14**], among other places.

Diffie-Hellman is an interactive protocol. Initially, Alice and Bob, who want to communicate securely with each other, both know the prime modulus p and the base g. These parameters are public, and are known to an eavesdropper Eve. Alice and Bob want to keep their communications secret from Eve. In a run of the protocol, they do the following:

- Alice generates her private key a, and her public key $A = g^a \bmod p$.
- Bob generates his private key b, and his public key $B = g^b \bmod p$.
- Alice sends A to Bob over their insecure channel. Bob sends B to Alice. (As discussed in lecture 2, Alice and Bob may get each others' keys by some other means, such as from a directory. This doesn't alter the core mathematical operations of the protocol).
- Alice calcuates the shared secret $S = B^a \bmod p = g^{ab} \bmod p$. Bob calculates $S = A^b \bmod p = g^{ab} \bmod p$.

They can now use the shared secret S as a seed to derive the keys for a symmetric cryptosystem, and engage in secure communications.

Note that Diffie-Hellman actually depends on a slightly different problem from the discrete logarithm problem itself:

Definition: Let p be a prime number, and g, a, b be integers in the range $[2, p-1]$. The *Computational Diffie-Hellman problem over* $\mathbb{Z}_p^*$, also known simply as the *Diffie-Hellman problem*, is the problem, given p, g, $g^a \bmod p$ and $g^b \bmod p$, of calculating $g^{ab} \bmod p$.

Clearly, an attacker who can solve the discrete log problem can also solve the Diffie-Hellman problem. It is not the case that in all groups there is a known reduction in the other direction; in particular, in $\mathbb{Z}_p^*$ no reduction is known of.

1.2.2. *ElGamal Encryption.* When Diffie-Hellman was first proposed, it was felt to be slightly unsatisfactory that it couldn't be used directly to encrypt a message. (In practice, Diffie-Hellman is used to agree on symmetric keys, and algorithms like RSA that could directly encrypt a message are generally used to transport symmetric keys, so nowadays the distinction between key exchange and public-key encryption algorithms is not seen as particularly important in usability terms). The ElGamal cryptosystem, a slight variant on Diffie-Hellman, addresses this perceived issue. As before, p and g are public parameters of the system. Now, Bob wants to send a secure message to Alice.

Before the protocol starts, Alice generates her private key a, and her public key $A = g^a \bmod p$. She places the public key A in a public directory. Bob wants to send Alice a message m securely.

Encryption —.

- Bob generates a random number k in the range $[2, p-1]$. This is known as the *ephemeral key.*
- Bob retrieves A and calculates the shared secret $S = A^k \bmod p = g^{ka} \bmod p$ and the 'hint' $r = g^k \bmod p$.
- The ciphertext is the pair $(r, s = S * m \bmod p)$

Decryption —.

- Alice receives (r, s).
- Alice calculates $S = r^a \bmod p = g^{ka} \bmod p$.
- Alice retrieves m as $m = s * S^{-1} \bmod p$.

Here, "$*$" represents multiplication.

The idea of ElGamal encryption is to generate an ephemeral shared secret and combine it with the message in some reversible way. On decryption, the recipient generates the same secret and disentangles it from the message.[1]

[1]Multiplication is not the only way that S and m could be combined: for example, XOR is more efficient than multiplication and is tempting for that reason. However, XOR leaks information about the top bits of m. To see why this is, consider the case where the binary representation of p starts

$$1001\ldots.$$

Now we know that $S < p$, so S cannot start with

$$111\ldots.$$

Therefore an attacker who sees s can rule out the possibility that certain bit patterns occur at the start of m.

Note that in ElGamal encryption, the ephemeral key k must be disposed of after the ciphertext is generated. If it were to leak, an attacker could read the message.

1.2.3. *ElGamal Signatures and DSA.* Finally, we consider digital signature algorithms based on the discrete log problem. The first such algorithm was based on an insight of Taher ElGamal about the interaction between the additive group of the exponents and the multiplicative group of the bases [**9**] – a similar insight to the one underlying RSA. The basic design admits of many variations (for example, [**31**]); the most widely-used is the US Government's Digital Signature Algorithm (DSA), which is standardized in [**10, 14**], among other places.

We here describe ElGamal's original algorithm. As before, p and g are known public parameters of the system, and Alice has a private key a and a public key $A = g^a \bmod p$.

Signing —.

- Alice hashes the message M to produce the message representative m
- Alice generates an *ephemeral keypair* $(k, r = g^k \bmod p)$.
- Alice solves for s the following equation:

$$ar + ks = m \quad \Rightarrow \quad s = (m - ar)/k \bmod (p-1)$$

- Alice transmits the message M and, the pair (r, s) as her signature.

Verification —.

- Bob receives (M, r, s) and retrieves Alice's public key A.
- Bob hashes M to produce m.
- Using the relationship

$$A^r.r^s = g^{ar}.g^{ks} = g^{ar+ks},$$

Bob performs the check

$$A^r.r^s \stackrel{?}{=} g^m \bmod p$$

If the left hand side equals the right hand side, Bob accepts the signature. Otherwise, he rejects it.

The security of the ephemeral key k is of even greater importance in ElGamal signatures than it is in ElGamal encryption. Anyone who discovers k now knows k, r, s and e, and can solve the resulting equation to recover the private key a. If the same k is used on two different messages m_1, m_2, k is immediately revealed as $(m_1 - m_2)/(s_1 - s_2) \bmod (p-1)$, again allowing the recovery of the private key. (If the same k is used twice, this will be immediately apparent because it will result in the same r in the two signatures). Finally, recent research [**13, 26, 27, 4**], to be described in Lecture 5 of this series, demonstrates that if there is a known bias in the generation of k, so that some values occur more often than others, an attacker can exploit this over a transcript of signatures to recover a.

In fact, in order for ElGamal encryption not to leak some information about the message, the message must be randomized in some reversible way before encryption. This fascinating topic is dealt with in more depth in lecture 4.

1.3. Speed And Security of Discrete Log-based Cryptosystems over $\mathbb{Z}_p^*$. All discrete logarithm problems fall to brute force: successively calculate $g, g^2, g^3 \ldots$ until you obtain A; then the current power of g is the discrete log a. However, there are more efficient methods than this. How much more efficient depend on the group in which the discrete logarithm of interest is set.

For example, for the group formed by $\mathbb{Z}_p^*$ under addition, recovering the discrete log is extremely easy: to solve

$$A = a.g \bmod p,$$

we simply calculate

$$a = A.g^{-1} \bmod p.$$

In this section, we explore the difficulty of the discrete log problem over $\mathbb{Z}_p^*$, and introduce some other groups in which the discrete log problem is even more difficult.

1.3.1. *Discrete Logarithms Over A Field: Index Calculus.* The standard method for breaking discrete logarithms over a field such as $\mathbb{Z}_p^*$ is known as the *index calculus.* It is due to many authors, but was first described for the group $\mathbb{Z}_p^*$ by Adleman [**1**]. The idea is first to express a number of small primes as powers of the base g, and then to attempt to find a multiple of the public key A which is easily expressible as a function of these small primes. Once this is done, the discrete log, $a = \log_g A$, can be recovered. In more detail, the attack (over $\mathbb{Z}_p^*$) proceeds as follows:

Building a Factor Base —.

(1) Select a set S of small primes, $S = \{p_1, p_2, \ldots, p_l\}$.
(2) Until "enough" relations have been collected:
   (a) Select a random integer k and calculate $x = g^k \bmod p$.
   (b) See if x, considered as an integer in the range $[0, p-1]$ can be written as a product of the members of S.
   (c) If this is possible, we have a relation of the form

$$g^k = \prod_{i=1}^{l} p_i^{c_i} \quad \Rightarrow \quad k = \sum_{i=1}^{l} c_i \log_g p_i (\bmod q).$$

   This relation gives a linear equation in the l variables $\{\log_g p_i\}$.
   (d) Once we have slightly more than l relations of this form, end this loop.
(3) Solve the relations obtained in the previous step to obtain $\{\log_g p_i\}$. This is the 'factor base'.

Solving for a —.

(1) Select a random integer k and calculate $x = g^k.A \bmod p$.
(2) See if x can be written as a product of the members of S:

$$x = \prod_{i=1}^{l} p_i^{c_i}.$$

   If it cannot, return to step 1.
(3) Calculate a as $a = \sum_{i=1}^{l} c_i \log_g p_i - k \bmod n$.

Of course, *any* number x can be expressed as a product of powers of the $\{p_i\}$. In fact, any number can be expressed as a power of a single p_i, if it lies in the group generated by that p_i. So why is the index calculus method effective?

It's effective because, if x can be expressed as a product of powers of small primes, there's an efficient way of obtaining this expression:

(1) For each p_i:
   (a) Set $c_i = 0$
   (b) Set $x' = x/p_i \bmod p$.
   (c) If $x' < x$, set $x = x'$, set $c_i = c_i + 1$, and go back to step 1b.
   (d) Otherwise, move on to the next p_i.
(2) If $x = 1$, output x as $\prod_i p_i^{c_i}$. Otherwise, output "could not express x in terms of $\{p_i\}$."

The running time for the above algorithm for any given x is clearly bounded above by $\sum_i \log_{p_i} p$. Therefore, the running time of the index calculus as a whole depends on this time, and on the chance that a randomly chosen x can in fact be expressed as a product of powers of the $\{p_i\}$ using the above algorithm. Therefore, as given here, the index calculus method has a typical running time of

$$O(e^{c(\log n)^{1/2}(\log\log n)^{1/2}}).$$

Improvements due to Gordon [**11**] and Schirokauer [**30**] yield a running time of

$$O(e^{c(\log n)^{1/3}(\log\log n)^{2/3}}),$$

similar to the running time of the General Number Field sieve method for factoring integers. This is faster than $e^{c\log n}$ for any c, and so the running time is referred to as "subexponential".

1.3.2. *Discrete Logarithms Over A Generic Group: Pollard's Algorithms.* .

The index calculus algorithm described in the previous section makes use of the log-time algorithm for expressing a number x as a product of powers of small numbers. We now look at a setting in which the index calculus is of much less use: prime-order subgroups of multiplicative groups.

Recall the multiplicative group $\mathbb{Z}_{11}^*$, presented in figure 1. This is a group of order 10. The subgroup of $\mathbb{Z}_{11}^*$ of order 5 consists of the group elements generated by the even powers of α: $\{1, 3, 4, 5, 9\}$. Note that these integers, plus 0, do not form a field – in other words, the set

$$\{0, 1, 3, 4, 5, 9\}$$

is not closed under addition mod 11. Also note that, although this particular prime-order subgroup contains small elements (such as 3), in general if a subgroup has order q and the main group has order $(p-1)$, the chance that any given small element of the main group is an element of the subgroup is $q/(p-1)$. As we will see later, for cryptographic security we will generally pick p, q such that there is a vanishingly small chance that any small element of the main group will be in the subgroup.

In the absence of small elements, we cannot use the subexponential-time index calculus method to recover discrete logarithms. In this section, we therefore consider methods for solving the discrete logarithm problem in "generic" groups, which is to say groups which have no exploitable structure.

The most straightforward approach to solving

$$y = g^x$$

in a cyclic group is simply to search through all possible values of $0 \le x < q$, where q is the order of the group. The running time of a brute force search is therefore about $O(q)$. The "baby-step giant-step" algorithm attributed to Shanks reduces this to $O(\sqrt{q})$, but also requires $O(\sqrt{q})$ storage. We here describe the Pollard-rho algorithm due to Pollard [**29**], which runs in time $\sqrt{q}$ (a parallelized version, so that using m processors gives a speedup of a factor of m, is described in [**37**]) and requires very little storage.

We now describe the Pollard-rho algorithm. The aim, given a base g and a target y in a cyclic group of order q, is to express y as g^x for known $x < q$.

(1) Set $x_0 = 1$, $a_0 = 0$, $b_0 = 0$, $i = 0$. a and b will track powers of g and y.
(2) Define the following method for generating the next value of x_j as follows:
   - If $x_j < p/3$, set $x_{j+1} = x_j * g$; set $a_{j+1} = a_j + 1$; set $b_{j+1} = b_j$.
   - If $p/3 \leq x_j < 2p/3$, set $x_{j+1} = x_j^2$; set $a_{j+1} = 2a_j$; set $b_{j+1} = 2b_j$.
   - If $2p/3 \leq x_j$, set $x_{j+1} = x_j * y$; set $a_{j+1} = a_j$; set $b_{j+1} = b_j + 1$.
(3) Until terminate:
   (a) Increment i.
   (b) Calculate x_i, a_i, b_i from $x_{i-1}, a_{i-1}, b_{i-1}$ by applying the above algorithm to x_{i-1}.
   (c) Calculate x_{2i}, a_{2i}, b_{2i} from $x_{2i-2}, a_{2i-2}, b_{2i-2}$ by applying the above algorithm twice to x_{2i-2}.
   (d) If $x_i = x_{2i}$, terminate and return the current values of x_i, a_i, b_i, x_{2i}, a_{2i}, b_{2i}.
(4) Return $x = (b_{2i} - b_i)/(a_i - a_{2i}) \bmod q$.

The Pollard-rho algorithm combines two observations. First, we assume that the method for "stepping" x_i essentially selects points at random from the group. Then, by the birthday paradox, after about $\sqrt{q}$ points have been selected, we expect that one point will have been selected twice. By storing all points generated to date, we could spot this collision as soon as it happened; however, this would require $O(\sqrt{q})$ storage. This is where we use the second observation, known as *Floyd's cycle-finding algorithm.* Assume that $x_j = x_{j+k}$. Then once $i > j$ (which implies $2i > j$), both $x - i$ and x_{2i} can be looked on as moving around a track of length k. At every iteration, x_{2i} moves two steps around the track and x_i moves one step; so we can see that x_{2i} catches up with x_i by one step on every iteration, and that in no more than k additional iterations we will have found an i for which $x_i = x_{2i}$. Once $x_i = x_{2i}$ the final step follows from

$$g^{a_i} y^{b_i} = g^{a_{2i}} y^{b_{2i}} \ .$$

1.3.3. *Performance Improvements Based on The Use of Small Subgroups.* In the two previous sections, we've looked at the discrete log problems in groups with an underlying field structure and groups where the underlying structure cannot be exploited. In the first case, there is a subexponential-time algorithm, the index calculus algorithm, to solve the discrete log problem. In the second, the best known algorithm is exponential time.

We can make use of this observation to speed up operations for cryptosystems based on the discrete log problem over $\mathbb{Z}_p^*$. Consider the case where q, a prime, divides $p - 1$:

$$q | (p - 1).$$

Now we can pick g to be a generator, not of all of $\mathbb{Z}_p^*$, but of the subgroup of order q:

$$g^q = 1 \bmod p.$$

Equivalent Symmetric Key Length (bits)	Length of p (bits)	Length of q (bits)
60	513	107
70	704	125
80	1230	141
100	1937	189
128	3273	240

TABLE 2. Sizes of main group and prime-order subgroup for equivalent security

This is of use because we can now select the private keys to lie in the range $[2, q-1]$ instead of $[2, p-1]$. The end result of this is that we can speed up calculations by, typically, a factor of 6-10 for realistic cryptosystems [**31**]. Table 2, based on [**21**], gives the appropriate bit lengths for p and q to give equivalent security.[2]

In practice, for 80-bit ("industrial-strength") security, it is standard practice to take p of size 1024 bits and q of size 160 bits. This means that exponentiations using the square-and-multiply method take about 160 squares and 80 multiplies, instead of the 1024 squares and 512 multiplies that would be necessary if private keys and other exponents in the system were taken in the range $[2, p-1]$. As the required security level gets higher, the speedup due to these techniques becomes even more pronounced.

Now, to generate parameters, instead of picking a large prime p, we can follow the following recipe:

(1) Pick a prime q, such that solving the discrete log problem over a group of order q using the Pollard-rho algorithm takes long enough to satisfy our security needs.
(2) Generate a prime p, satisfying the criteria:
  - $q|(p-1)$
  - p is sufficently large that solving the discrete log problem over $\mathbb{Z}_p^*$ using the index calculus method takes long enough to satisfy our security needs.
(3) Pick a random element $\alpha \in \mathbb{Z}_p^*$.
  (a) Set $g = \alpha^{(p-1)/q}$.
  (b) If $g \neq 1$, pick another α and repeat. Otherwise, continue.
(4) Output the modulus p, the small subgroup order q, and the small subgroup generator g.

The method used to find the generator g of the small subgroup uses the fact that all members (except the identity) of a prime-order group are generators of that group. Because $(p-1)/q$ is a multiple of the orders of all the other subgroups of $\mathbb{Z}_p^*$, raising any α to this power will result in a group element which is a non-trivial

[2]The paper [**21**] assumes ongoing improvement in index calculus techniques and compares breaking times for symmetric systems and discrete logs at various points in the future. Table 2 gives breaking times with present knowledge, and so differs slightly from the figures in [**21**]. Another recent paper [**35**], using a different cost metric, gives shorter lengths for p to get equivalent symmetric security levels.

Power	Value
α_{13}	703
$(\alpha_{13})^2$	117
$(\alpha_{13})^3$	310
$(\alpha_{13})^4$	236
$(\alpha_{13})^5$	803
$(\alpha_{13})^6$	706
$(\alpha_{13})^7$	1003
$(\alpha_{13})^8$	661
$(\alpha_{13})^9$	1166
$(\alpha_{13})^{10}$	288
$(\alpha_{13})^{11}$	669
$(\alpha_{13})^{12}$	675
$(\alpha_{13})^{13}$	1

TABLE 3. The subgroup of order 13 mod 1223, generated by $\alpha_{13} = 703$.

member only of the subgroup of order q. The chance that $\alpha^{(p-1)/q} = 1$ is the chance that a random group element is already 1 in the subgroup of order q – in other words, $1/q$ – so for sufficiently large q this algorithm will almost always work first time.

1.3.4. *Attacks Based on the Use of Small Subgroups.* In the previous section, we have examined how small subgroups can be used to speed up operations with no loss in security. Because evil is more interesting than good [**17**], we now turn to examine attacks based on the use of small subgroups.

The core idea of these attacks is that if an attacker can force a legitimate user to use an incorrect base, they will make the victim perform calculations, not in the correct subgroup, but in a subgroup of the attacker's own choosing. There are two aspects to this attack: first, a relatively trivial one, which allows the attacker to guess the session key with less effort than would otherwise be the case; second, a considerably more serious one which reveals the victim's private key.

We'll illustrate the attacks with toy examples over $\mathbb{Z}^*_{1223}$. This group has order 1222, which factorizes thus:

$$1222 = 2 * 13 * 47$$

Assume that all operations take place in the subgroup of order 47, which is generated by $\alpha_{47} = 408$ (as a side note, we obtained this generator using the recipe in section 1.3.3: $408 = 2^{1222/47} \bmod 1223$). The public parameters are therefore

$$p = 1223, \quad q = 47, \quad g = 408.$$

There are two other subgroups: the subgroup of order 2 consisting of $\{1, 1222\}$, and the subgroup of order 13, whose elements are listed in table 3. These are of use to the attacker, but not to Alice.

Alice generates her private and public keys in the large subgroup as follows:

- Private key $a = 22$ (random number mod 47)
- Public exponent $A = g^a \bmod p = 408^{22} \bmod 1223 = 348$.

Now she wants to engage in Diffie-Hellman key exchange with Bob. However, Mallory, an active attacker who can interfere with Alice and Bob's line, can remove

Alice		Mallory		Bob
Sends A	$\overset{348}{\longrightarrow}$			
		Intercepts A, replaces with 1	$\overset{1}{\longrightarrow}$	
			$\overset{B}{\longleftarrow}$	Calculates $S = 1^b = 1$; sends B
	$\overset{1}{\longleftarrow}$	Intercepts B, replaces with 1		
Calculates $S = 1^a = 1$				

TABLE 4. Mallory forces the shared secret to be 1.

all security from the communication trivially. The communication flow is illustrated in table 4. By taking both Alice and Bob's real public keys, and replacing them with the trivial group element 1, Mallory is able to force the shared secret to be 1.

Although real, this attack is more of a tiresome prank than an attack, and easy to work around by out-of-band means: for example, when Alice receives B, she could simply call Bob and ask if the public key he sent was the one she received. Alternatively, a CA could certify Bob's public key, as described in lecture 2. Both of these simple, infrastructure-level expedients prevent Mallory from mounting this type of man-in-the-middle attack.

But what if Mallory isn't eavesdropping and interfering in communications, but a trusted member of the system? If so, he can circumvent countermeasures based on checking the ownership of the key and mount an attack that allows him to recover Alice's key wholesale.

The attack, due originally to Lim and Lee [**23**], proceeds in several stages.

(1) Mallory gets the CA to certify two invalid "public keys": $\alpha_2 = 1222$, and $\alpha_{13} = 703$. These keys generate the subgroups of order 2 and 13, respectively.

(2) Mallory engages in a Diffie-Hellman key exchange with Alice, sending her α_2 as his public key.
   (a) Alice calculates $S = (\alpha_2)^a = 1222^{22} \bmod p = 1$.
   (b) Alice encrypts a message with S and returns it to Mallory.
   (c) By trying both $S = 1$ and $S = 1222$, the only possibilities, Mallory can determine that $S = 1$. Therefore, $a = 0 \bmod 2$.
   (d) Mallory continues with the exchange, using $S = 1$. Alice cannot tell that anything suspicious is happening.

(3) Now, Mallory engages in a Diffie-Hellman key exchange with Alice, sending her α_{13} as his public key.
   (a) Alice calculates $S = (\alpha_{13})^a = 703^{22} \bmod p = 1166$.
   (b) Alice encrypts a message with S and returns it to Mallory.
   (c) Mallory brute-force searches through the 13 possibilities and determines that $S = 1166$. Therefore, $a = 9 \bmod 13$.
   (d) Mallory continues with the exchange, using $S = 1166$.

(4) Mallory uses the Chinese Remainder Theorem to find a satisfying $a = 0 \bmod 2$ and $a = 9 \bmod 13$. Possible values of a are $\{22, 48, \dots\}$. Since 22 is the only possible value less than 47, he knows Alice's private key $a = 47$. He can now listen to any future conversations Alice has with anyone.

As described above, the attack depends on Mallory and Alice being on line, and Mallory being able to determine Alice's value of S in real time. If this is the case, Mallory must interact with Alice once for every subgroup he knows a generator for – in the case above, twice, once for $\mathcal{G}_2$ and once for $\mathcal{G}_{13}$. However, the attack can be extended even to non-interactive uses of discrete log systems, such as ElGamal encryption. In this case, the number of messages Mallory must send Alice is roughly the sum of the orders of the subgroups he knows generators for. The attack proceeds as follows:

(1) For each subgroup $\mathcal{G}_i$ with order q_i generated by α_i:
   (a) For each $1 \leq k < q_i$:
      (i) Mallory generates an ElGamal ciphertext with α_i as the 'hint' and α_i^k as S, and sends it to Alice.
      (ii) If Alice responds as if she's decrypted the message correctly, Mallory knows that Alice's key $a = k \bmod q_i$.
(2) Mallory uses the CRT to recombine all the partial values for a into the value for $a \bmod q$.

This version of the attack demonstrates two important design principles in cryptography – that any information leakage, even of whether or not a message decrypted correctly, may be of use to an opponent, and that all users should be careful to check any assumptions they may be making about the cryptographic material they use.

In the next section we discuss how to prevent these small subgroup attacks.

1.3.5. *Protection against Small Subgroup Attacks.* The small subgroup attacks described in the previous section are a class of attacks unique to discrete logarithm-based cryptosystems. Although similar attacks apply to ElGamal-like signature algorithms [**2**], the attacks against key exchange algorithms (and their straightforward extension to encryption algorithms) are probably more frightening, because they can lead to your private key being discovered even if the key itself, and all the operations you perform with it, are valid.

The following methods protect against small subgroup attacks. Here the public key is assumed to lie in a subgroup $\mathcal{G}_q$ of prime order q in a larger group $\mathcal{G}$ of order p.

- Only use p which does not have harmful small subgroups: for example, $p = 2qr + 1$, where r is a prime $> q$.
- On receipt of a public key X, calculate X^q in $\mathcal{G}$. If the result is not 1, reject the key. This guarantees that $X \in \mathcal{G}_q$.
- In situations where you would use your private key x to calculate h^x for some h, instead calculate $h^{x.p/q}$ and reject if the answer is 1. This method, known as *cofactor multiplication*, guarantees that the result of the exponentiation is in $\mathcal{G}_q$.
- Require that any "public key" received be certified by a third party which you trust to have carried out a validity check on it.

The choice of countermeasure will depend on the resources available, and the availability of a trusted third party. The countermeasure based on the use of only ps of the correct form depends on being able to choose p (and we'll see that there is a similar attack in the elliptic curve case which applies even if the elliptic curve group being used has no small subgroups). The efficiency of the calculation-based countermeasures depends on the relative sizes of p/q and q; if one of these quantities is much smaller than the other, the countermeasure using that quantity will be preferred. Note, though, that in general both of these calculation-based countermeasures will at least double the time required to carry out a Diffie-Hellman calculation – there will be one exponentiation required by the protocol itself, and one additional exponentiation for the countermeasure. Also note that protection against small subgroup attacks, as described here, may be covered by various US and international patents.

In this section we have described some of the more popular algorithms based on the discrete log problem in finite groups. We have looked at "passive" attacks involving key recovery by attacking the group that the key lies in. We have also described the uses of smaller subgroups, both to speed up operations and to enable new and interesting attacks. In the next section we will turn to cryptosystems based on the discrete logarithm problem on elliptic curves, which offer improvements in both performance and bandwidth over classical discrete log systems.

2. Elliptic Curve Cryptosystems

As we've already discussed, any group can have a discrete log problem defined over it. For cryptographic purposes, the harder this discrete log problem is, the better. Over the integers $\mathbb{Z}_p^*$, the best known algorithms are subexponential. We now turn to discuss the Elliptic Curve embodiment of the discrete log problem, for which (in all but a few niche cases) the best known algorithms are exponential in the key size. This allows us to achieve 80 bits of security with only about 160 bits of keying material, as opposed to the 1024 or more bits required by the classical discrete log problem.

The use of elliptic curves in cryptography was proposed independently by Koblitz [**19**] and Miller [**25**].

2.1. Elliptic Curve Arithmetic.

Elliptic curve points are a pair of values (x, y) satisfying an equation cubic in x and quadratic in y. However, x and y need not be integers, or even real numbers; they may instead lie in the field $GF(2^m)$ (the field of polynomials with binary coefficients) or in any other field. The choice of field significantly affects the efficiency of elliptic curve operations. For ease of exposition, however, we will initially only describe elliptic curve arithmetic where the underlying field is $\mathbb{Z}_p$.

For p an odd prime, the points on an elliptic curve are all points with integer coefficients (x, y), $x, y \in \mathbb{Z}_p$, which satisfy the equation

$$y^2 = x^3 + ax + b$$

where $a, b \in \mathbb{Z}_p$ and $4a^3 + 27b^2 \neq 0 \bmod p$. Additionally, there is one extra point, the "point at infinity" $\mathcal{O}$, which plays the role of the additive identity in the elliptic curve group. Figure 1 illustrates an elliptic curve over the reals $\mathbb{R}$. Table 5 lists those points that lie on the curve $y^2 = x^3 - 5x + 8$ over the field $\mathbb{Z}_{19}$.

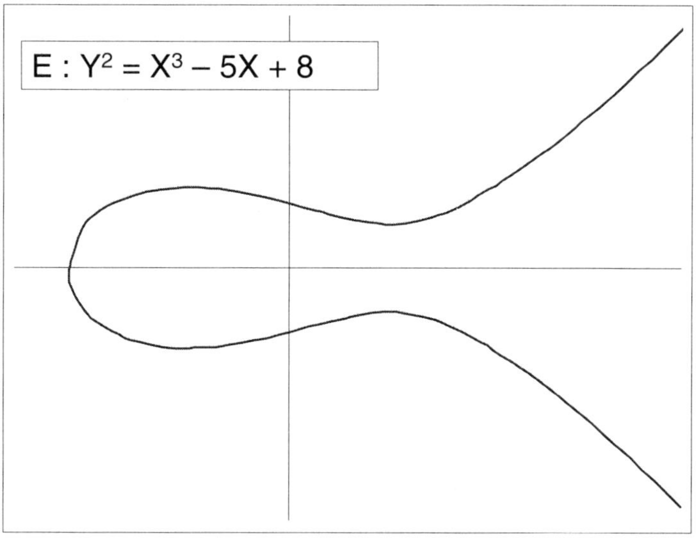

FIGURE 1. An elliptic curve.

$(1,2)$	$(1,17)$	$(2,5)$	$(2,14)$
$(3,1)$	$(3,18)$	$(6,2)$	$(6,17)$
$(8,9)$	$(8,10)$	$(11,7)$	$(11,12)$
$(12,2)$	$(12,17)$	$\mathcal{O}$	

TABLE 5. Points on $y^2 = x^3 - 5x + 8 \bmod 19$

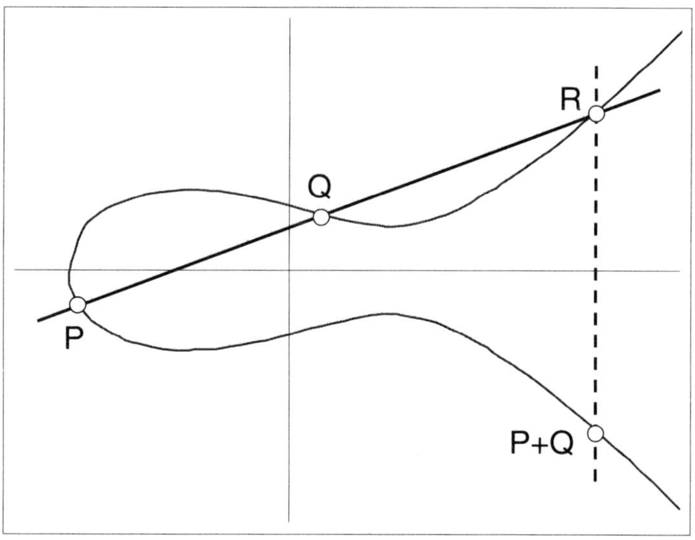

FIGURE 2. Point Addition.

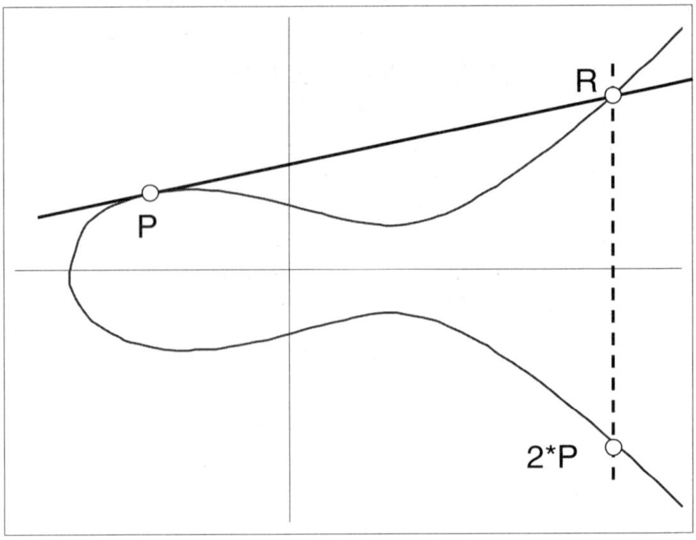

FIGURE 3. Point Doubling.

Point Addition: There is a rule, called the *chord-and-tangent rule*, for adding two points on an elliptic curve. This rule is easy to describe, and easy to illustrate geometrically (see figure 2 – this of course illustrates addition where the underlying finite field is $\mathbb{R}$, rather than $\mathbb{Z}_p$, but the visualization is useful). To add two points $P = (x_1, y_1)$ and $Q = (x_2, y_2)$:

- Draw a straight line through P and Q, and extend it to (x_3, y_3), the third point where it hits the curve. (A property of elliptic curves is that any straight line intersects the curve three times or less).
- Define $R = P + Q$ as $(x_3, -y_3)$.

The minus sign in $(x_3, -y_3)$ ensures that it is not generally true that if $(P+Q) = R$, then $R + Q = P$ (alternatively, it ensures that $P + Q + R = 0$ if and only if P, Q, R lie on a straight line). We will shortly see that this sign allows us to define an additive identity for the whole curve, making it into a group.

Point Doubling: The chord-and-tangent rule gives the following geometric method for adding a point $P = (x_1, y_1)$ to itself. See figure 3 for a graphical description of point doubling.

- Draw the tangent to the curve at the point P. This will intersect the curve at one other point $Q = (x_2, y_2)$.
- Define $2P$ as $(x_2, -y_2)$.

The Point At Infinity and Additive Inverses: The point $P = (x_1, y_1)$ has as its additive inverse the point $-P = (x_1, -y_1)$. A line drawn through P and $-P$ will intersect the curve at no other point. We therefore define the point at infinity $\mathcal{O}$ as the result of adding any point to its inverse. See figure 4 for an illustration.

It can easily be seen geometrically that $P + \mathcal{O} = P$. The line through $\mathcal{O}$ and P drops vertically through P, intersecting the curve again at $(x_1, -y_1)$. "Minusing" the y-coordinate returns (x, y). Thus $\mathcal{O}$ is the additive identity for the whole curve.

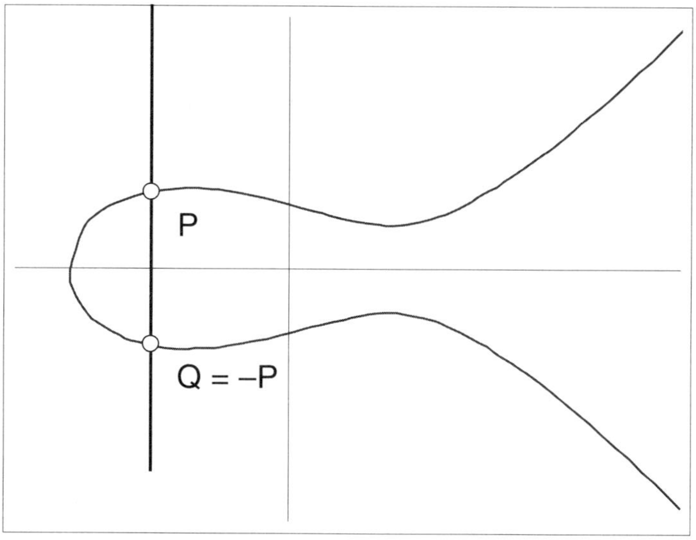

FIGURE 4. The Point At Infinity.

It is necessary for such an identity to exist in order for the points on the curve to form a group.

Formulas for Point Addition and Doubling. A precise recipe for adding two distinct points $P = (x_1, y_1)$ and $Q = (x_2, y_2)$ on an elliptic curve $E : y^2 = x^3 + Ax + B$ is:

$$\begin{array}{lll} \text{set} & \lambda & = \dfrac{y_2 - y_1}{x_2 - x_1}; \\ \text{set} & \nu & = y_1 - \lambda x_1; \\ \text{set} & x_3 & = \lambda^2 - x_1 - x_2; \\ \text{set} & y_3 & = \lambda x_3 + \nu; \\ \text{then} & P + Q & = (x_3, -y_3). \end{array}$$

A precise recipe for doubling a point $P = (x_1, y_1)$ on an elliptic curve $E : y^2 = x^3 + Ax + B$ is:

$$\begin{array}{lll} \text{set} & \lambda & = \dfrac{3x_1^2 + a}{2y_1}; \\ \text{set} & \nu & = y_1 - \lambda x_1; \\ \text{set} & x_3 & = \lambda^2 - 2x_1; \\ \text{set} & y_3 & = \lambda x_3 + \nu; \\ \text{then} & 2P & = (x_3, -y_3). \end{array}$$

Similar formulas can be defined for point addition and doubling on elliptic curves defined over any other underlying finite field. A curious feature of these formulas is that the results of addition and doubling depend only on a and not on b.

2.2. Order of Curves and Points, and the Elliptic Curve Discrete Logarithm Problem. The points on an elliptic curve E form a group under addition, and we can therefore define the Elliptic Curve Discrete Logarithm Problem. Before doing this, it's useful to define a couple of other terms.

Order of a Curve: The *order of a curve* E, denoted $\#E(\mathbb{F}_p)$, is the number of points on that curve.

Order of a Point: The *order of a point* P *on the curve* E is the smallest integer n such that nP (P added to itself n times) is the point at infinity $\mathcal{O}$. Note that n will always divide $\#E(\mathbb{F}_p)$.

The Elliptic Curve Discrete Logarithm Problem: Let E be an elliptic curve, let P be a point on that curve of order n, and let k be an integer in the range $[2, n-1]$. The *Elliptic Curve Discrete Logarithm Problem* is the problem, given E, P, n and $Q = kP$, to recover k.

There is a large class of elliptic curves for which no method is known to use the structure of the group to help solve the Elliptic Curve Discrete Log Problem (or ECDLP). On these curves, the best algorithms to break the ECDLP are the generic algorithms described in section 1.3.2: the baby-step giant-step, Pollard rho, and lambda algorithms, which have running time $O(\sqrt{n})$. An interesting issue, and one we won't touch on in these lectures, is the question of how to generate elliptic curves E such that $\#E(\mathbb{F}_p)$ is large, and has a large prime factor n. Once we have such a curve, it is easy to find a point that generates the large prime-order subgroup by a similar method to that used in the ordinary discrete log case: simply take a random point R, calculate

$$P = (\#E(\mathbb{F}_p)/n).R,$$

and accept P as a generator of this subgroup (also known as the "base point") if P is not $\mathcal{O}$. For further details on curve generation and point counting on a curve, the reader is referred to [**16, 20, 32**].

2.2.1. *Why is there no index calculus for elliptic curves?* There is currently no known index calculus-like method for solving the ECDLP. An insight into why this might be the case comes from considering the fact that the elliptic curve point addition and doubling formulas involve an inversion in the underlying field. Inversion in a field is an operation which doesn't respect "smallness": the inverse of a small value is not, in general, a small value itself (for example, in $\mathbb{F}_{19}$, the inverse of 2 is 10). This implies that even if we were to have a definition of a "small" elliptic curve point (for example, some bound on both x and y), there would be no guarantee that adding two small points, or doubling a small point, would give a small point as the result. So designing a logarithmic-time algorithm to express a point as a sum of multiples of other points, the core of the index calculus algorithm, is very difficult.

This is not to rule out the possibility that a useful mapping might be found from an elliptic curve group to a group in which the index calculus, or an even simpler method, might be applied. Nevertheless, it is fair to say that since the introduction of elliptic curve cryptography there have been insights into solving the ECDLP in special cases, but essentially no progress in solving the general case of the ECDLP. It remains the most promising setting for discrete log-based cryptosystems with short key sizes.

2.3. ECC algorithms: ECDH, ECDSA. Having defined the Elliptic Curve Discrete Log Problem, we now review the Diffie-Hellman and DSA algorithms in their elliptic curve settings.

2.3.1. *ECDH.* The Elliptic Curve analog of Diffie-Hellman is a simple transfer of Diffie-Hellman to the elliptic curve group setting. It was first proposed, independently, by Koblitz [**19**] and Miller [**25**]. Systems based on ECDH are standardized in [**33, 41, 14, 15**].

Assume that Alice and Bob share the domain parameters $D = (E, G, n)$, and that Alice has the key pair $(a, A = aG)$ and Bob has the key pair $(b, B = bG)$. To agree on a shared secret S, Alice and Bob do the following.

(1) Alice obtains Bob's public key B and calculates $S = aB = abG$.
(2) Bob obtains Alice's public key A and calculates $S = bA = abG$.
(3) Alice and Bob use S as their shared secret.

Since, in the case, S is an elliptic curve point, it may not be immediately obvious how to use it to protect data. A standard approach is to put the shared secret S through some hash function H and use the output as a symmetric key. Details of how this is done in practice may be found in [X9.63].

2.3.2. *ECDSA.* The Elliptic Curve Digital Signature Algorithm is a transfer of the DSA algorithm [**10**] to the elliptic curve setting, proposed by Scott Vanstone [**38**]. The transfer to the ECC setting involves some subtleties not present in the integer setting. It has been standardized in [**14, 40**] and in the most recent version of [**10**]. An excellent survey article is [**18**].

Signing and verification proceed as follows.

Signing —. To sign a message m, Alice with domain parameters $D = (E, G, n)$, associated keypair $(a, A = aG)$, and agreed hash function $H()$, does the following

(1) Select a random integer $k \in [1, n - 1]$.
(2) Compute the point $kG = (x_1, y_1)$ and the integer $r = x_1 \bmod n$. If $r = 0$ then go to step 1.
(3) Compute the integer $k^{-1} \bmod n$.
(4) Compute the integer $e = H(m)$.
(5) Compute the integer $s = k^{-1}(e + ar) \bmod n$. If $s = 0$ then go to step 1.
(6) Output the message m and the signature (r, s).

Verification —. Bob also knows the domain parameters D. Alice's public key $A = aG$, and the agreed hash function H. Having received the message m and the signature (r, s), he verifies it as follows:

(1) Verify that r and s are integers in the interval $[1, n - 1]$.
(2) Compute $e = H(m)$.
(3) Compute the integer $w = s^{-1} \bmod n$.
(4) Compute the integers $u_1 = ew \bmod n$ and $u_2 = rw \bmod n$.
(5) Compute the point $X = u_1G + u_2A = (x_1, y_1)$. If $X = \mathcal{O}$, reject the signature.
(6) Compute the integer $v = x_1 \bmod n$.
(7) Accept the signature if and only if $v = r$.

Notes: If elliptic curve operations are being performed over a finite field rather than over an integer, the quantities x_1 in signing and verification must be converted from field elements to integers. Likewise, the output of the hash function H will typically be a bit string or octet string rather than an integer, and must be converted

b	$\#E(\mathbb{F}_{19})$	b	$\#E(\mathbb{F}_{19})$	b	$\#E(\mathbb{F}_{19})$
0	20	7	22	14	14
1	27	8	15	15	16
2	24	9	23	16	20
3	20	10	17	17	16
4	24	11	25	18	13
5	26	12	18		
6	16	13	24		

TABLE 6. Number of points on the curve $y^2 = x^3 - 5x + b$ over $\mathbb{F}_{19}$ for different values of b.

to an integer before it can be used. These conversion methods must be agreed on before signing takes place. Standard conversion methods can be found in [**41**].

Why ECDSA works: Similar to ElGamal signatures, the signer is demonstrating the ability to solve an equation of the form

$$ar - ks = e \bmod n,$$

where a is the private key, and k and r are linked through the appropriate discrete log problem. In this case, though, the relationship between k and r is more complicated than $r = g^k \bmod p$. If we express this as $r = C(kG)$, where $C()$ is the conversion function that maps from an elliptic curve point to an integer, we see that in verification, Bob is checking

$$\begin{aligned} C((e/s)G + (r/s)A) &= r, \\ \Rightarrow C((e + ar)/sG) &= r, \\ \Rightarrow C(kG) &= r, \end{aligned}$$

as required. (Note that, as written here, verification requires only two point multiplications, while the description of ElGamal signatures in section 1.2.3 implied that verification required three exponentiations. In fact, the DSA variant of ElGamal requires only two exponentiations, not three. Additionally, we will soon see a method which can be used to make those two point multiplications or exponentiations not much more expensive than a single point multiplication or exponentiation).

2.4. Small subgroup attacks on ECC. One advantage that elliptic curve cryptosystems appear to have over standard discrete log systems is that the prime order subgroup generated by the base point P is very close to the size of the entire group. (For curves such as those specified in [**40**], $\#E/q$ is typically as low as 4). The absence of these other small subgroups should make it harder for an attacker to mount an attack based on choosing a series of false base points $\{P'\}$, of the type described in section 1.3.4. Additionally, the fact that the cofactor $\#E/q$ is so small means that it is always practical to protect against small subgroup attacks using cofactor multiplication, as described in section 1.3.5.

However, even though useful small subgroups (to the attacker) may not exist on the curve E itself, an attacker may still be able to force an honest user to operate in a small-order group. The key observation here is that, as noted in section 2.1, the formulas for point addition and doubling on a curve

$$y^2 = x^3 + ax + b$$

depend *only* on a, and not on b, while the order of the curve depends on both a and b (see table 6 for an example). So if Mallory wants to obtain Alice's private key, defined over the curve $E : y^2 = x^3 + ax + b$, Mallory does the following (attack originally due to Antipa *et al* [**3**]):

- Assembles a set of curves, $\{E'_i\}$, such that:
  (1) All the curves $\{E'_i\}$ are defined over the same underlying field and have the same value for a as E does.
  (2) Each curve E'_i has an order divisible by one or more small primes $\{p_{i,j}\}$.
  (3) The product of all the distinct $p_{i,j}$s is about q, q the order of the genuine base point on E.
- For each distinct $p_{i,j}$:
  (1) Finds a generator $P'_{i,j}$ of a subgroup on E'_i with order $p_{i,j}$.
  (2) Engages in a Diffie-Hellman key exchange with Alice, presenting $P'_{i,j}$ as his public key.
  (3) From this, using the methods of section 1.3.4, obtains $a \bmod p_{i,j}$.
- Recombines all the values for $a \bmod p_{i,j}$ to obtain $a \bmod q$.

Therefore, when implementing cryptosystems over elliptic curves, it is vital to make sure that a received public key lies on the stated curve and not on another one. The best way to do this is simply to check that the point (x, y) satisfies the curve equation $y^2 = x^3 + ax + b$. Note that this "curve validation" method may be covered by patents.

2.5. ECC implementation. One of the major attractions of elliptic curves is that the keys are considerably smaller than the keys required from classical discrete log based systems to get the same level of security. Because of this, much attention has been paid recently to issues of efficient implementation of elliptic curve cryptography, particularly on constrained devices. This section reviews some of the ways that elliptic curve based techniques can be used to obtain particularly fast cryptosystems.

2.5.1. *Square-and-multiply becomes double-and-add.* Just as modular exponentiation by y can be implemented in about $3\log_2 y/2$ modular multiplications, so multiplication of an elliptic curve point P by an integer n can be implemented in about $3\log_2 n/2$ additions and doubles. The simple algorithm is:

(1) Set $Y = \mathcal{O}$.
(2) Starting with the most significant bit of a, for each bit in turn:
  (a) Set $Y = 2Y$.
  (b) If the current bit of a is set, set $Y = Y + P$.
(3) Output Y.

Note that in elliptic curve arithmetic doubling and addition are much more distinct operations than squaring and multiplication are over the integers, and their speeds may be very different depending on the underlying field and the implementation. Full strategies for optimizing elliptic curve implementations must take this into account.

2.5.2. *Shamir's trick.* A nice trick due to Shamir can be used to speed up any calculation of the form

$$Y = aG_1 + bG_2$$

(or, in the standard discrete log setting, $y = g_1^a g_2^b \bmod p$). We consider the bitwise representation of the integers a and b, prepending 0 bits if necessary to the shorter to make them the same length. The algorithm is then:

(1) Set $Y = \mathcal{O}$. Store $H = G_1 + G_2$.
(2) Starting with the most significant bits of a and b, for each bit in turn:
  (a) Set $Y = 2Y$.
  (b) If the current bit of a and the current bit of b are both set, set $Y = Y + H$.
  (c) If only the current bit of a is set, set $Y = Y + G_1$.
  (d) If only the current bit of b is set, set $Y = Y + G_2$.
(3) Output Y.

This algorithm is considerably faster than calculating aG_1, bG_2 separately. For a, b of bit length l, the separate calculations would require approximately $2l$ doublings and l additions. The combined calculation requires only l doublings and $3l/4$ additions.

2.5.3. *Precomputation of multiples of known base.* For the case where all point multiplications are to be done on a known base point G, it is possible to trade off memory use for improved performance. Two very straightforward methods for multiplying G by an integer a are as follows:

Low-Memory Method:

(1) Pre-calculate and store G, $2G$, $3G$
(2) Set $Y = \mathcal{O}$.
(3) For each set of two bits in a:
  (a) Set $Y = 4Y$.
  (b) Depending on the value of the current two bits, set $Y = Y$, $Y + G$, $Y + 2G$, or $Y + 3G$.
(4) Output Y.

For a of bit length l, this will typically take l point doubles and $3l/8$ (instead of $l/2$) point additions.

High-Memory Method:

(1) Pre-calculate and store G, $2G$, $4G$, $\ldots$, $2^{l-1}G$.
(2) Set $Y = \mathcal{O}$.
(3) For each $i < l$, if a AND 2^i, $Y = Y + 2^i G$.

For a of bit length l, this will require no point doubles and typically $l/2$ point additions, but at the cost of storing l points.

The techniques above are simple, but hint at the possbilities for optimisation. More sophisticated methods are described in [**5, 22**].

2.5.4. *Avoiding Inversions: Projective Geometry.* Recall the elliptic curve point addition formula for points $P = (x_1, y_1)$ and $Q = (x_2, y_2)$:

$$\lambda = \frac{y_2 - y_1}{x_2 - x_1}; \quad x_3 = \lambda^2 - x_1 - x_2; \quad y_3 = -\lambda(x_3 - x_1) - y_1.$$

Note that every point addition requires an inversion over the underlying finite field; it is easy to check that the same is true for point doubling. Inversions modulo p are typically much more expensive than multiplications modulo p. Using standard parameters [**34**], an inversion can take 50-100 times as long as a multiplication on the same underlying prime field, and about 10 times as long as a multiplication on a binary field [**12, 6**] (see section 2.5.5 for more about implementing elliptic curves over binary fields).

It would clearly help if we could cut down the number of inversions necessary to add or double points. This can be done, at little cost in additional memory, using *projective geometry.*

When a projective coordinate representation is used, an elliptic curve point is represented not as the pair (x, y) but as the triple (X, Y, Z). Elliptic curve point addition using projective coordinates is defined as follows:

Conversion to Projective Form: A point (x, y) is converted to projective form (X, Y, Z) by setting

$$X = x, \quad Y = y, \quad Z = 1.$$

Point Addition with Projective Form: Two points (X_1, Y_1, Z_1) and (X_2, Y_2, Z_2) are added in projective representation to obtain (X_3, Y_3, Z_3) as follows:

(1) Set $u = Y_2Z_1 - Y_1Z_2$
(2) Set $v = X_2Z_1 - X_1Z_2$
(3) Set $A = u^2Z_1Z_2 - v^3 - 2v^2X_1Z_2$
(4) Set $X_3 = vA$
(5) Set $Y_3 = u(v^2X_1Z_2 - A)v^3Y_1Z_2$
(6) Set $Z_3 = v^3Z_1Z_2$.

Point Doubling with Projective Form: A point (X_1, Y_1, Z_1) is doubled in projective representation to obtain (X_3, Y_3, Z_3) as follows:

(1) Set $s = Y_1Z_1$
(2) Set $B = X_1Y_1s$
(3) Set $w = aZ_1^2 + 3X_1^2$
(4) Set $h = w^2 - 8B$
(5) Set $X_3 = 2hs$
(6) Set $Y_3 = w(4B - h) - 8Y_1^2s^2$
(7) Set $Z_3 = 8s^3$

Conversion from Projective Form: A point in projective form (X, Y, Z) is converted to a point in standard form (x, y) by setting

$$x = X/Z, \quad y = Y/Z.$$

It can be seen that projective form requires many more field operations than standard ("affine") form. Nevertheless, the time saved by avoiding the inversions more than cancels out the time required for the additional multiplications, particularly on machines with large wordsize. The results of [**12, 6**] are obtained using projective representations; these papers, and [**7**], are recommended for an in-depth discussion of the issues skimmed in this section.

2.5.5. *Choice of basis type: Binary Finite Fields.* We have dealt up till now with elliptic curves over $\mathbb{F}_p$. However, elliptic curve operations in cryptography are frequently performed over another field, $\mathbb{F}_{2^m}$. Elements of $\mathbb{F}_{2^m}$ can be considered to be binary polynomials of degree $m - 1$ or less. Addition in $\mathbb{F}_{2^m}$ is simple XOR of the two elements. Multiplication requires an object which plays a similar role to that played by the prime modulus in $\mathbb{F}_p$. This object is an *irreducible polynomial of degree* m (a polynomial with no factors of smaller degree). Reducing modulo such a polynomial is similar to reducing modulo a prime p. Note that the fields obtained by different choices of polynomial are isomorphic to each other, so the only effect of a particular choice of polynomial is on efficiency, not on the underlying field structure.

The use of $\mathbb{F}_{2^m}$ as an underlying field may have several advantages over the use of a prime field:

- Because all bits are considered independently, and all operations on those bits are modulo 2, the carry bit is never used. This is useful particularly on constrained devices (for example, those with eight-bit processors, which find multi-precision arithmetic particularly difficult).
- The irreducible polynomial f used as a modulus can be chosen to have very few non-zero terms, and for those non-zero terms to be of low exponent. This cuts down the number of bit operations necessary to reduce mod f. For example, NIST recommend the use of the modulus $x^{167} + x^6 + 1$ for $\mathbb{F}_{2^{167}}$, $x^{163} + x^7 + x^6 + x^3 + 1$ for $\mathbb{F}_{2^{163}}$.

On Pentium-based machines, these advantages are outweighed by the fact that the Pentium chip is optimized for big-integer operations. On more constrained devices, the advantages of $\mathbb{F}_{2^m}$ over $\mathbb{F}_p$ are more pronounced. A useful study of different techniques for optimizing performance over $\mathbb{F}_{2^m}$ can be found in [**12**]

2.5.6. *Choice of basis type: Gaussian Normal Basis.* There are many useful representations of the elements of $\mathbb{F}_{2^m}$, and one of these is the so-called *normal basis representation.* In this representation, instead of being considered polynomials of the form

$$a_0 + a_1 x + a_2 x^2 + \cdots + a_{m-1} x^{m-1},$$

elements are transformed into a polynomial of the form

$$a'_0\alpha + a'_1\alpha^2 + a'_2\alpha^4 + a'_3\alpha^8 \cdots + a'_{m-1}\alpha^{2^{m-1}}.$$

It is obvious by inspection that in this basis representation it is trivial to square an element: simply rotate it one place. Multiplication of field elements in this representation, however, can be cumbersome. However, it happens that the formula for point doubling for elliptic curves over $\mathbb{F}_{2^m}$ requires only squaring and addition, but no multiplication. In general, the use of Gaussian Normal Bases makes software implementations less efficient, but it can have great performance benefits in hardware.

2.5.7. *Optimal Extension Fields.* The best performance known for elliptic curve operations on desktop machines, however, is obtained using yet another underlying field for the point coordinates. This field is the *prime extension field* $\mathbb{F}_{p^m}$ (the name contrasts with the *binary extension field* $\mathbb{F}_{2^m}$). Here, the core idea is to take advantage of the underlying word size w of the machine in use, and use the facts that:

- integer operations on integers $\leq 2^w$ will tend to be extremely efficient, and
- reduction of an integer modulo a prime that is close to a power of 2 can be made extremely efficient.

Also, it turns out that inversions are very cheap in these fields. This further benefits the implementor, as explained in section 2.5.4; in fact, on a desktop machine, inversions over OEFs take only about four times as long as multiplications, compared to up to 40 times as long for other underlying fields [**36**]. This means that we can obtain good performance without having to use projective representation to avoid inversions.

Operation	Prime	OEF	Polynomial Basis
ECDSA Sign	9 ms	4 ms	20 ms
ECDSA Verify	30 ms	17 ms	60 ms
ECDH	30 ms	16 ms	63 ms

TABLE 7. Performance of elliptic curves over various finite fields in software

An example of a 192-bit Optimal extension field, for use on machines with a word size of 32 bits, is

$$\mathbb{F}_{p^m} = \mathbb{F}_p[x]/(x^6 - 2), \quad p = 2^{32} - 19.$$

Here, reduction modulo p can be implemented as a series of conditional adds of multiples of 19, and reduction modulo the polynomial $(x^6 - 2)$ involves simply doubling and adding 32-bit integers. Both of these operations are extremely efficient. Table 7, after [**36**], compares the performance of elliptic curves over OEFs to the performance over other base fields. The figures were obtained on a Sun SPARC workstation, but because comparing benchmarks obtained on different machines is difficult the table should be read with a view to the relative performance, rather than the absolute numbers.

3. Conclusion

We have surveyed cryptosystems based on both the discrete logarithm problem and the elliptic curve discrete logarithm problem. Elliptic curve systems, in particular, have many attractive properties compared to RSA: key generation is fast, key sizes are smaller, and there is a wealth of possibilities for efficient implementation. Against this, RSA has the property that public key operations can be made extremely fast; it also has the implementational advantage that there *aren't* so many possibilities for implementation, making interoperability easier to achieve. Nevertheless, with the current wealth of research being done on elliptic curve implementations and properties, it seems likely that they will be a permanent feature on the cryptographic landscape.

References

[1] L. M. Adleman, *A subexponential algorithm for the discrete logarithm problem with applications to cryptography*, Proceedings of the IEEE 20th Annual Symposium on Foundations of Computer Science, 55-60, 1979.

[2] R. Anderson, S. Vaudenay, *Minding your p's and q's*, In Kwangjo Kim and Tsutomu Matsumoto, editors, Advances in Cryptology – ASIACRYPT '96, volume 1163 of Lecture Notes in Computer Science, pages 26-35, Springer-Verlag

[3] A. Antipa, D. Brown, A. Menezes, R. Struik, S. Vanstone, *Validation of Elliptic Curve Public Keys* In Public Key Cryptography – PKC 2003, to appear.

[4] D. Bleichenbacher, 'On the generation of DSA one-time keys', 6th Workshop on Elliptic Curve Cryptography (ECC 2002), Proceedings to appear.

[5] E. Brickell, D. Gordon, K. McCurley, D. Wilson, *Fast exponentiation with precomputation*, Advances in Cryptology – Eurocrypt '92 LNCS 658 (1993) 200-207

[6] M. Brown, D. Hankerson, J. Hernandez, A. Menezes, *Software implementation of the NIST elliptic curves over prime fields*, Topics in Cryptology - CT-RSA 2001, Lecture Notes in Computer Science, 2020 (2001), 250-265

[7] H.Cohen, A.Miyaji and T.Ono, *Efficient Elliptic Curve Exponentiation using Mixed Coordinates*, Asiacrypt98, LNCS 1514, Springer-Verlag, pp.51-65, 1998.

[8] W. Diffie and M. Hellman. *New directions in cryptography.* IEEE Transactions on Information Theory, IT22(6): 644–654, November 1976.

[9] T. ElGamal. *A public key cryptosystem and a signature scheme based on discrete logarithms.* IEEE Transactions on Information Theory, IT31: pages 469–472, 1985.

[10] FIPS 186-2. *Digital Signature Standard.* Federal Information Processing Standards Publication 1862, 2000. Available from: http://csrc.nist.gov/

[11] D. M. Gordon, *Discrete logarithms in GF(p) using the number field sieve*, SIAM Journel on Discrete Mathematics, 6 (1993), 124-138.

[12] D. Hankerson, J. Hernandez, A. Menezes, *Software implementation of elliptic curve cryptography over binary fields*, Proceedings of CHES 2000, Lecture Notes in Computer Science, 1965 (2000), 1-24

[13] N. A. Howgrave-Graham and N. P. Smart, 'Lattice attacks on digital signature schemes', *Designs, Codes and Cryptography*, **23** (2001), 283–290.

[14] IEEE Std 1363-2000, *Standard Specifications for PublicKey Cryptography.* Institute of Electrical and Electronics Engineers, 2000. Information available from `http://grouper.ieee.org/groups/1363/`.

[15] IEEE P1363A. *Standard Specifications for PublicKey Cryptography – Amendment 1: Additional Techniques.* October, 2002, Working Draft 11bis. Information available from `http://grouper.ieee.org/groups/1363/`.

[16] T. Izu, J. Kogure, M. Noro, K. Yokoyama, *Efficient implementation of Schoof's algorithm*, Advances in Cryptology – AsiaCrypt '98 Lecture Notes in Computer Science 1514 (1999) Springer-Verlag 66-79.

[17] M. Jagger, *Sympathy for the Devil*, Beggar's Banquet, Decca SKL-4955, 1968.

[18] D. Johnson, A. Menezes, *The Elliptic Curve Digital Signature Algorithm (ECDSA)* Technical Report CORR 99-34, Dept. of C&O, University of Waterloo, 2000. Available from `http://www.cacr.math.uwaterloo.ca`.

[19] N. Koblitz. *Elliptic curve cryptosystems.* Mathematics of Computation, 48, pages 203–209, 1987.

[20] R. Lercier, *Finding good random elliptic curves for cryptosystems defined over* F_{2^m}, Advances in Cryptology – Eurocrypt '97, Lecture Notes in Computer Science 1223 (1197) Springer-Verlag 379-392.

[21] A. K. Lenstra, E. R. Verheul, *Selecting cryptographic key sizes*, Journal of Cryptography, vol. 14, no. 4, 2001, 255-293. Available from `http://www.cryptosavvy.com`.

[22] C.H. Lim and P.J.Lee, *More flexible exponentiation with precomputation*, Advances in Cryptology – Crypto '94, LNCS 839, 1994, 95-107.

[23] C.H. Lim and P.J. Lee. *A key recovery attack on discrete logbased schemes using a prime order subgroup.* In Advances in Cryptology: Crypto '97, pages 249–263, 1997.

[24] K. McCurley, *The discrete logarithm problem*, C. Pomerance, ed., Cryptology and Computational Number Theory, volume 42 of Proceedings of Symposia in Applied Mathematics, 49-74, American Mathematical Society, 1990.

[25] V. Miller. *Uses of elliptic curves in cryptography.* In Advances in Cryptology: Crypto '85, pages 417–426, 1985.

[26] P. Q. Nguyen, 'The dark side of the hidden number problem: Lattice attacks on DSA', *Proc. Workshop on Cryptography and Computational Number Theory*, Singapore 1999, Birkhäuser, (2001), 321–330.

[27] P. Q. Nguyen and I. E. Shparlinski, 'The insecurity of the Digital Signature Algorithm with partially known nonces', *J. Cryptology*, **15** (2002), 151–176.

[28] A. Odlyzko, *Discrete logarithms: The past and the future*, Designs, Codes, and Cryptography 19 (2000), pp. 129-145. Reprinted in Towards a Quarter-Century of Public Key Cryptography, N. Koblitz, ed., Kluwer, 2000, pp. 59-75. Available from `http://www.dtc.umn.edu/~odlyzko/doc/crypto.html`.

[29] J. Pollard. *Monte Carlo methods for index computation mod p.* Mathematics of Computation, 32, pages 918–924, 1978.

[30] O. Schirokauer, *Discrete Logarithms and Local Units*, Philosophical Transactions of the Royal Society of London A, 345 (1993), 409-423.

[31] C.P. Schnorr. *Efficient signature generation by smart cards.* Journal of Cryptology, 4, pages 161-174, 1991.

[32] R. Schoof. *Elliptic curves over finite fields and the computation of square roots mod p.* Mathematics of Computation, 44, pages 483–494, 1985.

[33] SEC 1, *Elliptic Curve Cryptography* Standards for Efficient Cryptography Group, Version 1.0, September, 2000. Available from `http://www.secg.org/secg_docs.htm`.

[34] SEC 2, *Recommended Elliptic Curve Domain Parameters* Standards for Efficient Cryptography Group, Version 1.0, September, 2000. Available from `http://www.secg.org/secg_docs.htm`.

[35] R.D. Silverman, *A Cost-Based Security Analysis of Symmetric and Asymmetric Key Lengths* RSA Labs Bulletin 13, available from `http://www.rsasecurity.com/rsalabs/bulletins/index.html`.

[36] N. Smart, *A comparison of different finite fields for use in elliptic curve cryptosystems*, Technical report CSTR-00-0007, University of Bristol, 2000. Available from `http://www.cs.bris.ac.uk/Tools/Reports/Abstracts/2000-smart.html`.

[37] P.C. van Oorschot and M. Wiener. *Parallel collision search with applications to hash functions and discrete logarithms.* 2nd ACM Conference on Computer and Communications Security, pages 210-218, ACM Press. 1994.

[38] S. Vanstone, *Responses to NIST's Proposal*, Communications of the ACM, 35, July 1992 50-52. American National Standards Institute,

[39] ANSI X9.42-2001, *Public Key Cryptography for the Financial Services Industry: Agreement of Symmetric Keys Using Discrete Logarithm Cryptography*, American National Standards Institute, 2001.

[40] ANSI X9.62–1999, *Public Key Cryptography for the Financial Services Industry: The Elliptic Curve Digital Signature Algorithm (ECDSA)*, American National Standards Institute, 1999

[41] ANSI X9.63–2001, *Public Key Cryptography for the Financial Services Industry: Key Agreement and Key Transport Using Elliptic Curve Cryptography* American National Standards Institute, 2001.

NTRU CRYPTOSYSTEMS, 5 BURLINGTON WOODS, BURLINGTON, MA 02144
E-mail address: `wwhyte@ntru.com`

Proceedings of Symposia in Applied Mathematics
Volume **62**, 2005

Towards Faster Cryptosystems, II

William D. Banks

Abstract. We discuss three cryptosystems, *NTRU*, *SPIFI*, and *ENROOT*, that are based on the use of polynomials with restricted coefficients.

Introduction

In this paper, we consider three cryptosystems that are based on the use of polynomials with restricted coefficients and over a finite ring $\mathcal{R}$. For cryptographic purposes, polynomials with restricted coefficients offer many attractive features, including resistance to lattice attacks and other security risks, very modest storage requirements, and competitive computational speed. The cryptosystems described below, namely *NTRU*, *SPIFI*, and *ENROOT*, utilize polynomials with restricted coefficients in different ways, and these constructions have met with varying levels of success in the cryptographic community. Our aim in this paper is not to imply that these particular cryptosystems are optimal in any sense. Instead, we simply hope to illustrate the elegance and simplicity of their design features and perhaps promote the development of the next generation of fast cryptosystems based on polynomials.

1. The NTRU Cryptosystem

The *NTRU Public Key Cryptosystem* is based on ring theory, and its underlying security relies on the difficulty of solving certain lattice problems when the dimension of the given lattice is sufficiently large. In practical implementations of the NTRU protocol, many of the polynomials that are used have coefficients lying in the set $\{0, \pm 1\}$; this means that multiplication in the underlying ring $\mathcal{R}$ can be performed very efficiently, which contributes significantly to the overall performance. Thus, NTRU provides a competitive alternative to cryptosystems based on RSA or Diffie-Hellman. For a more complete account of NTRU, the reader is referred to original paper [**11**] and other related articles that can be found at the NTRU website (`http://www.ntru.com`).

1991 *Mathematics Subject Classification.* Primary 54C40, 14E20; Secondary 46E25, 20C20.
Key words and phrases. Cryptography, polynomials, number theory.
The author was supported in part by NSF Grant # DMS-0070628.

1.1. The NTRU Protocol. The original version of NTRU depends on three integer parameters (N, p, q) and four sets $\mathcal{L}_f$, $\mathcal{L}_g$, $\mathcal{L}_\phi$ and $\mathcal{L}_m$ of polynomials with integers coefficients and degree at most $N-1$, which are naturally viewed as subsets of the ring $\mathcal{R} = \mathbb{Z}[x]/(x^N - 1)$. The symbol $*$ is used to denote the operation of multiplication in the ring $\mathcal{R}$. The parameters p and q need not be prime numbers (indeed, q is often chosen to be a power of 2 for obvious reasons), but one does require that $\gcd(p, q) = 1$. The basic NTRU protocol consists of the following three steps:

- **Key Creation.** *Bob* creates a public key h by selecting two polynomials $f \in \mathcal{L}_f$ and $g \in \mathcal{L}_g$. The polynomial f should satisfy the additional requirement that it have inverses modulo p and modulo q. These are denoted by F_p and F_q, respectively, so that

$$f * F_p \equiv 1 \pmod{p} \qquad \text{and} \qquad f * F_q \equiv 1 \pmod{q}.$$

Bob's public key is the polynomial

$$h \equiv F_q * g \pmod{q}.$$

Bob only needs to retain f as his private key, although in practice *Bob* would also want to store the polynomial F_p since this is needed for every decryption.

- **Encryption.** To encrypt a message $m \in \mathcal{L}_m$ to *Bob*, *Alice* randomly chooses a polynomial $\phi \in \mathcal{L}_\phi$. Using *Bob*'s public key h, she then computes

$$e = p\phi * h + m \pmod{q}$$

and transmits e to *Bob*.

- **Decryption.** *Bob* has received e from *Alice*. To decrypt, *Bob* first computes

$$a = f * e \pmod{q},$$

choosing the coefficients of a to lie in the interval between $-q/2$ and $q/2$. *Bob* then recovers the message m by computing

$$m = F_p * a \pmod{p}.$$

To see why the decryption works, we observe that in the last step, *Bob* computes the polynomial

$$\begin{aligned} a = f * e \pmod{q} &\equiv f * (p\phi * h + m) \pmod{q} \\ &\equiv p\phi * (f * F_q) * g + f * m \pmod{q} \\ &\equiv p\phi * g + f * m \pmod{q}. \end{aligned}$$

For appropriate choices of the input parameters, the polynomial

$$G = p\phi * g + f * m \in \mathcal{R}$$

will (almost certainly) have coefficients that all lie in the interval $-q/2$ to $q/2$, hence *Bob* recovers exactly the polynomial G after completing the first calculation.

Reducing G modulo p, *Bob* recovers the polynomial $f * m \pmod{p}$. Then, after multiplying by F_p (the inverse of f modulo p), he obtains *Alice*'s message m.

We remark that the protocol described here has been generalized to work over an arbitrary ring $\mathcal{R}$. In this more general setting, the parameters p and q can be any ideals in $\mathcal{R}$ such that $(p, q) = (1)$.

1.2. Parameter Selection and Efficiency. For the most current recommended parameter sets for NTRU, and an overview of the security analysis, we refer the reader to [**14**].

In practical implementations of NTRU, the most time consuming part of the encryption and decryption steps is multiplication in the ring $\mathcal{R}$; encryption involves the computation of one product $r * h \pmod{q}$, while decryption requires that two products $a = f * e \pmod{q}$ and $F_p * a \pmod{p}$ be computed. In the key creation step, the most time consuming part is the computation of the inverses F_p and F_q. Ordinarily, *Bob* will store F_p along with his private key f in order to avoid the recalculation of F_p each time an encrypted message is sent. To speed up both the key creation and encryption, *Bob* can choose the element f to have the special form $f = 1 + pf_1$ with $f_1 \in \mathcal{R}$. In this case, $F_p = 1$, so it is not necessary to compute the inverse of f modulo p in the key creation step, and the second multiplication in the decryption step is eliminated. This also eliminates the need to store F_p. However, if *Bob* does choose to work with elements f of this form, then since the underlying lattice is changed, special care is required in the parameter selection in order to avoid to potential lattice attacks.

The space of messages $\mathcal{L}_m$ consists of all polynomials modulo p; if p is odd, it is generally convenient to choose

$$\mathcal{L}_m = \{m \in \mathcal{R} \mid m \text{ has coefficients lying between } -(p-1)/2 \text{ and } (p-1)/2\},$$

while for $p = 2$ or $p = 2 + X$, $\mathcal{L}_m$ consists of polynomials with $\{0, 1\}$ coefficients. The other sample spaces $\mathcal{L}_f$, $\mathcal{L}_g$ and $\mathcal{L}_\phi$ also depend on the form of p, and are generally chosen to have the form

$$\mathcal{L}_f = \mathcal{L}(d_f), \qquad \mathcal{L}_g = \mathcal{L}(d_g), \qquad \mathcal{L}_\phi = \mathcal{L}(d),$$

or

$$\mathcal{L}_f = \mathcal{L}(d_f, d_f - 1), \qquad \mathcal{L}_g = \mathcal{L}(d_g, d_g), \qquad \mathcal{L}_\phi = \mathcal{L}(d, d),$$

where for all $d_1, d_2 \geq 1$, $\mathcal{L}(d_1)$ consists of all polynomials $F \in \mathcal{R}$ with exactly d_1 coefficients equal to $+1$ and the remaining coefficients equal to 0, and $\mathcal{L}(d_1, d_2)$ consists of all polynomials $F \in \mathcal{R}$ with exactly d_1 coefficients equal to $+1$, exactly d_2 coefficients equal to -1, and the remaining coefficients equal to 0.

We observe that any element of $\mathcal{R}$ modulo p can be encoded with about $N \log p$ bits. Indeed, to encode the coefficient at each position requires about $\log p$ bits, and there are N position altogether. Hence, the private key length is about $2N \log p$ bits. Similarly, the public key length is about $N \log q$ bits. For security equivalent to 1024-bit RSA (or a symmetric cipher with an 80-bit key), the following choices have been recommended:

$$(N, p, q) = (251, 2 + X, 128), \quad \mathcal{L}_f = \mathcal{L}(72), \quad \mathcal{L}_g = \mathcal{L}(72), \quad \mathcal{L}_\phi = \mathcal{L}(72),$$

which gives a private key size of 251 bits and a public key size of 1757 bits (further optimizations reduce the private key size to 192 bits; see [**13**]). For security equivalent to 2048-bit RSA (110-bit symmetric), the following choices are recommended:

$$(N,p,q) = (347, 2+X, 256), \quad \mathcal{L}_f = \mathcal{L}(64), \quad \mathcal{L}_g = \mathcal{L}(173), \quad \mathcal{L}_\phi = \mathcal{L}(64),$$

which after optimization has a private key size of 184 bits and a public key size of 2776 bits. For security equivalent to 4096-bit RSA (160-bit symmetric), the following choices are recommended:

$$(N,p,q) = (503, 2+X, 256), \quad \mathcal{L}_f = \mathcal{L}(420), \quad \mathcal{L}_g = \mathcal{L}(251), \quad \mathcal{L}_\phi = \mathcal{L}(170),$$

which has a private key size of 480 bits and a public key size of 4024 bits.

We remark that by working mostly with polynomials whose coefficients lie in $\{0,1\}$ or $\{0,\pm 1\}$, multiplication in $\mathcal{R}$ is very fast and efficient. Hence, even the most time consuming aspect of the NTRU protocol is greatly improved by the use of polynomials with restricted coefficients.

1.3. Some Security Issues. Here we briefly discuss a few issues of security; for a complete analysis of NTRU security, the reader is referred to [**14**] (see also [**11**]).

1.3.1. *Brute force attacks.* To recover the private key f, an attacker *Attila* can apply a brute force attack by trying all possible $f \in \mathcal{L}_f$ and testing whether $f * h \pmod q$ has small entries (i.e., lies in $\mathcal{L}_g$). Alternatively, *Attila* can try all possible $g \in \mathcal{L}_g$ and test whether $g * h^{-1} \pmod q$ has small entries (i.e., lies in $\mathcal{L}_f$). In practice one usually has $\#\mathcal{L}_g < \#\mathcal{L}_f$, so the key security is determined by $\#\mathcal{L}_g$, while the individual message security is determined by $\#\mathcal{L}_\phi$. There is a meet-in-the-middle attack due to Odlyzko, which cuts the search time by the usual square root (assuming a sufficient amount of storage); thus one finds that

$$\begin{aligned} \text{Key Security} &= \sqrt{\#\mathcal{L}_g} = \frac{1}{d_g!}\sqrt{\frac{N!}{(N-2d_g)!}}, \\ \text{Message Security} &= \sqrt{\#\mathcal{L}_\phi} = \frac{1}{d!}\sqrt{\frac{N!}{(N-2d)!}}. \end{aligned}$$

For instance, in a moderate security implementation of NTRU, with $N = 107$, $d_g = 12$ and $d = 5$, the key security is about 2^{50}, while the individual message security is about $2^{26.5}$.

1.3.2. *Multiple transmission attacks.* If *Alice* sends the same message m several times using the same public key h but different random ϕ's, the attacker *Attila* will be able to recover a large part of the message. For suppose *Alice* transmits $e_j \equiv \phi_j * h + m \pmod q$ for $j = 1, \ldots, r$. *Attila* can then compute $(e_j - e_1) * h^{-1} \pmod q$, obtaining $(\phi_j - \phi_1) \mod q$ for each j. But the coefficients of the ϕ's are so small that *Attila* recovers exactly $\phi_j - \phi_1$, and he can use this to recover many of the coefficients of ϕ_1. If r is of moderate size, then *Attila* will recover enough of ϕ_1 to be able to test the remaining coefficients by brute force, and therefore he can recover m. Thus, multiple transmissions are not advised.

1.3.3. *Malleability and information leakage.* The multiple transmission attack mentioned above is one of many similar attacks on "raw" NTRU. For example, encrypted messages are trivially *malleable*: an attacker can add or subtract 1 to any coefficient of e and there is a good chance that the decrypted m will have 1 added to or subtracted from the same coefficient. In addition, there is at least one bit of *information leakage*: due to the existence of the ring homomorphism

$$(a * b)(1) = a(1)b(1) \quad \forall a, b \in \mathcal{R},$$

a ciphertext e leaks $m(1)$ through $m(1) = e(1) - \phi(1)h(1)$ (note that in the parameter sets above, $\phi(1)$ is a public parameter of the system). A sensible encryption scheme must prevent this type of attack.

Therefore, to insure security, the NTRU primitive must be combined with a secure message processing scheme (similar to the way RSA must be combined with OAEP). In this scheme, *Alice* must combine m with some one-time randomness b in some reversible way to obtain the blinded message m' (this will ensure that $m(1)$ is hidden, and that even if the same m is encrypted twice, a different m' will be encrypted every time). Then she uses m and b to derive ϕ, using a hash function which can be guaranteed to remove mathematical structure from the relationship between m' and ϕ. Finally, she calculates the ciphertext $e = p\phi * h + m'$. On decryption, *Bob* recovers m', extracts m and b from it, regenerates ϕ and checks that $p\phi * h + m'$ is equal to the received e. This construction prevents both information leakage and the adaptive chosen ciphertext attacks described in lecture 4.

1.3.4. *Lattice attacks.* Very briefly, NTRU's security against lattice attacks is derived from the large dimension of the underlying lattice. Initial experiments using lattice reduction techniques such as LLL indicate that the time $t(N)$ needed to break an NTRU cryptosystem with parameter N grows like $N \log N$, i.e., faster than exponential. By extrapolating $t(N)$ from small values of N, one obtains the estimated breaking times and equivalent security levels given in section 1.2.

2. The SPIFI Identification Scheme

In this section, we describe the *SPIFI identification scheme*, we can be defined for an arbitrary finite ring $\mathcal{R}$; see [**2**] and [**3**]. The polynomials used in the SPIFI protocol are taken to have only a few nonzero coefficients, hence particular values of these polynomials can be computed very rapidly, and the storage requirements remain quite modest.

2.1. Notation and Definitions. Throughout this section and the next, $\mathcal{R}$ denotes an arbitrary finite (unitary) ring with $\mathcal{R}^\times$ its multiplicative group of units. We denote by N a fixed multiple of the exponent $\exp(\mathcal{R}^\times)$ of $\mathcal{R}^\times$; then $a^{N+1} = a$ for all $a \in \mathcal{R}^\times \cup \{0\}$. We assume that any element of $\mathcal{R}$ can be encoded using about $\log(\#\mathcal{R})$ bits, where as usual $\log x$ denotes the binary logarithm of $x > 0$.

To illustrate our ideas, we occasionally consider two important special cases referred to as the "$\mathbb{F}_q$-case" and the "$\mathbb{Z}_M$-case." In the $\mathbb{F}_q$-case, $\mathcal{R} = \mathbb{F}_q$ is the finite field q elements, where q is a fixed prime power; in this case, one can take $N = \exp(\mathcal{R}^\times) = q - 1$. In the $\mathbb{Z}_M$-case, $\mathcal{R} = \mathbb{Z}/M\mathbb{Z}$ is the ring of congruence classes with respect to a fixed RSA modulus $M = p\ell$, where p and ℓ are (large) prime numbers; in this case, one can either take $N = \varphi(M) = (p-1)(\ell-1)$, where φ is the *Euler function*, or $N = \lambda(M) = \mathrm{lcm}(p-1, \ell-1)$, where λ is the *Carmichael function*. With any of the choices above, we have $\log(\#\mathcal{R}) \approx \log(\#\mathcal{R}^\times) \approx \log N$.

Let d be a fixed positive integer. For any fixed subset $\mathcal{S} \subseteq \mathcal{R}$, we say that a polynomial $f(x_1, \ldots, x_d) \in \mathcal{R}[x_1, \ldots, x_d]$ is an *$\mathcal{S}$-polynomial* if every coefficient of f belongs to $\mathcal{S}$. Any expression of the form $ax_1^{e_1} \ldots x_d^{e_d}$ is said to be *monomial* with *coefficient* a and *exponent* $(e_1, \ldots, e_d)$. Finally, we say that a polynomial $f(x_1, \ldots, x_d) \in \mathcal{R}[x_1, \ldots, x_d]$ is τ*-sparse* if f has at most τ nonzero coefficients.

2.2. A Hard Problem. The hard problem underlying the SPIFI scheme can be stated as follows:

> *Given $2m$ arbitrary elements $\alpha_1, \ldots \alpha_m, \beta_1, \ldots, \beta_m \in \mathcal{R}$ and a set $\mathcal{S} \subseteq \mathcal{R}$ of small cardinality, it is not feasible to find a τ-sparse $\mathcal{S}$-polynomial $f(x) \in \mathcal{R}[x]$ of degree $\deg(f) \le N$ with $f(\alpha_j) = \beta_j$ for each $1 \le j \le m$, provided that N is of "medium" size relative to the choices of $m \ge 1$, the cardinality $\#\mathcal{S}$, and the parameter $\tau \ge 3$.*

More precisely, one expects that if m, $\mathcal{S}$ and τ are fixed, then the problem requires exponential time as $N \to \infty$.

For example, let p be a prime, and consider the case where $\mathcal{R}$ is the finite field $\mathbb{F}_p$ with p elements. Let $a_{ij} \equiv \alpha_j^i \pmod p$ and $b_j \equiv \beta_j \pmod p$ be chosen so that $0 \le a_{ij}, b_j \le p-1$ for $i = 0, \ldots, p-1$ and $j = 1, \ldots, m$. Then in this simplified situation, the hard problem above is still equivalent to the problem of finding a feasible solution to the *integer programming problem*

$$\sum_{i=0}^{p-1} x_i \varepsilon_i a_{ij} + y_j p = b_j, \qquad j = 1, \ldots, m, \qquad \sum_{i=0}^{p-1} \varepsilon_i \le \tau,$$

where $y_j \in \mathbb{Z}$, $x_i \in \mathcal{S}$, and $\varepsilon_i \in \{0, 1\}$ for all i and j.

2.3. The SPIFI Protocol. We fix the ring $\mathcal{R}$ and some integer parameters $k \ge 1$ and $r, s, t \ge 3$; this information is made *public*. The value of N is kept *private*. Since only *Alice* needs to know this value, the choice of the ring $\mathcal{R}$ and the value of N can be made by *Alice*.

To avoid a certain well known attack on the scheme (see **[1]** and the comments below), we also require that $\mathcal{R}$ contains elements of multiplicative order in the interval $[0.5N^{1/4}, 2N^{1/4}]$. Although this imposes certain number theoretic limitations on the ring $\mathcal{R}$ and the integer N, in practice these constraints are easily satisfied.

The SPIFI protocol consists of an initial set-up, or signature creation, and a verification procedure.

2.3.1. *SPIFI Signature Creation.* To create a digital signature, *Alice* uses the following algorithm:

- **Step 1.** *Alice* selects at random k distinct elements $a_0, \ldots a_{k-1} \in \mathcal{R}^\times$, where a_0 has a multiplicative order in the interval $[0.5N^{1/4}, 2N^{1/4}]$.

- **Step 2.** *Alice* selects a random $\lceil t/2 \rceil$-sparse $\{0,1\}$-polynomial $f_1(x) \in \mathcal{R}[x]$ with $\deg(f_1) \le N$ and $f_1(a_0) \in \mathcal{R}^\times$. Next, she selects at random a $\lfloor t/2 \rfloor$-sparse $\{0,1\}$-polynomial $f_2(x) \in \mathcal{R}[x]$ with $\deg(f_2) \le N$, $f_2(a_0) \ne 0$ and $f_2(a_0) \ne -f_1(a_0)$.

- **Step 3.** *Alice* computes the quantity $A = -f_2(a_0)f_1(a_0)^{-1}$ and creates the polynomial $f(x) = Af_1(x) + f_2(x)$. Then f is a t-sparse $\{0,1,A\}$-polynomial with $\deg(f) \le N$, and $f(a_0) = 0$. The polynomial f is *Alice*'s private key.

- **Step 4.** *Alice* computes the numbers $C_j = f(a_j)$ for $j = 1, \ldots, k-1$.

- **Step 5.** *Alice* publishes the set of values $\{A, a_0, \ldots a_{k-1}, C_1, \ldots, C_{k-1}\}$ as her public key.

2.3.2. *SPIFI Verification Protocol.* In order for *Alice* to verify her identity to *Bob*, the following algorithm is used:

- **Step 1.** (Commitment) *Alice* selects a random r-sparse $\{0,1\}$-polynomial $g(x) \in \mathcal{R}[x]$ with $\deg(g) \le N$ and $g(0) = 0$. She then computes the numbers
$$D_j = g(a_j), \qquad j = 1, \ldots, k-1,$$
and sends the sum $D = D_1 + \ldots + D_{k-1}$ to *Bob*.

- **Step 2.** (Challenge) *Bob* selects a random s-sparse $\{0,1,B\}$-polynomial $h(x) \in \mathcal{R}[x]$ of degree $\deg(h) \le N$ and sends h to *Alice*. Here $B \notin \{0,1,A\}$.

- **Step 3.** (Response) *Alice* computes
$$F(x) \equiv f(x)g(x)h(x) \pmod{x^{N+1} - x}$$
and sends the polynomial F and $\{D_1, \ldots, D_{k-1}\}$ to *Bob*.

- **Step 4.** (Verification) *Bob* computes
$$E_j = h(a_j), \qquad j = 1, \ldots, k-1,$$
and verifies that
$$D_1 + \ldots + D_{k-1} = D$$
that $F(x)$ is an rst-sparse $\{0,1,A,B,AB\}$-polynomial of degree at most N, that $F(a_0) = 0$, and that $F(a_j) = C_jD_jE_j$ for $j = 1, \ldots, k-1$.

Of course, there is a chance that the constructed polynomial $F(x)$ is not a $\{0,1,A,B,AB\}$-polynomial due to collisions; however, if rst is substantially smaller than N, then this chance is negligible (and in this case, *Alice* and *Bob* can repeat the procedure).

2.4. Efficiency. As mentioned earlier, the sparsity of the polynomials plays a dual role in that it not only guarantees the computational efficiency of this scheme, but it also means that the storage requirements are minimal.

Using only (naive) repeated squaring, one can compute the power a^e for any $a \in \mathcal{R}$ and $0 \le e \le N$ in about $2 \log N$ arithmetic operations in $\mathcal{R}$ in the worst case, or in about $1.5 \log N$ arithmetic operations "on average"; see Section 1.3 of [**4**], Section 4.3 of [**5**], or Section 2.1 of [**6**]. Consequently, any τ-sparse polynomial

$f(x) \in \mathcal{R}[x]$ of degree at most N can be evaluated at any point using only $O(\tau \log N)$ arithmetic operations in $\mathcal{R}$.

If $0 \in \mathcal{S} \subseteq \mathcal{R}$, then any τ-sparse $\mathcal{S}$-polynomial $f(x) \in \mathcal{R}[x]$ of degree at most N can be encoded with about $\tau \log(N \cdot \#\mathcal{S} - N)$ bits. To do this, we have to identify at most τ positions at which f has a nonzero coefficient. The encoding of each position requires about $\log N$ bits, and for each such position, about $\log(\#\mathcal{S} - 1)$ bits are then required to determine the corresponding element of $\mathcal{S}$. For example, the signature must encode rst positions of the polynomial F (corresponding to its nonzero coefficients), which takes about $rst \log N$ bits. Each position requires two additional bits to distinguish between the possible nonzero coefficients 1, A, B and AB. The encoding of $D_1, \ldots, D_{k-1}$ and their sum D requires about $k \log(\#R)$ bits. Consequently, the total signature size is about $rst \log(4N) + k \log(\#\mathcal{R})$ bits.

Putting everything together, after simple calculations we derive that (using the naive repeated squaring exponentiation)

- the *initial set-up* takes $O(kt \log N)$ arithmetic operations in $\mathcal{R}$;
- the *private key size* is about $t \log(2N)$ bits;
- the *public key size* is about $k(\log(\#\mathcal{R}) + \log(\#\mathcal{R}^\times))$ bits;
- *signature generation*, that is, computation of the polynomial F, the elements D_j, $j = 1, \ldots, k-1$, and their sum D, takes $O(rst)$ arithmetic operations with integer numbers in the range $[0, 2N]$ and $O((k-1)r \log N)$ arithmetic operations in $\mathcal{R}$;
- the *signature size* is about $rst \log(4N) + k \log(\#\mathcal{R})$ bits;
- *signature verification*, that is, computation of $D_1 + \ldots + D_{k-1}$, $F(a_j)$ and the products $C_j D_j E_j$, $j = 1, \ldots, k-1$, takes about $O(krst \log N)$ arithmetic operations in $\mathcal{R}$.

We remark that the practical and asymptotic performance of the SPIFI scheme can be improved if one uses more sophisticated algorithms to evaluate powers and sparse polynomials; see [**4, 5, 6, 16, 18**].

2.5. Some Security Issues. Here we briefly discuss a few issues of security; for a complete analysis of SPIFI security, the reader is referred to [**3**].

2.5.1. *Faking the key.* It is clear that recovering or faking the private key (that is, finding a t-sparse $\{0, 1, A\}$-polynomial polynomial $\widetilde{f}(x) \in \mathcal{R}[x]$ with $\widetilde{f}(a_0) = 0$ and $\widetilde{f}(a_j) = C_j$ for $j = 1, \ldots, k-1$) or faking the signature (that is, finding a rst-sparse $\{0, 1, A, B, AB\}$-polynomial $\widetilde{F}(x) \in \mathcal{R}[x]$ with $\widetilde{F}(a_0) = 0$ and $\widetilde{F}(a_j) = C_j D_j E_j$ for $j = 1, \ldots, k-1$) are both versions of the hard problem mentioned in Section 2.2. Hence the security of the SPIFI scheme relies on the difficulty of solving the hard problem in a computationally feasible manner.

2.5.2. *Factorization attacks.* Note that without the reduction

$$f(x)g(x)h(x) \pmod{x^{N+1} - x},$$

one possible attack might be via polynomial factorization. In any practical implementation of this scheme, one should make sure that both f and g have terms of degree greater than $N/2$ so there are some reductions in the Response step. On the other hand, even without the reduction modulo $x^{N+1} - x$, the factorization attack would not be likely to succeed because of the large degrees of the polynomials involved. All known factorization algorithms (as well as their important components such as irreducibility testing and the greatest common divisor algorithms) do not take any special advantage of sparsity or structure of the coefficients; see [**5, 17**]. Moreover, the first factor that any of these algorithms would find is the trivial one, i.e., the factor $(x-a_0)$. But the quotient $F(x)/(x-a_0)$ is most likely neither sparse nor an $\mathcal{S}$-polynomial for any small set $\mathcal{S}$. Finally, we remark that if one works in the setting of a ring $\mathcal{R}$ that is *not* a field (such as the $\mathbb{Z}_M$-case), then the problem of factorization becomes much more complicated, so this type of attack is even less likely to succeed.

2.5.3. *Lattice attacks.* One might also consider lattice attacks. In particular, one can try to select a rt-sparse $\{0,1,A\}$-polynomial $e(X) \in \mathcal{R}[x]$ with $e(a_0) = 0$, compute

$$D_j = e(a_j)C_j^{-1}, \qquad j = 1, \dots, k-1,$$

and then send these values together with

$$F(x) \equiv e(x)h(x) \pmod{x^{N+1} - x}$$

to the verifier. In principal, this attack could succeed since finding such a polynomial e is type of knapsack problem. But since the dimension of the corresponding lattice is equal to the (very large) degree N of the polynomials involved, any such attack seems completely infeasible at this time. With current technology, one can reduce lattices of degrees only in the hundreds, while in any practical implementation of the SPIFI scheme the lattices will have dimension N, which is roughly the size of an RSA modulus.

2.5.4. *Discrete logarithm attacks.* One might also attempt to construct such a polynomial e by solving the discrete logarithm in $\mathcal{R}$ to base a_0 (see [**1**]). But a_0 has been specifically selected to have an order that is small enough to defeat this threat. In fact, the basic SPIFI protocol can be modified slightly to avoid all attacks of this type. Specifically, one requests that for each of the polynomials $f(x)$, $g(x)$ and $h(x)$, the sum of the degrees of the monomials is divisible by the integer N. In this case, the same fact also holds for $F(x)$. Indeed, if an s-sparse polynomial and a t-sparse polynomial have monomials of degrees $n_1, \dots, n_s$ and $m_1, \dots, m_t$, respectively, with

$$\sum_{i=1}^{s} n_i \equiv 0 \pmod N \qquad \text{and} \qquad \sum_{j=1}^{t} m_j \equiv 0 \pmod N$$

then their product has st monomials $n_i + m_j$, $i = 1, \dots, s$, $j = 1, \dots, t$ (unless a collision occurs, which is very unlikely). Then

$$\begin{aligned} \sum_{i=1}^{s}\sum_{j=1}^{t}(n_i + m_j) &= \sum_{i=1}^{s}\left(tn_i + \sum_{j=1}^{t} m_j\right) \\ &= t\sum_{i=1}^{s} n_i + s\sum_{j=1}^{t} m_j \equiv 0 \pmod N \end{aligned}$$

as claimed. With this additional constraint, the discrete logarithm attack from [**1**] can only succeed with probability $1/N$, since in the collection of rt-sparse $\{0,1,A\}$-polynomials $e(X) \in \mathcal{R}[x]$ with $e(a_0) = 0$, the sum of the degrees of the monomials are uniformly distributed modulo N.

2.6. Remarks. Although using composite moduli might add some additional security features to the SPIFI scheme, the security is not compromised in the $\mathbb{Z}_M$-case even when the factorization $M = p\ell$ is known. In fact, in the case where the modulus is a (sufficiently large) prime, that is, in the $\mathbb{F}_q$-case, the scheme is quite secure.

It has turned out that *Alice* must make some commitment about the values of $D_1, \ldots, D_{k-1}$ before she receives the polynomial h from *Bob*, otherwise there is a very simple attack on the scheme. On the other hand, sending the whole set to *Bob* before he selects his polynomial h has its own dangers as well. Sending the sum $D = D_1 + \ldots + D_{k-1}$ is just one of many possible ways for *Alice* to undertake some commitments about the values of $D_1, \ldots, D_{k-1}$. Another way is to just send about half of the bits of $D_1, \ldots, D_{k-1}$ in the Commitment step and then send the remaining bits in the Response step. This latter method seems to improve on the overall security against an on-line attack.

Finally, we mention that the SPIFI scheme can be modified so that the value $N = \varphi(M)$ or $\lambda(M)$ (see Section 2.1) remains a secret known only to *Alice*. Indeed, *Alice* can choose g in Step 1 of the verification protocol so that the reduction modulo $x^{N+1} - x$ that occurs in Step 3 produces a polynomial whose degree is not "too close" to N. In fact, "on average" it should be about $N(1 - 1/2rst)$ for the SPIFI scheme and about $N(1-1/2R)$ for the ENROOT scheme (see Section 3 below) since the corresponding polynomials are rst-sparse and R-sparse, respectively. Thus, in the case that $N = \varphi(M)$, the degree of F gives a worse approximation to N than the value of M itself, at least if $M = p\ell$ is a product of two primes of roughly the same order.

3. The ENROOT Cryptosystem

In this section, we describe the *ENROOT cryptosystem* for an arbitrary finite ring $\mathcal{R}$; see [**7**] and [**3**]. Since the polynomial ring $\mathcal{R}[x_1, \ldots, x_d]$, where $d \geq 2$ is fixed in this construction, it is often convenient to employ vector notation, writing $f(\vec{x})$ for $f(x_1, \ldots, x_d)$, $\mathcal{R}[\vec{x}]$ for $\mathcal{R}[x_1, \ldots, x_d]$, etc.

3.1. A Hard Problem. Our one-way functions are based on the following hard problem:

> *Given the τ-sparse polynomials $f_1(\vec{x}), \ldots, f_d(\vec{x}) \subset \mathcal{R}[\vec{x}]$ of degree at most N, it is not feasible to find an element $\vec{a} = (a_1, \ldots, a_d) \in \mathcal{R}^d$ with $f_j(\vec{a}) = 0$ for $j = 1, \ldots, d$, provided that N is sufficiently large relative to the choices of $d \geq 2$ and $\tau \geq 3$.*

Again, we expect that if one fixes the number $d \geq 2$ and the sparsity $\tau \geq 3$, then the problem requires exponential time as $N \to \infty$ (see Section 3.4 below).

3.2. The ENROOT Protocol. We fix the ring $\mathcal{R}$ and the integers $d > \ell \geq 3$, $s_j, t_j \geq 3$, $j = 1, \ldots, d$ such that $t_1 = \ldots = t_\ell$. This information is made *public*. The value of N may be kept *private*. In fact, only *Bob* needs this value so the choice of the ring $\mathcal{R}$ and the value of N is made by *Bob*.

The ENROOT protocol consists of the following three steps:

- **Key Creation.** *Alice* selects d random elements $a_1, \ldots, a_d \in \mathcal{R}^\times$ which become her *private key*.

  Next, *Alice* randomly selects d polynomials $h_j(\vec{x}) \in \mathcal{R}[\vec{x}]$, of degree at most $\#\mathcal{R}$, containing at most $t_j - 1$ monomials, $j = 1, \ldots, d$, such that the first ℓ polynomials $h_1(\vec{x}), \ldots, h_\ell(\vec{x})$ have the same set $\mathcal{E}$ of exponents of their monomials. Finally, *Alice* publishes the polynomials $f_j(\vec{x}) = h_j(\vec{x}) - h_j(\vec{a})$ for $j = 1, \ldots, d$ as her *public key*, where $\vec{a}$ is the vector $(a_1, \ldots, a_d) \in (\mathcal{R}^\times)^d$.

- **Encryption.** To send a message $m \in \mathcal{R}$, *Bob* selects d random polynomials $g_j(\vec{x}) \in \mathcal{R}[\vec{x}]$ of degree at most N, containing at most $s_j - 1$ monomials such that one monomial has an exponent from the set $\mathcal{E}$ and having nonzero constant coefficients. *Bob* then computes the reduction $F(\vec{x})$ of the polynomial

$$m + f_1(\vec{x})g_1(\vec{x}) + \ldots + f_d(\vec{x})g_d(\vec{x})$$

  modulo the ideal in $\mathcal{R}[\vec{x}]$ generated by $\{x_1^{N+1} - x_1, \ldots, x_d^{N+1} - x_d\}$, and he sends $F(\vec{x})$ to *Alice*.

- **Decryption.** To decrypt the message, *Alice* simply computes $F(\vec{a}) = m$.

3.3. Efficiency. The sparsity of the polynomials involved again provides computational efficiency for this scheme. Using repeated squaring, one can compute the monomial $a_1^{e_1} \ldots a_d^{e_d}$ for any $(a_1, \ldots, a_d) \in \mathcal{R}^d$ and $0 \le e_j \le \#\mathcal{R}$, $j = 1, \ldots, d$, in about $O(d \log(2\#\mathcal{R}))$ arithmetic operations in $\mathcal{R}$. Consequently, any τ-sparse polynomial $f(\vec{x}) \in \mathcal{R}[\vec{x}]$ of degree at most $\#\mathcal{R}$ can be evaluated at any point in $\mathcal{R}^d$ in about $O(\tau d \log(2\#\mathcal{R}))$ arithmetic operations in $\mathcal{R}$.

We remark that any τ-sparse polynomial $f(\vec{x}) \in \mathcal{R}[\vec{x}]$ of degree at most $\#\mathcal{R}$ can be encoded with about $\tau((d+1)\log(\#\mathcal{R}))$ bits. To do this, we have to identify at most τ monomials for which f has a nonzero coefficient. The encoding of each monomial $x_1^{e_1} \ldots x_d^{e_d}$ requires about $d \log(\#\mathcal{R})$ bits, and for each such monomial about $\log(\#\mathcal{R})$ bits are then required to encode the coefficient.

Let us set

$$T = \sum_{j=1}^{d} t_j, \qquad S = \sum_{j=1}^{d} s_j, \qquad R = \sum_{j=1}^{d} t_j s_j, \qquad Q = (d+1)\log(\#\mathcal{R}).$$

Then, after simple calculations, we derive that (using the naive repeated squaring exponentiation)

- *generation of the public key*: producing the vector $\vec{a}$ requires $O(d \log(\#\mathcal{R}))$ random bits; to construct the polynomials $h_j(\vec{x})$ requires the generation of another $(T-d)Q$ random bits; the computation of the $h_j(\vec{a})$, $j = 1, \ldots, d$, takes $O(Td \log(2\#\mathcal{R}))$ arithmetic operations in $\mathcal{R}$;
- the *private key size* is about $d \log(\#\mathcal{R}) + (T - d)Q$ bits;
- the *public key size* is about TQ bits;
- *cost of encryption*: to construct the polynomials $g_j(\vec{x})$ requires the generation of about $d \log(\#\mathcal{R}) + (S - d)Q$ random bits; the computation of the polynomial $F(\vec{x})$ requires about R arithmetic operations in $\mathcal{R}$ plus Rd additions in $\mathbb{Z}/N\mathbb{Z}$;

- the *size of the encrypted message* is about RQ bits;
- the *cost of decryption*: the evaluation of $F(\vec{a}) = m$ takes $O(Rd\log(2N))$ arithmetic operations in $\mathcal{R}$.

In the $\mathbb{F}_q$-case, the above scheme can be accelerated if *Alice* sets $e_1 = 1$, selects a random element $a \in \mathcal{R}^\times$ and $d-1$ random exponents $e_2, \dots, e_d \in \mathbb{Z}/(q-1)\mathbb{Z}$, and defines $\vec{a}$ as $(a^{e_1}, \dots, a^{e_d}) \in (\mathcal{R}^\times)^d$. Again we mention that the performance of the ENROOT algorithm can be improved if one uses more sophisticated algorithms to evaluate powers and sparse polynomials; see [**4, 5, 6, 16, 18**]. Another possible way to improve performance is to use at Step 4 only $k < d$ randomly selected polynomials from the set $\{f_1, \dots, f_d\}$. For the same level of security, there will be a trade-off between the complexity of Step 2 (hence the size of the private key) and the complexity of Step 4.

3.4. Security Considerations. The obvious way to attack the ENROOT cryptosystem is to try to find a simultaneous solution to the system of polynomial equations

$$f_j(\vec{x}) = 0, \qquad j = 1, \dots, d, \tag{3.1}$$

which amounts to solving the hard problem in Section 3.1. All known algorithms to solve systems of polynomial equations of total degree n require (regardless of sparsity) an amount of time that is polynomial in n (that is, exponential time with respect to the bit length of n); see [**8, 17**]. Since the degrees of the polynomials in (3.1) will be very large in practical implementations (about the size of N), this attack is totally infeasible.

Another possibility is to simply "guess" a solution. One expects that a system of τ-sparse polynomial equations in d variables of high degree over $\mathcal{R}$ will have very few zeros if $d \ge 2$, even though the number of zeros of a polynomial over an arbitrary ring is not necessarily bounded by the degree. Working heuristically, if we view the vector of polynomials $\vec{f}(\vec{x}) = (f_1(\vec{x}), \dots, f_d(\vec{x}))$ as defining a "random" map $\vec{f} : \mathcal{R}^d \to \mathcal{R}^d$, then the expected number of roots common to all of the polynomials $f_j(\vec{x})$ (that is, the cardinality of the kernel of $\vec{f}$) is given by

$$\frac{1 - \#\mathcal{R}^{d(1-\#\mathcal{R}^d)}}{1 - (1 - \#\mathcal{R}^{-d})^{\#\mathcal{R}^d}} \approx \frac{1}{1 - e^{-1}} \approx 1.5819,$$

hence this brute force attack will take roughly $0.245\#\mathcal{R}^d$ trials "on average" to succeed. For arbitrary rings, we expect the choice $d \ge 2$ will provide the 2^{90} level of security against this attack if N is at least 50 bits long.

Although it is tempting to choose $d = \ell = 1$, in this case there are more sophisticated attacks that provide some information about *Alice*'s private key. One of these is based upon consideration of the difference set of the powers of monomials occurring in the polynomial $F(x)$. Indeed, if

$$f(x) = \sum_{i=1}^{t} A_i x^{n_i} \qquad \text{and} \qquad g(x) = \sum_{j=1}^{s} B_i x^{m_j}$$

are the polynomials selected by *Alice* and *Bob*, respectively, with $n_1 = m_1 = 0$ (and such that the sets $\{n_1, \dots, n_t\}$ and $\{m_1, \dots, m_s\}$ have a reasonably large intersection) then $F(x)$ contains at most $\tau \le st$ monomials $C_\nu x^{r_\nu}$, where

$$r_\nu \equiv n_i + m_j \pmod{N}, \qquad \nu = 1, \dots, \tau,$$

for some $i = 1, \dots, t$ and $j = 1, \dots, s$.

Consequently, finding the repeated elements in the difference set

$$\Delta = \{r_\nu - r_\eta \pmod N \mid \nu, \eta = 1, \dots, \tau\},$$

may reveal some information about the polynomial $f(x)$.

In addition, if $d = 1$, one can also compute the greatest common divisor of $f(x)$ with $x^{N+1} - x$. Since this polynomial will have lower degree than f in general, it would be easier to find a root from a theoretical standpoint. Although it is not clear how to do this in an amount of time that is polynomial in the sparsity rather than in the degree of $f(x)$, it remains a potential threat.

On the other hand, these attacks on ENROOT fail when $d > \ell \geq 2$. Indeed, the first attack may help to gain some information about the total set of monomials in all of the polynomials $f_1, \dots, f_d$, but it does not provide any information about the individual polynomials since it is impossible to determine which monomial comes from which product $f_j g_j$, $j = 1, \dots, d$. In order to try all possible partitions into d groups of $s_j t_j$ monomials, $j = 1, \dots, d$, needs to examine

$$\mathcal{P} = \frac{R!}{(s_1 t_1)! \dots (s_d t_d)!} \tag{3.2}$$

total combinations. In particular, the most interesting case is when $s_1, \dots, s_d$ are of approximately the same size as well as $t_1, \dots, t_d$, that is, when $s_j \sim s$ and $t_j \sim t$ for $j = 1, \dots, d$. In this case

$$\log \mathcal{P} \sim st(d \log d),$$

hence the number $\mathcal{P}$ of combinations to consider grows exponentially with respect to all parameters, provided that $d > \ell \geq 2$.

The second attack fails as well since the notion of greatest common divisor for multivariate polynomials is not defined, and taking resolvents to reduce to one variable is too costly.

However the case $d = 2$ is still not secure. Indeed, in this case we have either $d = \ell = 2$ or $\ell = 1$. In either case there are very simple linear algebra attacks which do not apply when $d > \ell \geq 2$ which we believe to be completely secure against the aforementioned attacks. There are some other alternative ways to guarantee that there are sufficiently many common elements in the sets of exponents of monomials of $f_1, \dots, f_d$. In particular, the first few monomials of each polynomial $h_1, \dots, h_d$ can be selected the same exponents.

Finally, we remark that the ENROOT cryptosystem is probably secure against lattice attacks for the same reason that the SPIFI scheme is secure (see Section 2.5): most lattice attacks would necessarily be based on lattices of dimension equal to the cardinality of $\#\mathcal{R}$, and in practical implementations this number would be very large.

References

[1] F. Bao, R. H. Deng, W. Geiselmann, C. Schnorr, R. Steinwandt and H. Wu, 'Crytoanalysis of two sparse polynomial based cryptosystems', *Proc. Int. Conf. on Public Key Cryptography, PKC'2001, Lect. Notes in Comp. Sci.*, Springer-Verlag, Berlin, 2001, to appear.

[2] W. Banks, D. Lieman and I. E. Shparlinski, 'An identification scheme based on sparse polynomials', *Lect. Notes in Comp. Sci.*, Springer-Verlag, Berlin, **1751**, 68–74.

[3] W. Banks, D. Lieman, I. Shparlinski, and V. To, "Cryptographic applications of sparse polynomials over finite rings," in *Proceedings of ICISC2000 (Seoul)*, Lecture Notes in Comput. Sci. **2015**, Springer-Verlag, Berlin (2001).

[4] H. Cohen *A course in computational algebraic number theory*, Springer-Verlag, Berlin, 1997.

[5] J. von zur Gathen and J. Gerhard, *Modern computer algebra*, Cambridge Univ. Press, Cambridge, 1999.

[6] D. M. Gordon, 'A survey of fast exponentiation methods', *J. Algorithms*, **27** (1998), 129–146.

[7] D. Grant, K. Krastev, D. Lieman and I. E. Shparlinski, 'A public key cryptosystem based on sparse polynomials', *Proc. International Conference on Coding Theory, Cryptography and Related Areas, Guanajuato, 1998*, Springer-Verlag, Berlin, 2000, 114–121.

[8] M.-D. A. Huang and Y.-C. Wong, 'Solving systems of polynomial congruences modulo a large prime', *Proc. 37 IEEE Symp. on Found. of Comp. Sci.*, 1996, 115–124.

[9] J. Hoffstein, B. S. Kaliski, D. Lieman, M. J. B. Robshaw and Y. L. Yin, 'A new identification scheme based on polynomial evaluation', *US Patent*, No. **No. 6076163**, 2000.

[10] J. Hoffstein, D. Lieman and J. H. Silverman, 'Polynomial Rings and Efficient Public Key Authentication', *Proc. the International Workshop on Cryptographic Techniques and E-Commerce*, City University of Hong Kong Press, to appear.

[11] J. Hoffstein, J. Pipher and J. H. Silverman, 'NTRU: A ring based public key cryptosystem', *Lect. Notes in Comp. Sci.*, Springer-Verlag, Berlin, **1433** (1998), 267–288.

[12] J. Hoffstein and J. H. Silverman, 'Polynomial rings and efficient public key authentication II', *Proc. the International Workshop on Cryptography and Computational Number Theory, Singapore, 1999*, Birkhäuser, to appear.

[13] J. Hoffstein and J. H. Silverman, 'Optimizations for NTRU', *Public Key Cryptography and Computational Number Theory, Warsaw, 2000*, available from `http://www.ntru.com`.

[14] N. Howgrave-Graham, J. H. Silverman, A. Singer, and W. Whyte, 'Choosing Parameter Sets for NTRUEncrypt with NAEP and SVES-3', *Proceedings of CT-RSA 2005*; expanded version available from `http://www.ntru.com`.

[15] A. Knopfmacher and J. Knopfmacher, 'Counting polynomials with a given number of zeros in a finite field', *Linear and Multilinear Algebra*, **26** (1990), 287–292.

[16] N. Pippenger, 'On the evaluation of powers and monomials', *SIAM J. Comp.*, **9** (1980), 230–250.

[17] I. E. Shparlinski, *Finite fields: Theory and computation*, Kluwer Acad. Publ., Dordrecht, 1999.

[18] A. C.-C. Yao, 'On the evaluation of powers', *SIAM J. Comp.*, **5** (1976), 100–103.

Department of Mathematics, University of Missouri, Columbia, Missouri 65211
E-mail address: `bbanks@math.missouri.edu`

Proceedings of Symposia in Applied Mathematics
Volume **62**, 2005

Playing "Hide-and-Seek" with Numbers: The Hidden Number Problem, Lattices and Exponential Sums

Igor E. Shparlinski

ABSTRACT. We give a survey of recent results on the *hidden number problem* introduced by Boneh and Venkatesan in 1996 and its numerous generalizations. Many of the results in this area are based on a rather surprising combination of two celebrated number theoretic techniques: bounds of *exponential sums* and *lattice basis reduction* algorithms, which are briefly outlined as well. We also describe several cryptographic applications and outline some possible directions for further research.

1. Preliminaries

1.1. Introduction. It has been discovered by Boneh and Venkatesan [**18, 19**] that studying the bit security problem for the *Diffie–Hellman secret key* naturally leads to a problem of recovering an unknown integer a from several most (or least) significant bits of residues of the products at modulo a large prime p. The multipliers t are known but are very weakly "controlled" and cannot be chosen in advance. These multipliers can however be arranged to be random elements of a subgroup of the unit group in the finite field of p elements.

This problem, called the *hidden number problem*, has since proved to have a wide spectrum of applications and appeared in a number of other questions, related and unrelated to cryptography.

The proposed in [**18, 19**] approach has revealed very interesting links with *lattice basis reduction* algorithms. This method alone is usually enough to design heuristic algorithms, however, it is rarely enough to derive rigorous results. So, in [**50**], yet another powerful number theoretic technique, the method of *exponential sums*, has been brought into this area. In fact several other number theoretic results have made their way into this area too. For example, quite unexpectedly, even results on the *Waring problem* in finite fields have turned out to be relevant, see [**115, 117**], where this link has been discovered and exploited (it has also proved to be useful for some other applications, see [**29, 116**]).

1991 *Mathematics Subject Classification.* Primary 11H09, 11T23, 11T71, 11Y16; Secondary 68Q25, 94A60.

Here we try to describe the hidden number problem in its most general form and also give a detailed account of various concrete cases which have been studied in the literature. We also give a brief outline of underlying number theoretic techniques and hope that this survey may contribute to further cross-fertilization among mathematics, computer science and cryptography.

1.2. Generic Hidden Number Problem. In the most general form the *hidden number problem*, **HNP**, can be described as follows. Let us consider a parametric family of maps

$$f_\beta : \mathcal{D} \to \mathcal{V}, \qquad \beta \in \mathcal{A},$$

between two algebraic domains $\mathcal{D}, \mathcal{V}$ depending on a parameter β (which could be a vector) from a certain set of possible parameters $\mathcal{A}$.

> Generic-**HNP**: *Given some partial information about the values $f_\alpha(t) \in \mathcal{V}$ for several test values of t, selected uniformly at random from some subset $\mathcal{T} \subseteq \mathcal{D}$, find α.*

We are interested in finding an efficient (usually polynomial time) algorithm to recover α which uses as few as possible (usually polynomially many) test points $t \in \mathcal{T}$.

We remark that the functions f_α are usually easily invertible; thus, having an exact value of $f_\alpha(t)$ for one $\alpha \in \mathcal{A}$ is enough for recovering t. As well, having $f_\alpha(t)$ for one $t \in \mathcal{T}$ is enough for recovering α. Therefore, the difficulty of this problem lies not in the difficulty of inverting $f_\alpha(t)$ (as a function of either α or t) as in many other cryptographic situations, but rather in the difficulty of collecting together partial information provided for distinct values of $t \in \mathcal{T}$.

Typically (but not always) the domains $\mathcal{D}$ and $\mathcal{V}$ are finite fields or residue rings.

There is certainly no general approach to the Generic-**HNP** in its full generality. However, for different choices of the sets $\mathcal{A}, \mathcal{D}, \mathcal{T}, \mathcal{V}$, the family $\{f_\beta \mid \beta \in \mathcal{A}\}$ and the type (and amount) of information revealed about $f_\alpha(t)$, one gets different instances of this problem and each of them requires a somewhat individual approach. Typically, the values of the "evaluation" points t are exactly given, although the situation when only some partial information about them is available is of interest and has several important applications. One can also consider the case when the values of t can be chosen by the algorithm itself rather than selected at random from $\mathcal{T}$. Usually in this case one can get much stronger results than in the case when there is no control over the values of t, For example, several strong results about hard core bits of the RSA function and discrete logarithm have been obtained by using these variants of the **HNP**, see [**43, 44, 47, 58**].

Finally, one can also imagine the situation when one or both of the domains $\mathcal{D}, \mathcal{V}$ are not known. For instance, it may be known that $\mathcal{D} = \mathcal{V} = \mathbb{F}_p$ for some unknown prime p but the test values t as well as some information about $f_\alpha(t)$ are both described in terms which do not involve p, for example, both are given as some integer numbers. Problems of this type seem to be especially hard, however some of them succumb to quantum algorithms, see [**57**].

So, as one can easily see, there is large variety of possible types of the **HNP**. Nevertheless, some general strategies have recently been developed.

The main, but not the only, area of applications of the problems considered here is cryptography. Several recent notions of security measure the robustness of a cryptographic scheme in terms of the chances a malicious adversary has of retrieving any information other than that explicitly given away by the scheme. In particular, it is of great importance to be able to measure the amount of "secret bits" of certain secret primitives associated with the scheme (such as bits of the message or bits of the exchanged secret key) accessible, with a certain probability, to a potential attacker.

The **HNP** approach has proved to be a valuable tool in this area. For instance, this approach has been used to prove certain bit security results for the Diffie-Hellman key exchange system [**18, 48, 49, 50**] and the Shamir message passing scheme [**18, 51**], as well as for the XTR and LUC cryptosystems [**85, 108**]. It has also been used to design provable attacks on the Digital Signature Scheme [**95**] and its modifications, including the Nyberg–Rueppel scheme [**32**], which are provably insecure under certain conditions. Elliptic curve variants of the above schemes are also accessible for studying by this method [**17, 96**].

Here we give a brief survey of some special cases of this problem, mainly those which admit polynomial time algorithms. We also outline various applications of these results and pose some open problems.

We have already mentioned that bounds of exponential sums and lattice basis reduction algorithms are principal ingredients of most of our results. Besides some of them use bounds for the number of solutions of various equations over finite fields.

We remark, that although most of the problems which are discussed in this paper have cryptographic motivation and interpretation they have also found a number of applications to other areas, such as pseudorandom number generators, correcting noisy oracles for polynomials and exponential functions, and non-approximability results for permanent and some other linear algebra functions.

1.3. Notation. Throughout this paper $\log z$ denotes the binary logarithm of $z > 0$. As usual, for a prime power q we denote by $\mathbb{F}_q$ the finite field of q elements. Given a prime p we assume that $\mathbb{F}_p$ consists of elements $\{0, 1, \dots, p-1\}$.

For integers s and $m \geq 1$ we denote by $\lfloor s \rfloor_m$ the remainder of s on division by m. Given an integer m and $\ell > 0$, we denote by $\mathrm{MSB}_{\ell,m}(x)$ any integer u such that

$$\left| \lfloor x \rfloor_m - u \right| \leq m/2^{\ell+1}.$$

Roughly speaking, $\mathrm{MSB}_{\ell,m}(x)$ gives ℓ most significant bits of the remainder of x modulo m. However, this definition is more flexible and suits better our purposes. In particular we remark that ℓ in the above inequality need not be an integer.

We need to recall the notion of *discrepancy*, one of the most important technical tools of our approach. The discrepancy of an N-element sequence

$$\Gamma = \{\gamma_1, \dots, \gamma_N\}$$

of elements of the interval $[0, 1]$ is defined as

$$\mathcal{D}(\Gamma) = \sup_{J \subseteq [0,1]} \left| \frac{A(J, N)}{N} - |J| \right|, \tag{1.1}$$

where the supremum is extended over all subintervals J of $[0, 1]$, $|J|$ is the length of J, and $A(J, N)$ denotes the number of points γ_n in J for $1 \leq n \leq N$.

All the necessary background in the theory of finite fields can be found in [**86**] and the necessary background in cryptology can be found in [**90**].

1.4. Acknowledgment. The author would like to thank Ricardo Dahab, Isabel González Vasco and Arne Winterhof for a patient and careful reading which helped to correct a number of minor inaccuracies in the original version of the paper and for many fruitful discussions. During the preparation of this paper, the author was supported in part by ARC grant DP0211459.

2. Specializations of HNP

2.1. HNP over $\mathbb{F}_p$ — $\mathbb{F}_p$-HNP. We start with the $\mathbb{F}_p$-**HNP**, introduced by Boneh and Venkatesan in [**18**], which has originated the whole direction of research:

> $\mathbb{F}_p$-**HNP**: *Recover a number $\alpha \in \mathbb{F}_p$ such that for k elements $t_1, \ldots, t_k \in \mathbb{F}_p^*$, chosen independently and uniformly at random, we are given k pairs*
>
> $$(t_i, \mathrm{MSB}_{\ell,p}(\alpha t_i)), \qquad i = 1, \ldots, k,$$
>
> *for some $\ell > 0$.*

Using an ingenious reduction to the closest vector problem and a certain lattice basis reduction algorithm, Boneh and Venkatesan [**18**], motivated by applications to the bit security of the Diffie–Hellman secret key, designed a deterministic polynomial time algorithm which for $\ell = \left\lceil \log^{1/2} p \right\rceil + \lceil 2 \log\log p \rceil$ and $k = O(\log^{1/2} p)$ recovers α for almost all choices of $t_1, \ldots, t_k \in \mathbb{F}_p^*$.

In fact, using the full power of the presently known lattice basis reduction algorithms such as those given in [**1, 104**] and some results of [**65**], one can reduce the number of bits to a slightly smaller number which is $o(\log p)$, see Section 2.2.

Boneh and Venkatesan have also proposed an alternative approach [**19**] which even works with values of ℓ as little as $\ell = \lceil 2 \log\log p \rceil$, but the resulting algorithm is *non-uniform*. The latter means that although such an algorithm exists, designing it takes exponential time. In [**115**], the algorithm of [**19**] has been extended to subgroups of $\mathbb{F}_p^*$. Unfortunately this approach has not received as much attention as the algorithm of [**18**] and its real power and possible applications remain unclear.

2.2. HNP over Arbitrary Sets — $\mathcal{T}$-HNP. It has turned out that for many applications, including some results about the so-called bit security of Diffie-Hellman, Shamir and some other cryptosystems [**50, 51, 85, 108, 109, 115, 117**] and rigorous results on attacks (following the *heuristic* arguments of [**62, 94**]) on the Digital Signature Algorithm (DSA) and DSA-like signature schemes [**32, 95, 96**], the condition that t is selected uniformly at random from $\mathbb{F}_p$ is too restrictive. This has actually been the reason why the original application of the $\mathbb{F}_p$-**HNP** for establishing a bit security result for the Diffie–Hellman secret key given in [**18**], has a minor gap in the proof. In [**50**], using exponential sums, this gap has been closed and the result extended to the more general situation where the generating element of the corresponding Diffie–Hellman scheme is not necessarily a primitive root of $\mathbb{F}_p$. In fact, that paper shows that bounds of exponential sums from [**59, 73**], combined with the ideas of [**18**], allow to solve the analogue of the $\mathbb{F}_p$-**HNP** with the test points $t_1, \ldots, t_k$ chosen from a multiplicative subgroup $\mathcal{G} \subseteq \mathbb{F}_p^*$. The size of this subgroup can be quite small; we only need $\#\mathcal{G} \geq p^{1/3+\varepsilon}$ for any sufficiently large prime p and only $\#\mathcal{G} \geq p^{\varepsilon}$ for almost all primes p. Certainly, using more recent bounds of [**20**], one can easily show that the condition $\#\mathcal{G} \geq p^{\varepsilon}$ is sufficient for all (rather than almost all) primes p.

The application of the $\mathbb{F}_p$-**HNP** to the Shamir message passing scheme, given in [**18**], has a similar problem. Accordingly, using some other bounds of exponential sums, a corrected and generalized version of the result of [**18**] has been obtained in [**51**]. Again, the test points are chosen from a certain subset of $\mathbb{F}_p$ rather than from the whole field.

Similar arguments have also been used in [**109**] to establish a bit security result for the function g^{x^2}, which corresponds to the "diagonal case" of the Diffie–Hellman mapping $(g^x, g^y) \to g^{xy}$.

Yet another set of test points t arises in the attack on DSA. This has been developed in [**94**] (which also simplifies and improves the attack from [**62**]). However, both [**62**] and [**94**] contain only *heuristic* results. In fact, in [**95**] the following generalization of the $\mathbb{F}_p$-**HNP** and the problems considered in [**50, 51, 109**] has been formulated and studied.

> $\mathcal{T}$-**HNP**: *Recover a number $\alpha \in \mathbb{F}_p$ such that for k elements $t_1, \ldots, t_k \in \mathcal{T}$, chosen independently and uniformly at random from some given subset $\mathcal{T} \subseteq \mathbb{F}_p$, we are given k pairs*
>
> $$(t_i, \mathrm{MSB}_{\ell,p}(\alpha t_i)), \qquad i = 1, \ldots, k,$$
>
> *for some $\ell > 0$.*

Certainly not for every set $\mathcal{T}$ the corresponding $\mathcal{T}$-**HNP** can be solved. However, in [**95**] a very general sufficient condition has been described for which this problem can be solved by using the same technique as in the original work of Boneh and Venkatesan [**18**]. This condition is related to uniformity of distribution of $\mathcal{T}$ among the elements of $\mathbb{F}_p$.

We say that a finite sequence $\mathcal{T}$ of integers is Δ-*homogeneously distributed modulo* m if for any integer a with $\gcd(a, m) = 1$, the discrepancy of the sequence $\{\lfloor at \rfloor_p / m\}_{t \in \mathcal{T}}$, given by (1.1) is at most Δ.

It has been proved in [**95**] that if $\mathcal{T}$ is $2^{-\log^{1/2} p}$-homogeneously distributed modulo p then the $\mathcal{T}$-**HNP** can be solved in polynomial time with

$$\ell = \left\lceil c \left(\frac{\log p \log \log \log p}{\log \log p} \right)^{1/2} \right\rceil$$

for any constant $c > 0$ and $k = \lceil 3 \log p / \ell \rceil$.

This result has been used in [**32, 96**] to design an attack on the *elliptic curve DSA*, the *Nyberg–Rueppel* and other DSA-like signature schemes.

The condition of $2^{-\log^{1/2} p}$-homogeneous distribution is rather weak. Thus, for quite weakly uniformly distributed sets $\mathcal{T}$ there is a polynomial time algorithm for the $\mathcal{T}$-**HNP**. For instance, this condition is trivially satisfied for $\mathcal{T} = \mathbb{F}_p^*$, as in the $\mathbb{F}_p$-**HNP**, but also for the sets which arise in [**32, 50, 51, 95, 96**], in the much stronger form of $p^{-\delta}$-homogeneous distribution with some constant $\delta > 0$. In each case bounds of exponential sums have played the key role. For example, the results of [**50, 51**] use the bounds from [**59, 73**]. The results of [**32, 95**] also make use of the bounds from [**59, 73**], as well as of the Weil bound, see [**86**], and the Vinogradov method of estimating double sums. Finally, the proof of the main result of [**96**] follows the same scheme as in [**32, 95**], but makes use of the bound from [**70**] (instead of the bounds from [**59, 73**]).

In [**115, 117**], a new ingredient has been brought into the above approach when it applies to sequences for which the property of the $2^{-\log^{1/2} p}$-homogeneous distribution modulo p is not known. Quite often for such sequences it is possible to establish that the sequence formed by s-sums

$$\mathcal{T}^s = \{t_1 + \ldots + t_s \mid t_1, \ldots, t_s \in \mathcal{T}\} \tag{2.1}$$

is $2^{-\log^{1/2} p}$-homogeneously distributed for some polynomially bounded value of s, that is, for some $s = \log^{O(1)} p$. It is shown in [**117**] how the basic algorithm of [**18**] can be modified to work with such sequences. For example, in [**117**], using a very weak bound from [**71**] which however applies to very small subgroups, the bit security result of the Diffie–Hellman secret key of [**18, 50**] has been extended to subgroups of arbitrary size. It would be interesting to find other applications of this approach of amplifying the uniformity of distribution properties of the original sequence $\mathcal{T}$.

For sets in the residue ring $\mathbb{Z}_m$ modulo m one can also obtain similar results, however the algorithm has now two alternatives: it either recovers α or finds a nontrivial divisor of m, see Chapter 18 in [**110**].

2.3. HNP with Approximately Given Points — $\mathcal{T}$-Approx-HNP. In the above instances we assumed that the evaluation points are exactly given. However, it has turned out that for some applications, including bit security of the "timed-release crypto" introduced by Rivest, Shamir and Wagner [**102**] and "correcting" noisy exponentiation black-boxes, see [**61**] for more details, the following problem arises, where only some partial information about the evaluation points t is known.

> $\mathcal{T}$-Approx-**HNP**: *Recover a number $\alpha \in \mathbb{F}_p$ such that for k elements $t_1, \ldots, t_k \in \mathcal{T}$, chosen independently and uniformly at random from some given subset $\mathcal{T} \subseteq \mathbb{F}_p$, we are given k pairs*
>
> $$(\mathrm{MSB}_{\ell,p}(t_i), \mathrm{MSB}_{\ell,p}(\alpha t_i)), \qquad i = 1, \ldots, k,$$
>
> *and also* $\mathrm{MSB}_{\ell,p}(\alpha)$ *for some* $\ell > 0$.

In [**61**], a polynomial time algorithm has been designed which solves the $\mathcal{T}$-Approx-**HNP** (and its analogue in some residue rings, including the residue rings corresponding to RSA moduli). The algorithm works for all sets of cardinality $\#\mathcal{T} \geq p^{1/2+\delta}$ with some fixed $\delta > 0$. In the case $\mathcal{T} = \mathbb{F}_p^*$ the algorithm works with

$$\ell = \left\lceil \left(\frac{4}{5} + \varepsilon\right) \log p \right\rceil \qquad \text{and} \qquad k = \lceil 4\varepsilon^{-1}/5 \rceil$$

for any $\varepsilon > 0$. This result has been rigorously proved. The paper [**61**] also contains an outline of another approach, which (*heuristically*) should work with a slightly smaller value of $\ell = \lceil (3/4 + \varepsilon) \log p \rceil$. Thus for the $\mathcal{T}$-Approx-**HNP** one needs many more bits to be known. In fact it has been shown in [**61**] that this is unavoidable, and the factor $4/5$ cannot be replaced with any other constant $\vartheta < 1/2$. Surprisingly enough this negative result is also based on bounds of exponential sums.

2.4. HNP for the Trace over $\mathbb{F}_q$ — $\mathrm{Tr}_{\mathbb{F}_q/\mathbb{F}_p}$-$\mathcal{T}$-HNP. There are many possible generalizations of the $\mathcal{T}$-**HNP** to extension fields. However, in studying bit security of XTR, see [**80, 81**], and LUC, see [**12, 118**], the following problem has emerged:

Let $\mathbb{F}_q$ be an extension of degree $m \geq 1$ of $\mathbb{F}_p$, $q = p^m$. Accordingly, let $\mathrm{Tr}_{\mathbb{F}_q/\mathbb{F}_p}(z)$ denote the trace of $z \in \mathbb{F}_q$ in $\mathbb{F}_p$, that is,

$$\mathrm{Tr}_{\mathbb{F}_q/\mathbb{F}_p}(z) = z + z^p + \ldots + z^{p^{m-1}}.$$

$\mathrm{Tr}_{\mathbb{F}_q/\mathbb{F}_p}$-$\mathcal{T}$-**HNP**: *Recover a number $\alpha \in \mathbb{F}_q$ such that for k elements $t_1, \ldots, t_k \in \mathcal{T} \subseteq \mathbb{F}_q$, chosen independently and uniformly at random, we are given k pairs*

$$\left(t_i, \mathrm{MSB}_{\ell,p}\left(\mathrm{Tr}_{\mathbb{F}_q/\mathbb{F}_p}(\alpha t_i)\right)\right), \qquad i = 1, \ldots, k,$$

for some $\ell > 0$.

We remark that for the $\mathrm{Tr}_{\mathbb{F}_q/\mathbb{F}_p}$-$\mathcal{T}$-**HNP** even the case $\ell = \lceil \log p \rceil$, that is, when the values $\mathrm{Tr}_{\mathbb{F}_q/\mathbb{F}_p}(\alpha t_i)$, $i = 1, \ldots, k$, are exactly given, is not immediately trivial. Nevertheless, it is easy to see that with $\ell = \lceil \log p \rceil$, the $\mathrm{Tr}_{\mathbb{F}_q/\mathbb{F}_p}$-$\mathcal{T}$-**HNP** is essentially a linear algebra problem, see [**48**].

For the $\mathrm{Tr}_{\mathbb{F}_q/\mathbb{F}_p}$-$\mathcal{T}$-**HNP** one can easily obtain a general characterization of the sets $\mathcal{T}$ for which it can be solved in polynomial time, similar to the one given in [**95**] for the $\mathcal{T}$-**HNP**. However, only the case where $\mathcal{T} = \mathcal{G}$ is a multiplicative subgroup of $\mathbb{F}_q^*$ seems to have applications and thus this is the only case which has been studied, see [**85, 108**]. As the bounds of exponential sums from [**59, 73**] cannot be extended to $\mathbb{F}_q$, accordingly the algorithms of [**85, 108**] either apply to relatively large subgroups or to a substantially large number of bits. For example, the algorithm obtained in [**108**] needs a linear portion of bits to be known. In fact, instead of using bounds of exponential sums, the bound from [**25**] on the number of zeros of some sparse polynomials has been used in [**108, 111**].

The results of [**108**], at least in its part relevant to the applications to XTR and LUC, have been drastically improved in [**85**], where in several important cases, a polynomial time algorithm has been designed for the $\mathrm{Tr}_{\mathbb{F}_q/\mathbb{F}_p}$-$\mathcal{T}$-**HNP** with $\ell = \left\lceil \log^{1/2} p \right\rceil$. The method of [**85**] is based on a certain bound of exponential sums conjectured by Deligne in [**36**] (and proved in some special case). In the full generality, it has been proved by Katz [**66**] (the proof follows from Theorem 4.1.1 of [**66**] after some standard transformations). In fact, for the cases relevant to the XTR and LUC cryptosystems, simpler and more explicit statements are given in [**83**] and in Chapter 6 of [**84**], see [**85**] for more details.

It is quite plausible that the approach of [**115, 117**] can be applied to the $\mathrm{Tr}_{\mathbb{F}_q/\mathbb{F}_p}$-$\mathcal{T}$-**HNP** as well. In particular, one can probably use a very weak bound of [**106**] which however applies to very small subgroups of $\mathbb{F}_{2^n}$ (or any other finite field of small characteristic).

2.5. HNP with Chosen Test Points — $\mathcal{T}$-CTP-HNP. As we have already mentioned, in some scenarios, the test points $t \in \mathcal{T}$ can be chosen by the algorithm. This certainly allows us to obtain much more powerful results. Note that even if test points t can be chosen the set $\mathcal{T}$ itself may remain unknown. That is, for $t \in \mathcal{T}$ we are given some partial information about $f_\alpha(t) \in \mathcal{V}$ but for $t \notin \mathcal{T}$, we are given just an arbitrary (but fixed) response. Of course the hardness of this problem is due to the fact that we cannot immediately decide whether $t \in \mathcal{T}$ or not.

$\mathcal{T}$-CTP-**HNP**: *Recover a number $\alpha \in \mathbb{F}_p$ such that for some unknown subset $\mathcal{T} \subseteq \mathbb{Z}_m$ and k appropriately chosen test points*

$t_1, \dots, t_k \in \mathbb{Z}_m$, we are given k pairs

$$(t_i, u_i), \qquad i = 1, \dots, k,$$

where $u_i = \mathrm{MSB}_{\ell,m}(t_i)$ for some $\ell > 0$ if $t_i \in \mathcal{T}$ and u_i is an arbitrary element of $\mathbb{Z}_m$ otherwise (but always the same for the same value of t_i).

In particular, this problem arises in proving very strong bit security results of RSA in the "noisy" oracle model, see [**58**]. In fact, it is shown in [**58**] that for any set $\mathcal{T} \in \mathbb{Z}_m$ of cardinality $\mathcal{T} \geq (0.5 + \delta)m$ with some fixed $\delta > 0$ and $\ell = 1$ there is a polynomial time algorithm which either finds a factor of m or recovers α, see also Chapter 18 of [**110**]. A certain variant of this problem has also been considered in [**17**].

2.6. HNP in a Free Module over a Commutative Ring — Module-HNP. Let $\mathcal{R}$ be a commutative ring with identity and $\mathcal{M}$ a free module of dimension $n \geq 1$ over $\mathcal{R}$. Let $\mathrm{Hom}_{\mathcal{R}}(\mathcal{M}, \mathcal{R})$ denote the module of $\mathcal{R}$-linear homomorphisms of $\mathcal{M}$, see Section 2 of Chapter 3 of [**77**].

Let ψ be a certain fixed probability distribution on $\mathrm{Hom}_{\mathcal{R}}(\mathcal{M}, \mathcal{R})$.

It has been shown in [**48**] that some simple linear algebra arguments can be used to study the following problem:

Module-**HNP**: *Recover a number $\alpha \in \mathcal{M}$ such that for k elements $\tau_1, \dots, \tau_k \in \mathrm{Hom}_{\mathcal{R}}(\mathcal{M}, \mathcal{R})$, chosen independently at random according to the probability distribution ψ, we are given k pairs*

$$(\tau_i, \tau_i(\alpha)), \qquad i = 1, \dots, k.$$

The exact expression for the complexity of the algorithm of [**48**] depends on the complexity of linear algebra over $\mathcal{R}$ and on the density of singular matrices over $\mathcal{R}$.

2.7. HNP for Inversion Modulo p — $\mathbb{F}_p$-Inverse-HNP. Yet another type of the **HNP** has been introduced and studied in [**15**]:

$\mathbb{F}_p$-Inverse-**HNP**: *Recover a number $\alpha \in \mathbb{F}_p$ such that for k elements $t_1, \dots, t_k \in \mathbb{F}_p$, chosen independently and uniformly at random, we are given k pairs*

$$\left(t_i, \mathrm{MSB}_{\ell,p}\left(\frac{1}{\alpha + t_i}\right)\right), \qquad i = 1, \dots, k,$$

for some $\ell > 0$.

The most essential distinction of the $\mathbb{F}_p$-Inverse-**HNP** from the previously mentioned variants of the **HNP** is its non-linearity. Nevertheless, the authors of [**15**] have found a way to linearize this problem and construct two polynomial time algorithms which recover α, provided that ℓ is sufficiently large. One algorithm works with

$$\ell = \left\lceil \left(\frac{2}{3} + \varepsilon\right) \log p \right\rceil$$

for any $\varepsilon > 0$, and the authors claim that this algorithm can be rigorously analyzed and proved. The other algorithm of [**15**] needs fewer bits and works with

$$\ell = \left\lceil \left(\frac{1}{3} + \varepsilon\right) \log p \right\rceil,$$

however it is only *heuristic* and it is not clear how to prove that it always works correctly. Nevertheless the authors of [**15**] believe that the above bound is tight and thus α cannot be recovered in polynomial time for smaller values of ℓ.

We also remark that several interesting cryptographic applications of the $\mathbb{F}_p$-Inverse-**HNP** have been outlined in [**15**] and we complete agree with the authors of [**15**] that it deserves a further detailed study.

Quantum algorithms for this problem and also a more general problem for some parametric classes of rational functions over $\mathbb{F}_p$ have been developed in [**57**].

2.8. HNP on Elliptic Curves — EC-HNP. Certainly elliptic curves provide an interesting source of cryptographic applications. Accordingly, one can consider the following problem which has also been briefly mentioned firstly in [**18**] and then in [**15**].

Let $\mathcal{E}$ be an elliptic curve over $\mathbb{F}_p$. We also denote by $\mathcal{E}(\mathbb{F}_p)$ the group of $\mathbb{F}_p$-rational points on $\mathcal{E}$, including the point at infinity as identity. We use $\oplus$ for the group operation on $\mathcal{E}$. For a point $P \in \mathcal{E}(\mathbb{F}_p)$ we denote by $x(P)$ its x-component in a given fixed affine model of $\mathcal{E}$.

EC-**HNP**: *Recover a point $A \in \mathcal{E}(\mathbb{F}_p)$ such that for k points $T_1, \ldots, T_k \in \mathcal{E}(\mathbb{F}_p)$, chosen independently and uniformly at random, we are given k pairs*

$$(T_i, \mathrm{MSB}_{\ell,p}(x(A \oplus T_i))), \qquad i = 1, \ldots, k,$$

for some $\ell > 0$.

It is mentioned in [**15**] that the same linearization technique which applies to the $\mathbb{F}_p$-Inverse-**HNP** can be used for the EC-**HNP** and *heuristically* it should work with

$$\ell = \left\lceil \left(\frac{3}{5} + \varepsilon\right) \log p \right\rceil .$$

Also, it is claimed in [**15**] that a rigorous result is possible as well but with a much larger value of ℓ.

We remark that obtaining analogues of the bit security results from [**18, 50**] for the elliptic curve Diffie-Hellman scheme has been the primary motivation to consider the $\mathbb{F}_p$-Inverse-**HNP**. This motivation may not be so strong anymore because of the bit security results of [**17**] obtained by using very different ideas. Surprisingly enough for elliptic curves one can show that even one single bit of the elliptic curve Diffie–Hellman secret key is as secure as the whole key. The proof makes use of the whole family of certain twists of $\mathcal{E}$ and cannot been extended to the classical settings of the Diffie–Hellman scheme over $\mathbb{F}_p$. Nevertheless, the EC-**HNP** is very interesting on its own and certainly deserves more attention.

2.9. Polynomial HNP — Poly-HNP. It is natural to consider polynomials instead of linear functions as in the $\mathbb{F}_p$-**HNP**. In fact it makes sense to consider sparse polynomials of the form

$$f_\beta(X) = \sum_{j=1}^{s} \beta_j X^{e_j} \in \mathbb{F}_p[X]$$

where $\beta = (\beta_1, \ldots, \beta_s)$ is the coefficient vector and $e_1, \ldots, e_s$ are certain known exponents. Certainly the case of "dense" polynomials, $e_j = j$, $j = 1, \ldots, s$, is of interest as well. This leads to the following

Poly-**HNP**: *Recover a vector of coefficients* $\alpha \in \mathbb{F}_p^s$ *such that for* k *elements* $t_1, \ldots, t_k \in \mathbb{F}_p^*$, *chosen independently and uniformly at random, we are given* k *pairs*

$$(t_i, \mathrm{MSB}_{\ell,p}(f_\alpha(t_i))), \qquad i = 1, \ldots, k,$$

for some $\ell > 0$.

The case $\ell = \lceil \log p \rceil$, that is, when $f_\alpha(t_i)$, $i = 1, \ldots, k$ are exactly known, leads to a linear algebra problem. However the main difficulty is to show that the corresponding system of linear equations is non-singular, see [**48, 111**]. For smaller values of ℓ this problem has been studied in [**107, 116**].

The actual value of ℓ depends on the particular properties of the set of exponents $\{e_1, \ldots, e_s\}$ and can be as small as $(s \log p)^{1/2}$ for a very wide class of exponents. For a wider class of sets of exponents the algorithm of [**107**] requires

$$\ell = \left\lceil \left(1 - \frac{1}{s} + \varepsilon\right) \log p \right\rceil.$$

In [**116**], the technique of [**115, 117**] has been combined with certain bounds of exponential sums of [**28**] (which in turn generalize that of [**71**]). This has lead to very substantial improvements of some of the results of [**107**].

Finally, quantum algorithms for this and more general problems, which work for very small values of ℓ, sometimes for $\ell = 1 + \varepsilon$, and also for the case where p is not known, are given in [**57**].

A multiplicative analogue of the Poly-**HNP** has been considered in [**42**]. The problem is to recover a polynomial f of degree d over $\mathbb{F}_p$ or over $\mathbb{Z}$ given a black-box which for any t returns a multiple $m_t f(t)$ with some integer multiplicative "noise" $m_t \neq 0$. If $|m_t| \le M|t|^{(1-\varepsilon)/(d+2)}$ for some $M > 1$, the algorithm of [**42**] recovers $f(X) \in \mathbb{Z}[X]$ in polynomial time (polynomial in the degree and the bit size of the coefficients of f, ε^{-1} and $\log M$). A similar algorithm has also been obtained for $f(X) \in \mathbb{F}_p[X]$, provided that $|m_t| \le p^{(1-\varepsilon)/(d+2)^2}$ and p is large enough (thus in the $\mathbb{F}_p$ case the bound on $|m_t|$ is less generous). In fact such results can also be obtained in the case when the multipliers m_t are rational numbers with reasonably small numerators and denominators. Sparse polynomials can be studied as well. We remark however that for the approach of [**42**] it is essential to be able to choose the test points t is a special way, nominated by the algorithm, rather to have them at random. Thus obtaining an efficient algorithm in this case remains an important open problem.

Using bit strings derived from polynomial evaluations in $\mathbb{F}_p$ has been proposed as a pseudorandom generator in [**100**]. So the above results establish some limitations of this approach.

We also mention that the Poly-**HNP** is related to several other polynomial interpolation and approximation problems. In particular, it has links with *noisy polynomial interpolation* [**13, 55, 105, 120**], *testing, learning and reconstructing polynomials with noisy queries* [**3, 4, 31, 46, 64, 69**] and *sparse polynomial interpolation* [**26, 27, 53, 67, 76, 82, 87, 121, 122**].

2.10. HNP over Unknown Algebraic Number Fields — ANF-HNP. A **HNP** of a somewhat different spirit has recently been introduced and studied in [**112**]. To describe this problem we need to recall some basic facts of the theory of algebraic number fields.

Let $\mathbb{Z}_{\mathbb{K}}$ be the ring of integers of $\mathbb{K}$. We recall that the degree of a prime ideal p is the integer d such that the norm $\mathrm{Nm}(\mathsf{p}) = p^d$, where p is a rational prime number which is divisible by p, see Section 1 of Chapter 4 of [**93**]. It is also known that the residue ring $\mathbb{Z}_{\mathbb{K}}/\mathsf{p}$ is isomorphic to the finite field of p^d elements, $\mathbb{Z}_{\mathbb{K}}/\mathsf{p} \simeq \mathbb{F}_{p^d}$.

Let α be a root of an irreducible polynomial

$$F_\alpha(X) = f_n X^n + \ldots + f_1 X + f_0 \in Z[X], \quad f_n \neq 0,$$

which is the minimal polynomial of α over $\mathbb{Z}$. We denote by $\mathcal{P}_\alpha$ the set of all rational prime numbers p with $\gcd(p, f_n) = 1$ and which have a prime divisor p of first degree in $\mathbb{Z}_{\mathbb{K}}$. In particular, $\mathbb{Z}_{\mathbb{K}}/\mathsf{p} \simeq \mathbb{F}_p$ for $p \in \mathcal{P}_\alpha$.

It is known that p has a prime divisor p of first degree if and only if $F_\alpha(X)$ has a root modulo p, see Theorem 4.12 of [**93**].

We also remark that almost all prime ideals of $\mathbb{Z}_{\mathbb{K}}$ are of first degree, and the density of primes which are divisible by a prime ideal of first degree is $1/n$, see Theorem 7.11 of [**93**]. On the other hand, it is useful to recall that Corollary 2 of Proposition 7.10 of [**93**] shows that 'almost all' ideals are of the first degree.

Then for each prime number $p \in \mathcal{P}_\alpha$ and a prime ideal p of first degree which divides p, there exists an unique integer a, $0 \le a \le p-1$, such that $\alpha \equiv a \pmod{\mathsf{p}}$, where the congruence is considered in $\mathbb{Z}_{\mathbb{K}}$.

> ANF-**HNP**: *Recover a number* $\alpha \in \mathbb{K}$ *such that we are given* k *primes* $p_1, \ldots, p_k \in \mathcal{P}_\alpha$ *and* k *integers* $a_1, \ldots, a_k \in \mathbb{Z}$ *with* $\alpha \equiv a_i \pmod{\mathsf{p}_i}$, *where* p_i *is a prime ideal of first degree which divides* p_i, $i = 1, \ldots, k$.

It is shown in [**112**] that if for some constant $\tau > 0$ we have

$$p_1 \ldots p_k > 2^{\tau n^2 \log\log n / \log n} \left(\sum_{j=0}^{n} |f_j|^2 \right)^n,$$

then one can find α in randomized polynomial time (in $\log p_1, \ldots, \log p_k$ and n) with probability exponentially close to 1.

We remark that the ANF-**HNP** has been motivated by an idea of Amin Shokrollahi of using a hidden algebraic number field for an identification scheme. In fact, one of such possible schemes is briefly outlined in [**112**], see also Section 4.3.

2.11. Chinese Remaindering HNP — CR-HNP. The following problem is motivated by the series of papers [**14, 45, 54**].

Let $A > 0$ be a sufficiently large integer.

> CR-**HNP**: *Recover a number* $\alpha \in [0, A]$ *such that for* k *prime numbers* $p_1, \ldots, p_k$, *chosen independently and uniformly at random from the interval* $[2^{n-1}, 2^n]$, *we are given* k *pairs*
>
> $$(p_i, \mathrm{MSB}_{\ell, p_i}(\alpha)), \qquad i = 1, \ldots, k,$$
>
> *for some* $\ell > 0$.

In fact it is easy to see that one cannot find α exactly (for example, the provided information can both apply with high probability to α and to $\alpha + 1$).

A polynomial time algorithm to find a short interval containing all possible values of a has been given in [**113**]. A multiplicative analogue of the CR-**HNP** has been studied in [**114**].

2.12. Character Values HNP — χ-HNP. This problem has a somewhat different spirit and demonstrated how different could be the ways to provide some information about the target value.

Let χ be a nontrivial multiplicative character of $\mathbb{F}_p$. For example, for applications to pseudorandom number generators the case of the χ being the Legendre symbol is of special interest.

In fact it makes sense to consider monic square-free polynomials of the form

$$f_\beta(X) = \sum_{j=1}^{s} \beta_j X^j \in \mathbb{F}_p[X]$$

where $\beta = (\beta_1, \ldots, \beta_s)$ is the coefficient vector.

> χ-**HNP**: *Recover a vector of coefficients $\alpha \in \mathbb{F}_p^s$ such that for k elements $t_1, \ldots, t_k \in \mathbb{F}_p$, chosen independently and uniformly at random, we are given k pairs*
>
> $$(t_i, \chi(f_\alpha(t_i))), \qquad i = 1, \ldots, k.$$

The problem is of intrinsic interest and also has strong cryptographic motivation; sequences of values of quadratic characters have been considered as sources of cryptographically strong pseudorandom bits [**2, 16, 35, 37, 52, 56, 60, 88, 89, 101**]. It seems that even when $f_\beta(X) = X + \beta$ is a linear polynomial and the points $t_1, \ldots, t_k$ can be chosen by the algorithm (rather than random elements of $\mathbb{F}_p$) the problem is still extremely hard. However, in the above modification when the points $t_1, \ldots, t_k$ can be chosen by the algorithm, there are very efficient quantum algorithms [**33, 34, 103**]. It seems that [**103**] gives the best known deterministic algorithm. It is based on a somewhat subtle application of the Weil bound and takes about $O(p^{d+\varepsilon})$ steps. This improves slightly the brute force search which takes $O(p^{d+1+\varepsilon})$ steps and also an algorithm which is based on the "naive" use of the Weil bound, which leads to an algorithm requiring $O(p^{d+1/2+\varepsilon})$ steps. In any case, the χ-**HNP** and its modifications definitely deserve more attention.

3. How Does This Work?

3.1. Lattices and HNP. We explain the ideas underlying most of the above algorithms on the example of the $\mathbb{F}_p$-**HNP**. In fact we follow quite closely the pioneering paper [**18**].

Let $\{\mathbf{b}_1, \ldots, \mathbf{b}_s\}$ be a set of linearly independent vectors in $\mathbb{R}^s$. The set of vectors

$$L = \left\{ \sum_{i=1}^{s} n_i \mathbf{b}_i \mid n_i \in \mathbb{Z} \right\},$$

is called an s-dimensional full rank lattice. The set $\{\mathbf{b}_1, \ldots, \mathbf{b}_s\}$ is called a *basis* of L, and L is said to be spanned by $\{\mathbf{b}_1, \ldots, \mathbf{b}_s\}$.

One of the most fundamental problems in this area is the *closest vector problem*, **CVP**: given a basis of a lattice L in $\mathbb{R}^s$ and a target vector $\mathbf{u} \in \mathbb{R}^s$, find a lattice vector $\mathbf{v} \in L$ which minimizes the Euclidean norm $\|\mathbf{u} - \mathbf{v}\|$ among all lattice vectors. It is well know that **CVP** is **NP**-hard (see [**97, 98**] for references). However, its approximate version [**5**] admits a polynomial time algorithm which goes back to the lattice basis reduction algorithm of Lenstra, Lenstra and Lovász [**79**].

It has been remarked in Section 2.1 of [**91**] and then in Section 2.4 of [**97**] and Section 2.4 of [**98**] that combining [**104**] and [**65**] one can obtain the following statement which is somewhat stronger than that usually used in the literature. There exists a polynomial time algorithm which, given an s-dimensional full rank lattice L and a vector $\mathbf{r} \in \mathbb{R}^s$, finds a lattice vector $\mathbf{v}$ satisfying the inequality

$$\|\mathbf{v} - \mathbf{r}\| \le 2^{O\left(s \log^2 \log s / \log s\right)} \min\{\|\mathbf{z} - \mathbf{r}\|, \quad \mathbf{z} \in L\}. \tag{3.1}$$

One can also use a probabilistic analogue **[1]** of this result which gives a slightly better constant.

We are now prepared to sketch the main ideas of **[18]** to solve the **HNP**. Let $d \ge 1$ be integer. Given t_i, $u_i = \mathrm{MSB}_{\ell,p}(\alpha t_i)$, $i = 1, \dots, d$, we build the lattice $\mathcal{L}(p, \ell, t_1, \dots, t_d)$ spanned by the rows of the matrix:

$$\begin{pmatrix} p & 0 & \dots & 0 & 0 \\ 0 & p & \ddots & \vdots & \vdots \\ \vdots & \ddots & \ddots & 0 & \vdots \\ 0 & 0 & \dots & p & 0 \\ t_1 & t_2 & \dots & t_d & 1/2^{\ell+1} \end{pmatrix}.$$

and notice

$$\mathbf{w} = \left(\lfloor \alpha t_1 \rfloor_p, \dots, \lfloor \alpha t_d \rfloor_p, \alpha/2^{\ell+1}\right) \in \mathcal{L}(p, \ell, t_1, \dots, t_d).$$

This vector is very close to the *known* vector $\mathbf{u} = (u_1, \dots, u_d, 0)$ (at the distance of order $p2^{-\ell}$). Thus applying one of the lattice basis reduction algorithms one can *hope* to recover $\mathbf{v}$ and thus α. In order to make this algorithm *rigorous* one needs to show that (for almost all choices of $t_1, \dots, t_d \in \mathbb{F}_p$) there is no other lattice vector which is close to $\mathbf{u}$. Namely, taking into account the "stretching" factor in CVP, we have to show that there are very few d-tuples $(t_1, \dots, t_d) \in \mathbb{F}_p^d$ for which the lattice $\mathcal{L}(p, \ell, t_1, \dots, t_d)$ has a vector $\mathbf{v} \ne \mathbf{w}$ and such that

$$\|\mathbf{v} - \mathbf{u}\| \le p2^{-\ell} \exp\left(O\left(\frac{d \log^2 \log d}{\log d}\right)\right).$$

The last inequality implies that

$$\|\mathbf{v} - \mathbf{w}\| \le p2^{-\ell} \exp\left(O\left(\frac{d \log^2 \log d}{\log d}\right)\right) \tag{3.2}$$

which is our main tool.

Any vector $\mathbf{v} \in \mathcal{L}(p, \ell, t_1, \dots, t_d)$ is of the form

$$\mathbf{w} = \left(\beta t_1 - \lambda_1 p, \dots, \beta t_d - \lambda_d p, \beta/2^{\ell+1}\right),$$

with some integers β and $\lambda_1, \dots, \lambda_d$. Thus (3.2) implies that for all $i = 1, \dots, d$ we have

$$(\alpha - \beta)t_i \equiv y_i \pmod p \tag{3.3}$$

for some $y_i \in [-h, h]$ where

$$h = p2^{-\ell} \exp\left(O\left(\frac{d \log^2 \log d}{\log d}\right)\right).$$

The probability that for t, chosen uniformly at random from $\mathbb{F}_p^*$, we have $\gamma t \equiv y \pmod p$ with some $y \in [-h, h]$ satisfies the inequality

$$\Pr_{t \in \mathbb{F}_p^*}\left[\gamma t \equiv y \pmod p \mid y \in [-h, h]\right] \le \frac{2h}{p} \tag{3.4}$$

for any $\gamma \neq 0$.

Therefore the probability P that (3.3) holds for all $i = 1, \ldots, d$ and at least one $\beta \neq \alpha$, is at most

$$P \leq (p-1)\left(\frac{2h+1}{p}\right)^d \leq p(3h/p)^d = p2^{-\ell d} \exp\left(O\left(\frac{d^2 \log^2 \log d}{\log d}\right)\right).$$

Thus if

$$\ell = \left\lceil C \frac{\log^{1/2} p \log\log\log p}{\log\log p} \right\rceil \qquad \text{and} \qquad d = 2\left\lceil \frac{\log p}{\ell} \right\rceil$$

with some absolute constant $C > 0$ then the lattice basis reduction algorithm returns $\mathbf{v}$ with probability exponentially close to 1.

3.2. Discrepancy and HNP. Analyzing the above argument on easily sees that the inequality (3.4) is the only place where we used that t is selected uniformly at random from $\mathbb{F}_p^*$. However, for a Δ-homogeneously distributed modulo p sequence $\mathcal{T}$, the inequality (3.4) can be replaced with

$$\Pr_{t \in \mathcal{T}} [\gamma t = y \pmod p \mid y \in [-h, h]] \leq \frac{2h}{p} + \Delta$$

which is quite enough to finish the arguments, provided that Δ is reasonably small.

Moreover, the same scheme works modulo a composite number as well: for $\gcd(\alpha - \beta, m) = 1$ we use the above arguments. Otherwise either $\alpha \equiv \beta \pmod n$ or $m > \gcd(\alpha - \beta, n) > 1$ and we have a nontrivial divisor of m.

Finally, establishing the property of Δ-homogeneous distribution ultimately leads to studying exponential sums with elements of the sequence $\mathcal{T}$. In some applications $\mathcal{T}$ has a very nice and well-studied number-theoretic structure. Examples include, bit security results for the Diffie–Hellman, LUC and XTR and schemes, see [**18, 50, 85, 115, 117**], where $\mathcal{T}$ is just a subgroup of a multiplicative group of a finite field. Thus one can apply the variety of results readily available from [**36, 20, 59, 71, 72, 73, 99**]. On the other hand, in some applications the corresponding sequence $\mathcal{T}$ is rather intricate. Examples include, applications to DSA-like and Nyberg-Rueppel signature schemes, see [**32, 95, 96**], where one has to apply and combine several methods of estimation of exponential sums in order to establish the desired result.

3.3. Exponential Sums and HNP. Exponential sums provide a natural tool to study the discrepancy. In particular, the following statement goes back to pioneering works of Polya and Vinogradov on exponential sums and their applications, see Corollary 3.11 of [**99**]. Any sequence $\mathcal{T}$ of elements of $\mathbb{F}_p$ is Δ-homogeneously distributed modulo p with

$$\Delta = O\left(\frac{\log p}{\#\mathcal{T}} \max_{1 \leq c \leq p-1} \left|\sum_{t \in \mathcal{T}} \exp(2\pi i c t/p)\right|\right).$$

Thus to prove that the algorithm based on the arguments of Sections 3.1 and 3.2 apply to a certain sequence $\mathcal{T}$ and solves the $\mathcal{T}$-**HNP**, one needs nontrivial bounds of exponential sums with elements of this sequence.

Moreover, if such bounds are too weak to guarantee the desired level of uniformity of distribution, then one can consider the sequence of s-sums $\mathcal{T}^s$ given by (2.1). Namely, for the sequence $\mathcal{T}^s$ we have the Δ_s-homogeneous distribution modulo p with

$$\Delta_s = O\left(\frac{\log p}{(\#\mathcal{T})^s} \max_{1\le c\le p-1}\left|\sum_{t\in\mathcal{T}} \exp(2\pi ict/p)\right|^s\right).$$

Thus any gain against the trivial upper bound for the above exponential sums (which is just $\#\mathcal{T}$ of course), grows exponentially with s. This simple observation underlies the modifications of the scheme of [**18**] proposed in [**115, 117**].

In some cases, for example for proving bit security of the Diffie–Hellman key, see Section 4.1, the corresponding sequence $\mathcal{T}$ has a very nice number theoretic structure and one can use bounds of exponential sums which already exist in number theoretic literature. For example, for the aforementioned bit security results one can use the following breakthrough result of [**20**] which improves a series of previously known bounds [**59, 72, 73**]. For any $\varepsilon > 0$ there exists $\delta > 0$ such that for any element $g \in \mathbb{F}_p^*$ of multiplicative order $T \ge p^\varepsilon$ the bound

$$\max_{\gcd(c,p)=1}\left|\sum_{x=0}^{T-1} \exp(2\pi icg^x/p)\right| = O\left(T^{1-\delta}\right) \tag{3.5}$$

holds. In particular (3.5) immediately implies an improvement of the results of [**50**] and several other papers, which are based on weaker bounds [**59, 73**].

As we have remarked, in [**115, 117**] the s-fold sequence (2.1) for the subgroup $\mathcal{T} = \mathcal{G} \subseteq \mathbb{F}_p^*$ generated by g, has been considered together with the bound of [**71**]

$$\max_{\gcd(c,p)=1}\left|\sum_{x=0}^{T-1} \exp(2\pi icg^x/p)\right| \le T\left(1 - \frac{C(\varepsilon)}{(\log p)^{1+\varepsilon}}\right)$$

which holds for any

$$T \ge \frac{\log p}{(\log\log p)^{1-\varepsilon}},$$

where the constant $C(\varepsilon) > 0$ depends only on ε. The gain against the trivial bound T is extremely small, but for the s-fold sequence (2.1) with, say, $s = \log^{2+\varepsilon} p$ the gain is already quite substantial.

On the other hand, in some cases, the sequence $\mathcal{T}$ has a very artificial structure and obtaining bounds of the corresponding exponential sums becomes a rather challenging problem. For example, for the sequence (3.7), appearing in the attack of [**94, 95**] on DSA, such a bound is given in [**95**] by using a combination of the bounds of exponential sums with exponential functions from [**59, 73**] with the *Weil* bound, see [**86**], and the Vinogradov method of estimates of double sums.

We recall the DSA settings. Assume that q and p are primes with $q|p-1$ and that $g \in \mathbb{F}_p$ is a fixed element of multiplicative order q. Let $\mathcal{M}$ be the set of messages to be signed and let $h : \mathcal{M} \to \mathbb{F}_q$ be an arbitrary *hash-function*. They all (that is, p, q, g, $\mathcal{M}$, h) are *publicly* known.

The *secret key* is an element $\alpha \in \mathbb{F}_q^*$ which is known only to the signer.

To sign a message $\mu \in \mathcal{M}$, the signer chooses a random integer $k \in \mathbb{F}_q^*$ usually called the *nonce*, and which must be kept secret. We define the following two elements of $\mathbb{F}_q$:

$$r(k) = \left\lfloor \left\lfloor g^k \right\rfloor_p \right\rfloor_q, \qquad s(k,\mu) = \left\lfloor k^{-1}\left(h(\mu) + \alpha r(k)\right)\right\rfloor_q. \tag{3.6}$$

The pair $(r(k), s(k,\mu))$ is the *DSA signature* of the message μ with a nonce k.

The attack on the DSA which has been developed in [**94**] (and which simplifies and improves the attack from [**62**]) is based on solving the **HNP** with the sequence

$$\mathcal{T} = \left\{ \lfloor 2^{-\ell} r(k) s(k,\mu)^{-1} \rfloor_q \mid (k,\mu) \in \mathcal{S} \right\}, \tag{3.7}$$

where $\mathcal{S}$ is the set of pairs $(k,\mu) \in [1, q-1] \times \mathcal{M}$ with $s(k,\mu) \neq 0$.

Denote by W the number of solutions of the equation

$$h(\mu_1) = h(\mu_2), \qquad \mu_1, \mu_2 \in \mathcal{M}.$$

Thus $W/|\mathcal{M}|^2$ is the probability of *collision* and expected to be of order q^{-1} for any practically usable hash function.

In [**95**] the heuristic results of [**94**] have been made rigorous by proving a nontrivial upper bound of exponential sums with elements of the sequence (3.7). The main difficulty is that the double reduction in $r(k)$, modulo p and then modulo q, erases any number theoretic structure in the exponential function g^k. Using the new bound of [**20**] together with the arguments of [**95**] one can show that for any any $\varepsilon > 0$ there exists $\delta > 0$ and $g \in \mathbb{F}_p$ of multiplicative order $q \geq p^{\varepsilon}$ the bound

$$\max_{\gcd(a,q)=1} \left| \sum_{(k,\mu)\in\mathcal{S}} \exp\left(2\pi i a t(k,\mu)/q\right) \right| = O\left(W^{1/2} q^{3/2-\delta}\right) \tag{3.8}$$

holds.

As in the situation with [**50**], the paper [**95**] makes use of weaker bounds from [**59, 73**], which certainly have led to weaker results.

For the elliptic curve analogue of DSA one can use [**70**] instead of [**20, 59, 72, 73**], see [**96**]. In either case, these bounds are quite adequate for the purposes on [**95, 96**]. On the other hand, in the case of sequence appearing in the attack on the Nyberg-Rueppel signature scheme and some other DSA-like schemes, the bounds of [**32**] are not quite satisfactory and it would be very interesting to extend them to a wide class of parameters.

In fact, even if the sequence $\mathcal{T}$ is not known to be homogeneously distributed but at least admits a non-trivial upper bound for the number of its elements in an interval, one can still obtain some nontrivial results about the corresponding $\mathcal{T}$-HNP. For example, the algorithms of [**107, 108**] are based on the obtained in [**25**] upper bound

$$T \leq 2q^{1-1/(k-1)} D^{1/(k-1)} + O(q^{1-2/(k-1)} D^{2/(k-1)}),$$

on the number T of solutions of the equation

$$\sum_{i=1}^{t} a_i x^{\tau_i} = 0, \qquad x \in \mathbb{F}_q^*,$$

with coefficient $a_1, \ldots, a_k \in \mathbb{F}_q^*$, and exponents $\tau_1, \ldots, \tau_k \in \mathbb{Z}$ and

$$D = \min_{1\leq i\leq t} \max_{j\neq i} \gcd(\tau_j - \tau_i, q-1),$$

see also [**110**].

4. Applications

4.1. Bit Security of the Diffie–Hellman Key. We recall the problem which underlies the Diffie–Hellman key exchange system: given an element g of order τ modulo p, find an efficient algorithm to recover Diffie–Hellman secret key $K = \lfloor g^{xy} \rfloor_p$ from $\lfloor g^x \rfloor_p$ and $\lfloor g^y \rfloor_p$.

Typically, either $\tau = p - 1$ (thus g is a primitive root) or $\tau = q$, a large prime divisor of $p - 1$.

The sizes of p and τ are determined by the present state of art in the *discrete logarithm problem*. Typically, p is at least about 500 bits, τ is at least about 160 bits.

However after the common DH key $K = \lfloor g^{xy} \rfloor_p$ is established, only a small portion of bits of K will be used as a common key for some pre-agreed *private* key cryptosystem.

Thus a natural question arises: *Assume that finding K is infeasible, is it still infeasible to find certain bits of K?*

Boneh and Venkatesan [**18**] have found a very elegant link between the $\mathcal{T}$-**HNP** and the above problem.

Indeed, assume there is an efficient algorithm to find ℓ most significant bits of $\lfloor g^{xy} \rfloor_p$ from $X = \lfloor g^x \rfloor_p$ and $Y = \lfloor g^y \rfloor_p$. Then, given $A = \lfloor g^a \rfloor_p$ and $B = \lfloor g^b \rfloor_p$, one can select a random $u \in [0, \tau - 1]$ one can apply the above algorithm to A and $U = \lfloor Bg^u \rfloor_p$ getting

$$\mathrm{MSB}_{\ell,p}\left(g^{a(b+u)}\right) = \mathrm{MSB}_{\ell,p}\left(\alpha g_a^u\right)$$

where $\alpha = \lfloor g^{ab} \rfloor_p$ and $g_a = g^a$. Thus we have a special case of the **EHNP**. Unfortunately the paper [**18**] has a minor flaw in the proof of Theorem 2. To bridge this gap and to extend the result to the case of $\tau < p - 1$, weaker forms [**59, 73**] of the bound (3.5) have been used in [**50**]. The results of [**50**] have recently been improved and extended in several directions in [**10, 11, 49, 115, 117**].

4.2. Attack on the DSA and DSA-like Schemes. On the other hand, in some cases the corresponding exponential sums are new and require a separate study. As we have mentioned, in [**95**] the sequence arising in the attack on the DSA has been studied.

From the congruence

$$\alpha r(k) s(k,\mu)^{-1} \equiv k - h(\mu) s(k,\mu)^{-1} \pmod q$$

where $r(k)$ and $s(k,\mu)$ are given by (3.6), we see that if some most significant bits k are known then one can get some most significant bits of $\lfloor \alpha r(k) s(k,\mu)^{-1} \rfloor_q$ as well.

The attack on the DSA, which is based on this observation, has been developed in [**94**]. The heart of this attack is solving the $\mathcal{T}$-**HNP** with the sequence

$$\mathcal{T} = \left\{ r(k) s(k,\mu)^{-1} \mid \mu \in \mathcal{M}, k \in \mathbb{F}_q^* \text{ such that } s(k,\mu) \not\equiv 0 \pmod q \right\}. \tag{4.1}$$

In [**95**] the heuristic results of [**94**] have been made rigorous by estimating exponential sums (3.8) with the sequence (3.7). The main difficulty is to show the uniformity of distribution of the sequence (4.1). This is because the sequence $r(k)$, obtained as a result of double modular reduction, modulo two distinct primes, has now explicit number theoretic or algebraic structure. As we have mentioned before, a combination of several methods of the theory of exponential sums has been used in [**95**] to prove the necessary result.

Numerical tests have confirmed the efficiency of this attack, in fact only 3-4 known bits of k (for $O(\log q)$ distinct signatures) are enough to recover the private key α.

Here are several *practical implications* of this attack:

- Do not use **small** k (to cut the cost of exponentiation in $r(k)$).
- Protect your software/hardware against **timing/power attacks** when the attacker measures the time/power consumption and selects the signatures for which this value is smaller than "on average" – these signatures are likely to correspond to small values of k (because they correspond to faster exponentiation in $r(k)$, timing for other parts of the algorithm is about the same for all k and μ).
- Use quality **pseudorandom number generators** to generate k, biased generators are dangerous.
- Do not use **Arazi's cryptosystem** which combines the DSA and Diffie-Hellman key exchange protocol, it has been noticed in [**24**] that it leaks some information about k which can be used for this attack.
- Be careful with **CryptoLib** from **AT&T**: it always uses odd values of k, thus one bit is leaked immediately, a couple more and ....

A different attack on the DSA, although also using lattice basis reduction, is given in [**9**]. It requires many more bits of the nonce k but may apply to fewer signatures; in some cases to just one signature.

4.3. Attack on the Hidden Number Field Identification Scheme. It is well known that if we are given the residues of a rational number $\alpha = r/s \in \mathbb{Q}$ modulo sufficiently many rational primes $p_1, \dots, p_m$, which do not divide the denominator s, then the Chinese Remainder Theorem can be used to recover α. If α is an integer $\alpha \in \mathbb{Z}$ then the result is immediate, otherwise one needs to use continued fractions to recover α. For algebraic number fields the situation looks more complicated. Although the Chinese Remainder Theorem can easily be extended to these fields, the actual algorithm to recover $\alpha \in \mathbb{K}$ where $\mathbb{K}$ is a given algebraic number field, is not straightforward even if α is an algebraic integer. Having cryptographic applications in mind, one could assume that if the field $\mathbb{K}$ itself is unknown then the problem becomes intractable. One of the possible cryptographic scenarios could be fixing several algebraic numbers $\alpha_1, \dots, \alpha_k$ and then (using linear algebra) finding a system of k polynomials

$$H_i(X_1, \dots, X_k) \in \mathbb{Z}[X_1, \dots, X_k], \qquad i = 1, \dots, k,$$

of degree d with at most t coefficients (for reasonably small values of d, t and coefficient size) and such that

$$H_i(\alpha_1, \dots, \alpha_k) = 0, \qquad i = 1, \dots, k.$$

Making these polynomials public, one can prove the knowledge of the elements $\alpha_1, \dots, \alpha_k$ by giving their residues $a_1, \dots a_k$ modulo some prime ideal p. The verifier can easily check that

$$H_i(a_1, \dots, a_k) \equiv 0 \pmod{\mathsf{p}}, \qquad i = 1, \dots, k, \tag{4.2}$$

(because these polynomials are sparse). On the other hand the forgery attempt via solving the system of congruences (4.2) seems to be infeasible. In particular no known algorithm takes advantage of sparsity of the involved polynomials. In fact all known algorithms run in time polynomial in the $(d+1)^k$, thus exponential in k, see [**40, 41**].

Of course in this case the prime ideals which are used at each identification round in the above scheme should admit a description over $\mathbb{Q}$ and thus should not reveal (at least explicitly) any information about $\mathbb{K}$ (otherwise an attack based on the Chinese Remainder Theorem immediately applies). In particular, one can use prime ideals $\mathfrak{p}$ of first degree.

However, the results of [**112**] on the ANF-**HNP** show that even if the field $\mathbb{K}$ is unknown, using lattice basis reduction one can recover in polynomial time (separately for each $i \in \{1, \dots, k\}$) the minimal polynomial of α_i from sufficiently many rational integer residues of α_i modulo prime ideals.

4.4. Other Applications. We have already discussed several applications of the above variants of the **HNP**. Here we present a brief summary and classification of these and some other applications.

- Bit Security of
  - Diffie–Hellman Scheme: $\mathbb{F}_p$-**HNP**, $\mathcal{T}$-**HNP**, see [**10, 11, 18, 19, 49, 50, 117**].
  - El Gamal Cryptosystem: $\mathbb{F}_p$-**HNP**, $\mathcal{T}$-**HNP**, see [**18, 19, 50, 115, 117**].
  - Discrete Logarithm: $\mathcal{T}$-CTP-**HNP**, see [**58**].
  - RSA: $\mathcal{T}$-CTP-**HNP**, see [**17, 58, 110**].
  - Shamir Message Passing Scheme: $\mathbb{F}_p$-**HNP**, $\mathcal{T}$-**HNP**, see [**18, 19, 50**].
  - Elliptic Curve Diffie–Hellman Scheme: EC-**HNP**, $\mathcal{T}$-CTP-**HNP**, see [**11, 15, 17**].
  - XTR and LUC: $\mathrm{Tr}_{\mathbb{F}_q/\mathbb{F}_p}$-$\mathcal{T}$-**HNP**, see [**85, 108**].
  - Timed-Release Crypto: $\mathcal{T}$-Approx-**HNP**, see [**61**].
  - Triparty Key Exchange Based on Weil and Tate Pairings: $\mathrm{Tr}_{\mathbb{F}_q/\mathbb{F}_p}$-$\mathcal{T}$-**HNP**, see [**39**].
- Attacks on
  - DSA: $\mathcal{T}$-**HNP**, see [**95**].
  - Elliptic Curve DSA: $\mathcal{T}$-**HNP**, see [**96**].
  - Projective Elliptic Curve Diffie–Hellman Scheme: $\mathcal{T}$-**HNP**, see [**92**].
  - Nyberg-Rueppel Signature Scheme: $\mathcal{T}$-**HNP**, see [**32**].
  - MQV Cryptosystem: $\mathcal{T}$-**HNP**, see [**78**].
  - Arazi Cryptosystem: $\mathcal{T}$-**HNP**, see [**24**].
  - Hidden Number Field Identification Scheme: ANF-**HNP**, see [**112**].
- Pseudorandom Generators from
  - Diagonal Diffie–Hellman Map $g^x \to g^{x^2}$: $\mathcal{T}$-**HNP**, see [**109**].
  - Inversive Diffie–Hellman Map $g^x \to g^{1/x}$: $\mathcal{T}$-**HNP**, see [**61**].
  - Polynomials $x \to f(x)$: Poly-**HNP**, see [**42, 57, 100, 107, 116**].
  - Inversions $x \to 1/(x+a)$: $\mathbb{F}_p$-Inverse-**HNP**, see [**15, 57**].
  - Black-Box Finite Fields: Module-**HNP**, see [**48**].
  - Character Evaluation: χ-**HNP**, see [**33, 34, 103**].
- Reconstruction/Correction from

– Noisy Polynomial Evaluation: Poly-**HNP**, see [**42, 57, 107, 116**].
– Noisy Exponentiation: $\mathcal{T}$-Approx-**HNP**, see [**61**].
– Noisy Weil Pairing: $\mathcal{T}$-Approx-**HNP**, see [**61**].
– Noisy Chinese Remaindering: CR-**HNP**, see [**113**].

∘ Non-approximability of
– Permanents: $\mathcal{T}$-**HNP**, see [**29**].
– Sparse Determinants: $\mathcal{T}$-**HNP**, see [**29**].
– Hard Polynomials: $\mathcal{T}$-**HNP**, see [**29**].

5. Conclusion and Further Directions

There are certainly several possible directions for further research. In particular, for each **HNP** which we have considered, one can try to reduce the amount of supplied information (for example, the value of ℓ) at each test point t, even if this requires increasing the number k of the test points. Making rigorous some or all of the aforementioned heuristic results give rise to another natural class of problems. One can also consider modifications of the above problems where the test points can be chosen by the algorithm and the other extreme, where only partial information about each test point t is revealed (say, the $\mathcal{T}$-Approx-**HNP** is such a modification of the $\mathcal{T}$-**HNP**). All such variations are of interest and deserve to be studied.

It would also be very interesting to obtain, for each of these problems, some general description of possible sets $\mathcal{T}$ from which the test points can be selected in order to be able to solve the corresponding **HNP** in polynomial time. This has been done for the $\mathcal{T}$-**HNP** but still ought to be done for the other problems.

New problems can also be considered. For example, the Poly-**HNP**, $\mathbb{F}_p$-Inverse-**HNP** and EC-**HNP** can be included as special partial cases in the more general scenario of the **HNP** related to recovering a rational function from its approximations at several randomly chosen points. Studying analogues of the above problems for multivariate polynomials and rational functions is of ultimate interest as well.

One can also study an analogue of the CR-**HNP** where some partial information is given about a certain function of α modulo distinct primes, for example, $\mathrm{MSB}_{\ell,p_i}(\alpha)$ can be replaced with $\mathrm{MSB}_{\ell,p_i}(\alpha^{-1})$, where α^{-1} is computed modulo p_i, for each $i = 1, \ldots, k$.

Even though the scheme described in Section 4.3 has been broken by the algorithm for the ANF-**HNP** of [**112**], this idea of using a hidden algebraic number field, which is due to Amin Shokrollahi who generously shared it with the author, deserves more attention and further study.

It has been noticed in [**18**] that the $\mathbb{F}_p$-**HNP** resembles the predicting of the *linear congruential generator* problem, see [**21, 22, 23, 30, 38, 63, 74, 75**] (we also remark that the same applies to the $\mathcal{T}$-**HNP**). Moreover, the Poly-**HNP** and $\mathbb{F}_p$-Inverse-**HNP** have clear links with predicting *polynomial* and *inversive* pseudorandom number generators, see [**6, 7, 8**]. It would be very desirable to understand these links and interrelations better, this should lead to a series of new interesting results.

We have already mentioned several *quantum algorithms* which have been designed for certain types of the **HNP**, see [**33, 34, 57, 103**]. Extending the scope of such applications of quantum algorithms is a very interesting direction of research.

Finally, we believe that the approach of [**19**] definitely deserves more attention and further exploration, see [**115**]. The fact that it leads to so-called non-uniform algorithms may limit its practical value, but from the theoretical point of view the idea looks very attractive and fruitful.

References

[1] M. Ajtai, R. Kumar and D. Sivakumar, 'A sieve algorithm for the shortest lattice vector problem', *Proc. 33rd ACM Symp. on Theory of Comput.*, Crete, Greece, July 6-8, (2001), 601–610.

[2] M. Anshel and D. Goldfeld, 'Zeta functions, one-way functions, and pseudorandom number generators', *Duke Math. J.*, **88** (1997), 371–390.

[3] S. Ar, R. Lipton, R. Rubinfeld and M. Sudan, 'Reconstructing algebraic functions from erroneous data', *SIAM J. Comput.*, **28** (1999), 487–510.

[4] S. Arora and M. Sudan, 'Improved low-degree testing and its applications', *Proc. 29nd ACM Symp. on Theory of Comp.*, (1997), 485–495.

[5] L. Babai, 'On Lovász' lattice reduction and the nearest lattice point problem', *Combinatorica*, **6** (1986), 1–13.

[6] S. R. Blackburn, D. Gomez-Perez, J. Gutierrez and I. E. Shparlinski, 'Predicting the inversive generator', *Lect. Notes in Comp. Sci.*, Springer-Verlag, Berlin, **2898** (2003), 264–275.

[7] S. R. Blackburn, D. Gomez-Perez, J. Gutierrez and I. E. Shparlinski, 'Predicting nonlinear pseudorandom number generators', *Math. Comp.*, **74** (2005), 1471–1494.

[8] S. R. Blackburn, D. Gomez-Perez, J. Gutierrez and I. E. Shparlinski, 'Reconstructing noisy polynomial evaluation in residue rings', *J. of Algorithms*, (to appear).

[9] I. F. Blake and T. Garefalakis, 'On the security of the digital signature algorithm', *Designs, Codes and Cryptography*, **26** (2002), 87–96.

[10] I. F. Blake and T. Garefalakis, 'On the complexity of the discrete logarithm and Diffie-Hellman problems', *J. Compl.*, **20** (2004), 148–170.

[11] I. F. Blake, T. Garefalakis and I. E. Shparlinski, 'On the bit security of the Diffie-Hellman key', *Appl. Algebra in Engin., Commun. and Computing*, (to appear).

[12] D. Bleichenbacher, W. Bosma and A. K. Lenstra, 'Some remarks on Lucas-based cryptosystems', *Lect. Notes in Comp. Sci.*, Springer-Verlag, Berlin, **963** (1995), 386–396.

[13] D. Bleichenbacher and P. Q. Nguyen, 'Noisy polynomial interpolation and noisy Chinese remaindering', *Lect. Notes in Comp. Sci.*, Springer-Verlag, Berlin, **1807** (2000), 53–69.

[14] D. Boneh, 'Finding smooth integers in shorts intervals using CRT decoding', *J. Comp. and Syst. Sci.*, **64** (2002), 768–784.

[15] D. Boneh, S. Halevi and N. A. Howgrave-Graham, 'The modular inversion hidden number problem', *Lect. Notes in Comp. Sci.*, Springer-Verlag, Berlin, **2248** (2001), 36–51.

[16] D. Boneh and R. Lipton, 'Algorithms for black-box fields and their applications to cryptography', *Lect. Notes in Comp. Sci.*, Springer-Verlag, Berlin, **1109** (1996), 283–297.

[17] D. Boneh and I. E. Shparlinski, 'On the unpredictability of bits of the elliptic curve Diffie–Hellman scheme', *Lect. Notes in Comp. Sci.*, Springer-Verlag, Berlin, **2139** (2001), 201–212.

[18] D. Boneh and R. Venkatesan, 'Hardness of computing the most significant bits of secret keys in Diffie–Hellman and related schemes', *Lect. Notes in Comp. Sci.*, Springer-Verlag, Berlin, **1109** (1996), 129–142.

[19] D. Boneh and R. Venkatesan, 'Rounding in lattices and its cryptographic applications', *Proc. 8th Annual ACM-SIAM Symp. on Discr. Algorithms*, SIAM, 1997, 675–681.

[20] J. Bourgain and S. V. Konyagin, 'Estimates for the number of sums and products and for exponential sums over subgroups in fields of prime order', *Comptes Rendus Mathematique*, **337** (2003), 75–80.

[21] J. Boyar, 'Inferring sequences produced by pseudo-random number generators', *J. ACM*, **36** (1989), 129–141

[22] J. Boyar, 'Inferring sequences produces by a linear congruential generator missing low–order bits', *J. Cryptology* **1** (1989) 177–184.

[23] E. F. Brickell and A. M. Odlyzko, 'Cryptoanalysis: A survey of recent results', *Contemp. Cryptology*, IEEE Press, NY, 1992, 501–540.

[24] D. R. L. Brown and A. J. Menezes, 'A small subgroup attack on a key agreement protocol of Arazi', *Research Report CORR 2001-50*, Faculty of Math., Univ. Waterloo, Waterloo, (2001), 1–5.

[25] R. Canetti, J. B. Friedlander, S. V. Konyagin, M. Larsen, D. Lieman and I. E. Shparlinski, 'On the statistical properties of Diffie–Hellman distributions', *Israel J. Math.*, **120** (2000), 23–46.

[26] A. L. Chistov and M. Karpinski, 'Fast interpolation algorithms for sparse polynomials with respect to the size of coefficients', *Research Report 85109–CS*, Bonn Univ., 1994.

[27] M. Clausen, A. Dress, J. Grabmeier and M. Karpinski, 'On zero testing and interpolation of k-sparse multivariate polynomials over finite fields', *Theor. Comp. Sci.*, **84** (1991), 151–164.

[28] T. Cochrane, C. Pinner and J. Rosenhouse, 'Bounds on exponential sums and the polynomial Waring's problem $\bmod p$', *Proc. Lond. Math. Soc.*, **67** (2003), 319–336.

[29] B. Codenotti, I. E. Shparlinski and A. Winterhof, 'Non-approximability of the permanent of structured matrices over finite fields', *Comp. Compl.*, **11** (2002), 158–170.

[30] S. Contini and I. E. Shparlinski, 'On Stern's attack against secret truncated linear congruential generators', *Proc. 10th Aust. Conf. on Information Security and Privacy*, Brisbane, 2005, Lect. Notes in Comp. Sci., Springer-Verlag, Berlin, (to appear).

[31] D. Coppersmith and M. Sudan, 'Reconstructing curves in three (and higher) dimensional space from noisy data', *Proc. 35rd ACM Symp. on Theory of Comp.*, ACM, 2003, 136–142.

[32] E. El Mahassni, P. Q. Nguyen and I. E. Shparlinski, 'The insecurity of Nyberg–Rueppel and other DSA-like signature schemes with partially known nonces', *Lect. Notes in Comp. Sci.*, Springer-Verlag, Berlin, **2146** (2001), 97–109.

[33] W. van Dam, 'Quantum algorithms for weighing matrices and quadratic residues', *Algorithmica*, **34** (2002), 413–428.

[34] W. van Dam, S. Hallgren and L. Ip, 'Quantum algorithms for hidden coset problems', *Proc. 14th ACM-SIAM Symp. on Discr. Algorithms*, SIAM, 2003, 489–498.

[35] I. B. Damgård, 'On the randomness of Legendre and Jacobi sequences', *Lect. Notes in Comp. Sci.*, Springer-Verlag, Berlin, **403** (1990), 163–172.

[36] P. Deligne, *Cohomologie 'etale (SGA $4\frac{1}{2}$)*, Lect. Notes in Math., Springer-Verlag, Berlin, **569** (1977).

[37] C. Ding, 'Pattern distributions of Legendre sequences', *IEEE Trans. Inform. Theory*, **44** (1998), 1693–1699.

[38] A. M. Frieze, J. Håstad, R. Kannan, J. C. Lagarias and A. Shamir, 'Reconstructing truncated integer variables satisfying linear congruences', *SIAM J. Comp.*, **17** (1988), 262–280.

[39] S. D. Galbraith, H. J. Hopkins and I. E. Shparlinski, 'Secure bilinear Diffie-Hellman bits', *Lect. Notes in Comp. Sci.*, Springer-Verlag, Berlin, **3108** (2004), 370–378.

[40] J. von zur Gathen, 'Irreducibility of multivariate polynomials', *J. Comp. and Syst. Sci.*, **31** (1985), 225–264.

[41] J. von zur Gathen and E. Kaltofen, 'Factoring sparse multivariate polynomials', *J. Comp. and Syst. Sci.*, **31** (1985), 265–287.

[42] J. von zur Gathen and I. E. Shparlinski, 'Polynomial interpolation from multiples', *Proc. 15th ACM-SIAM Symposium on Discrete Algorithms*, SIAM, 2004, 1125–1130.

[43] M. Goldmann and M. Näslund, 'The complexity of computing hard core predicates', *Lect. Notes in Comp. Sci.*, Springer-Verlag, Berlin, **1294** (1997), 1–15.

[44] M. Goldman, M. Näslund and A. C. Russell, 'Complexity bounds on general hard-core predicates', *J. Cryptology*, **14** (2001), 177–195.

[45] O. Goldreich, D. Ron and M. Sudan, 'Chinese remaindering with errors', *IEEE Trans. Inform. Theory*, **46** (2000), 1330–1338.

[46] O. Goldreich, R. Rubinfeld and M. Sudan, 'Learning polynomials with queries: the highly noisy case', *SIAM J. Discr. Math.*, **13** (2000), 535–570.

[47] M. I. González Vasco and M. Näslund, 'A survey of hard core functions', *Proc. Workshop on Cryptography and Computational Number Theory, Singapore 1999*, Birkhäuser, 2001, 227–256.

[48] M. I. González Vasco, M. Näslund and I. E. Shparlinski, 'The hidden number problem in extension fields and its applications', *Lect. Notes in Comp. Sci.*, Springer-Verlag, Berlin, **2286** (2002), 105–117.

[49] M. I. González Vasco, M. Näslund and I. E. Shparlinski, 'New results on the hardness of Diffie-Hellman bits', *Proc. Intern. Workshop on Public Key Cryptography, Singapore, 2004*, Lect. Notes in Comp. Sci., Springer-Verlag, Berlin, **2947** (2004), 159–172.

[50] M. I. González Vasco and I. E. Shparlinski, 'On the security of Diffie–Hellman bits', *Proc. Workshop on Cryptography and Computational Number Theory*, Singapore 1999, Birkhäuser, (2001), 257–268.

[51] M. I. González Vasco and I. E. Shparlinski, 'Security of the most significant bits of the Shamir message passing scheme', *Math. Comp.*, **71** (2002), 333–342.

[52] L. Goubin, C. Mauduit and A. Sárközy, 'Construction of large families of pseudo-random binary sequences', *J. Number Theory*, **106** (2004), 56–69.

[53] D. Grigoriev, M. Karpinski and M. Singer, 'Computational complexity of sparse rational interpolation', *SIAM J. Comput.*, **23** (1994), 1–11.

[54] V. Guruswami, A. Sahai and M. Sudan, '"Soft-decision" decoding of Chinese remainder codes', *Proc. 41st IEEE Symp. on Found. of Comp. Sci.*, (2000), 159–168.

[55] V. Guruswami and M. Sudan, 'Improved decoding of Reed–Solomon and algebraic geometric codes', *IEEE Trans. Inform. Theory*, **45** (1999), 1757–1767.

[56] K. Gyarmati, 'On a pseudorandom property of binary sequences', *Ramanujan J.*, **8**, (2004), 289–302.

[57] S. Hallgren, A. Russell and I. E. Shparlinski, 'Quantum noisy rational function reconstruction', *Proc. of the 11th Annual International Computing and Combinatorics Conference*, Kunming, 2005, Lect. Notes in Comp. Sci., Springer-Verlag, Berlin, (to appear).

[58] J. Håstad and M. Näslund, 'The security of individual RSA and discrete log bits', *J. ACM*, **51** (2004), 187–230.

[59] D. R. Heath-Brown and S. V. Konyagin, 'New bounds for Gauss sums derived from kth powers, and for Heilbronn's exponential sum', *Ouart. J. Math.*, **51** (2000), 221–235.

[60] J. Hoffstein and D. Lieman, 'The distribution of the quadratic symbol in function fields and a faster mathematical stream cipher', *Proc. Workshop on Cryptography and Computational Number Theory, Singapore 1999*, Birkhäuser, 2001, 59–68.

[61] N. A. Howgrave-Graham, P. Q. Nguyen and I. E. Shparlinski, 'Hidden number problem with hidden multipliers, timed-release crypto and noisy exponentiation', *Math. Comp.*, **72** (2003), 1473–1485.

[62] N. A. Howgrave-Graham and N. P. Smart, 'Lattice attacks on digital signature schemes', *Designs, Codes and Cryptography*, **23** (2001), 283–290.

[63] A. Joux and J. Stern, 'Lattice reduction: A toolbox for the cryptanalyst', *J. Cryptology*, **11** (1998), 161–185.

[64] V. Kabanets and R. Impagliazzo, 'Derandomizing polynomial identity tests means proving circuit lower bounds', *Comp. Compl.*, **13** (2004), 1–46.

[65] R. Kannan, 'Algorithmic geometry of numbers', *Annual Review of Comp. Sci.*, **2** (1987), 231–267.

[66] N. M. Katz, *Gauss sums, Kloosterman sums, and monodromy groups*, Ann. of Math. Studies, **116**, Princeton Univ. Press, (1988).

[67] A. R. Klivans and D. A. Spielman, 'Randomness efficient identity testing of multivariate polynomials', *Proc. 33rd ACM Symp. on Theory of Comp.*, ACM, 2001, 216–223.

[68] E. Kiltz, 'A primitive for proving the security of every bit and about universal hash functions & hard core bits', *Preprint*, 2001.

[69] M. Kiwi, F. Magniez and M. Santha, 'Exact and approximate testing/correcting of algebraic functions: A survey', *Lect. Notes in Comp. Sci.*, Springer-Verlag, Berlin, **2292** (2002), 30–83.

[70] D. R. Kohel and I. E. Shparlinski, 'Exponential sums and group generators for elliptic curves over finite fields', *Lect. Notes in Comp. Sci.*, Springer-Verlag, Berlin, **1838** (2000), 395–404.

[71] S. V. Konyagin, 'On estimates of Gaussian sums and the Waring problem modulo a prime', *Proc. Math. Inst. Russian Acad. Sci.*, Moscow, **198** (1992), 111–124 (in Russian).

[72] S. V. Konyagin, 'Bounds of exponential sums over subgroups and Gauss sums', *Proc 4th Intern. Conf. Modern Problems of Number Theory and Its Applications*, Moscow Lomonosov State Univ., Moscow, 2002, 86–114 (in Russian).

[73] S. V. Konyagin and I. Shparlinski, *Character sums with exponential functions and their applications*, Cambridge Univ. Press, Cambridge, (1999).

[74] H. Krawczyk, 'How to predict congruential generators', *J. Algorithms*, **13** (1992), 527–545.

[75] J. C. Lagarias, 'Pseudorandom number generators in cryptography and number theory', *Proc. Symp. in Appl. Math.*, Amer. Math. Soc., Providence, RI, **42** (1990), 115–143.
[76] Y. N. Lakshman and B. D. Saunders, 'Sparse polynomial interpolation in non-standard bases', *SIAM J. Comp.*, **24** (1995), 387–397.
[77] S. Lang, *Algebra*, Addison-Wesley, MA, (1965).
[78] P. J. Leadbitter and N. Smart, 'Analysis of the insecurity of ECMQV with partially known nonces', *Lect. Notes in Comp. Sci.*, Springer-Verlag, Berlin, **2851** (2003), 240–251.
[79] A. K. Lenstra, H. W. Lenstra and L. Lovász, 'Factoring polynomials with rational coefficients', *Mathematische Annalen*, **261** (1982), 515–534.
[80] A. K. Lenstra and E. R. Verheul, 'The XTR public key system', *Lect. Notes in Comp. Sci.*, Springer-Verlag, Berlin, **1880** (2000), 1–19.
[81] A. K. Lenstra and E. R. Verheul, 'Key improvements to XTR', *Lect. Notes in Comp. Sci.*, Springer-Verlag, Berlin, **1976** (2000), 220–233.
[82] D. Lewin and S. Vadhan 'Checking polynomial identities over any field: Towards a derandomization?', *Proc. 30th ACM Symp. on Theory of Comp.*, ACM, 1998, 438-447.
[83] W.-C. W. Li, 'Character sums and abelian Ramanujan graphs', *J. Number Theory*, **41** (1992), 199–217.
[84] W.-C. W. Li, *Number theory with applications*, World Scientific, Singapore, (1996).
[85] W.-C. W. Li, M. Näslund and I. E. Shparlinski, 'The hidden number problem with the trace and bit security of XTR and LUC', *Lect. Notes in Comp. Sci.*, Springer-Verlag, Berlin, **2442** (2002), 433–448.
[86] R. Lidl and H. Niederreiter, *Finite fields*, Cambridge University Press, Cambridge, (1997).
[87] R. Lipton and N. Vishnoi, 'Deterministic identity testing for multivariate polynomials', *Proc. 14th ACM-SIAM Symp. on Discr. Algorithms*, SIAM, 2003, 756–760.
[88] C. Mauduit, 'Finite and infinite pseudorandom binary words', *Theor. Comp. Sci.*, **273** (2002), 249–261.
[89] C. Mauduit and A. Sárközy, 'On finite pseudorandom binary sequences 1: Measure of pseudorandomness, the Legendre symbol', *Acta Arith.*, **82** (1997), 365–377.
[90] A. J. Menezes, P. C. van Oorschot and S. A. Vanstone, *Handbook of Applied Cryptography*, CRC Press, Boca Raton, FL, 1996.
[91] D. Micciancio, 'On the hardness of the shortest vector problem', *PhD Thesis*, MIT, 1998.
[92] D. Naccache, N. Smart and J. Stern, 'Projective coordinates leak', *Cryptology ePrint Archive, Report 2003/191*, 2003, 1–11.
[93] W. Narkiewicz, *Elementary and analytic theory of algebraic numbers*, Polish Sci. Publ., Warszawa, (1990).
[94] P. Q. Nguyen, 'The dark side of the hidden number problem: Lattice attacks on DSA', *Proc. Workshop on Cryptography and Computational Number Theory*, Singapore 1999, Birkhäuser, (2001), 321–330.
[95] P. Q. Nguyen and I. E. Shparlinski, 'The insecurity of the Digital Signature Algorithm with partially known nonces', *J. Cryptology*, **15** (2002), 151–176.
[96] P. Q. Nguyen and I. E. Shparlinski, 'The insecurity of the elliptic curve Digital Signature Algorithm with partially known nonces', *Designs, Codes and Cryptography*, **30** (2003), 201–217.
[97] P. Q. Nguyen and J. Stern, 'Lattice reduction in cryptology: An update', *Lect. Notes in Comp. Sci.*, Springer-Verlag, Berlin, **1838** (2000), 85–112.
[98] P. Q. Nguyen and J. Stern, 'The two faces of lattices in cryptology', *Lect. Notes in Comp. Sci.*, Springer-Verlag, Berlin, **2146** (2001), 146–180.
[99] H. Niederreiter, *Random number generation and quasi–Monte Carlo methods*, SIAM, Philadelphia, (1992).
[100] H. Niederreiter and C. P. Schnorr, 'Local randomness in polynomial random number and random function generators', *SIAM J. Comp.*, **13** (1993), 684–694.
[101] R. Peralta, 'On the distribution of quadratic residues and nonresidues modulo a prime number', *Math. Comp.*, **58** (1992), 433–440.
[102] R. L. Rivest, A. Shamir and D. A. Wagner, 'Time-lock puzzles and timed-release crypto', *MIT Laboratory for Computer Science. Technical Report MIT-LCS-TR-684*, MIT, Massachusets, 1996, 1–9.
[103] A. C. Russell and I. E. Shparlinski, 'Classical and quantum algorithms for function reconstruction via character evaluation', *J. Compl.*, **20** (2004), 404–422.

[104] C. P. Schnorr, 'A hierarchy of polynomial time basis reduction algorithms', *Theor. Comp. Sci.*, **53** (1987), 201–224.

[105] M. A. Shokrollahi and H. Wasserman, 'List decoding of algebraic-geometric codes', *IEEE Trans. Inform. Theory*, **45** (1999), 432–437.

[106] I. E. Shparlinski, 'On exponential sums with sparse polynomials and rational functions', *J. Number Theory*, **60** (1996), 233–244.

[107] I. E. Shparlinski, 'Sparse polynomial approximation in finite fields', *Proc. 33rd ACM Symp. on Theory of Comput.*, Crete, Greece, July 6-8, (2001), 209–215.

[108] I. E. Shparlinski, 'On the generalised hidden number problem and bit security of XTR', *Lect. Notes in Comp. Sci.*, Springer-Verlag, Berlin, **2227** (2001), 268–277.

[109] I. E. Shparlinski, 'Security of most significant bits of g^{x^2}', *Inform. Proc. Letters*, **83** (2002), 109–113.

[110] I. E. Shparlinski, *Cryptographic applications of analytic number theory*, Birkhauser, 2003.

[111] I. E. Shparlinski, 'Security of polynomial transformations of the Diffie–Hellman key', *Finite Fields and Their Appl.*, **10** (2004), 123–131.

[112] I. E. Shparlinski and R. Steinfeld, 'Chinese remaindering for algebraic numbers in a hidden field', *Lect. Notes in Comp. Sci.*, Springer-Verlag, Berlin, **2369** (2002), 349–356.

[113] I. E. Shparlinski and R. Steinfeld, 'Noisy Chinese remaindering in the Lee norm', *J. Compl.*, **20** (2004), 423–437.

[114] I. E. Shparlinski and R. Steinfeld, 'Chinese Remaindering with multiplicative noise', *Theory of Comp. Sys.*, (to appear).

[115] I. E. Shparlinski and A. Winterhof, 'A nonuniform algorithm for the hidden number problem in subgroups', *Proc. Intern. Workshop on Public Key Cryptography, Singapore, 2004*, Lect. Notes in Comp. Sci., Springer-Verlag, Berlin, **2947** (2004), 416–424.

[116] I. E. Shparlinski and A. Winterhof, 'Noisy interpolation of sparse polynomials in finite fields', *Appl. Algebra in Engin., Commun. and Computing*, (to appear).

[117] I. E. Shparlinski and A. Winterhof, 'A hidden number problem in small subgroups', *Math. Comp.*, (to appear).

[118] P. J. Smith and C. T. Skinner, 'A public-key cryptosystem and a digital signature system based on the Lucas function analogue to discrete logarithms', *Lect. Notes in Comp. Sci.*, Springer-Verlag, Berlin, **917** (1995), 357–364.

[119] E. R. Verheul, 'Certificates of recoverability with scalable recovery agent security', *Lect. Notes in Comp. Sci.*, Springer-Verlag, Berlin, **1751** (2000), 258–275.

[120] H. Wasserman, 'Reconstructing randomly sampled multivariate polynomials from highly noisy data', *Proc. 9th ACM-SIAM Symp. on Discr. Algorithms*, SIAM, 1998, 59–67.

[121] K. Werther, 'The complexity of sparse polynomial interpolation over finite fields', *Appl. Algebra in Engin., Commun. and Comp.*, **5** (1994), 91–103.

[122] R. Zippel, *Effective polynomial computation*, Kluwer Acad. Publ., Dordrecht, (1993).

DEPARTMENT OF COMPUTING, MACQUARIE UNIVERSITY, SYDNEY, NSW 2109, AUSTRALIA
E-mail address: igor@ics.mq.edu.au

Index

ISBN 0-8218-3365-0

9 780821 833650